I Choose *the* Moon

MY JOURNEY FROM THE MIDWEST TO THE MIDDLE EAST

JONEA MOUNSEY

MINDSTIR MEDIA

Published by Mindstir Media, LLC
45 Lafayette Rd | Suite 181| North Hampton, NH 03862 | USA
1.800.767.0531 | www.mindstirmedia.com

Printed in the United States of America
ISBN-13:978-1-958729-15-1

Dedication

I dedicate this book to all of those who have bravely stood up for what is right when the crowd has chosen to look the other way.

And to the people of Iraq who have been misdiagnosed by the media. You have openly shared your kindness, trust, and amity.

In memory of

My dad, Jerry Tucker, the person I credit for giving me a sense of adventure and encouraging me to go over and above in everything I do.

Bob Titel, my admirable friend who made me promise
to write a book about my engaging adventures.

Randy Spearling, my soulmate, if only you had been forty years younger.

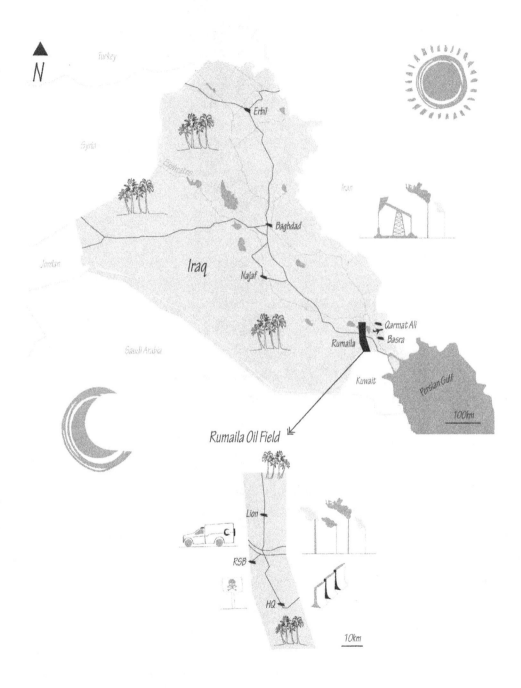

Turkey

N

Syria

Euphrates

Jordan

Iraq

Baghdad

Najaf

Saudi Arabia

Erbil

Iran

Qarmat Ali
Rumaila   Basra

Kuwait

Persian Gulf

100km

Rumaila Oil Field

Lion

RSB

HQ

10km

Contents

Finding Fortitude

The Moon Has a Story to Tell

"Adriana, hi, this is Jonea. After giving it some thought, I have decided to accept the position in Iraq."

The response came with a British accent. "Jonea, I'm happy to hear this. Welcome aboard." I had done it. I had found and secured my dream job. After ending the call, I started to reflect on the path that had led me here. I wondered how different my life could have been if I had made just one single decision differently.

Life is not supposed to be easy; otherwise, how can we measure real success? During the lowest point in my life, I made the decision that no matter what it took I would fight my way to happier times. My goal became to be a self-sufficient woman and free myself from the selfish, hard-hearted man I was married to.

In 1989, I enrolled in one single class at the local university. Earning my degree as a nurse would be my first step toward a new life and, finally, an achievement I could call my own. In February of the following year, I had my fourth child. It was after Jan was born that my relationship with my husband hit bottom. We had had rocky times off and on before, but when he accused me of sleeping with one of his friends this was the straw that broke the camel's back. He dreamed this up because our youngest child didn't look like the other kids. Jan looked more like me than the other three. My spouse's accusation absolutely crushed me.

One class at a time, I plodded along with my nursing degree while caring for four young kids and working part-time at my husband's business. I kept my head down, trying to steer clear of the ongoing emotional abuse. The arguments became more and more frequent. My husband agreed to join me in seeing a marriage counselor, but after a few sessions he quit going. I continued therapy for more than a year and a half.

Then one day while I was in a session, I mentioned to the counselor that my kids had asked me if I ever felt like divorcing Dad. The counselor paused and excused herself for a moment. She returned with the names of two divorce attorneys. "Jonea, it's your choice, but I think you've done all you can."

My heart had decided I was overstaying in a controlling and manipulative marriage. I was sick of being afraid—afraid of the what-ifs. What if I can't make it as a single mom? What if I'm making the wrong decision? What if this has a long-term emotional effect on the kids? It was time to stop second-guessing myself and take the leap. In my heart, I knew I'd be fine, but the mind is a powerful thing. My head had tried to convince me for the past year and a half that my children would starve and that I probably would end up broke and empty-handed.

Fourteen years of living with a despotic man had lowered my self-confidence and sense of who I was. A wife, a mom, the company secretary, the person who strived to keep everyone but herself happy (codependent), Jonea had gotten lost. Working in the office at my husband's company allowed him even more control over me.

My first courageous move was when I filed for divorce. Filing those papers was the scariest thing I've ever done. My mind raced and immediately questioned how I would make it on my own with four dependents to support.

The two years it took for the divorce to be finalized were dreadful. We had to wait for my spouse's business to get appraised, and he did his best to drag it out. In the meantime, he emotionally and financially punished me any way he could. While my electricity was cut off the week before Christmas, my ex was vacationing in Florida with his girlfriend. He hadn't bothered to pay my alimony on time, so I wasn't able to pay my bills. Overdue alimony became a frequent occurrence, so my parents generously supported us with grocery money from time to time so at least we didn't go hungry.

Before settling the divorce, I decided that the kids and I would move out of state. Despite being legally separated, remaining in the same city would not prevent the ongoing torment. I needed some space.

Knowing better than to let it slip that I planned to leave with the kids, I avoided mentioning my intentions to him until I figured out an escape plan. There would be hell to pay when the time came.

May 1995 was a memorable time. At age thirty-four, I graduated from college as a registered nurse. I was one of only four people in my immediate family to complete an advanced degree. My aunt (Dad's sister) and two of her children were the only others. The satisfaction of walking across the stage and receiving my diploma was measureless. I felt proud, grateful, and relieved. On top of this, it was awe-inspiring that my children were old enough to realize the accomplishment I had achieved. In the back of my mind, I knew I was influencing them for the better.

In that same month, the divorce became final. Hallelujah! I was starting to see some light at the end of the tunnel. These were two significant steps forward. With a degree in hand, I would finally have the means to support my family and stand on my own two feet.

I decided to take the kids on a road trip to Arizona during their summer break to celebrate the momentous occasion. The cash settlement from the divorce allowed me to afford the trip. It made sense to check out Arizona, as it was one of the places I was considering as our potential new home. I wanted the kids to have a say in where we moved to, and it was important to me that they felt heard. Plus, I needed to look into the job situation, search for housing, and find out if they had good schools. Another reason Phoenix topped the list was that I had family there. My cousins, Anita, Terry, and Dennis, and their families called Phoenix home, and I knew they would be supportive and happy if I ended up there.

I elected to rent a pop-up camper trailer, thinking it would be a fantastic way to travel with the kids. It would save money on hotels, add to our memorable adventures, and give us more outdoor time. The kids loved the idea of camping and were excited they would get to see the Grand Canyon and meet their Arizona cousins.

We had a blast, minus the occasional sibling spats. Our Arizona family kindly took us exploring, showing us a few local sights. There was so much to see and do, from major league sports teams, museums, hiking, and historical towns to tour.

Although it was bloody hot this time of year, with temperatures in the 110s, it really didn't seem that bad. Cousin Dennis's family had a pool, and the kids swam nearly every day. I found the worst part was getting into a hot car, with every surface scorching. Prior to this visit, I had been apprehensive about the extreme summer temperatures but now realized it wouldn't be that hard to acclimatize.

While we were in Phoenix, I wanted to look into what nursing jobs were available, understand the pay scale, and learn about benefits. Before our visit, I had lined up three interviews at different hospitals around the valley. In all three interviews, each facility told me the same thing, that Arizona traditionally only hires from their local pool of freshly degreed nurses. Still, they would be glad to hire me once I had a year of experience, but not as a new graduate nurse. It was reassuring to know there was a healthy job market within my profession.

The second thing I did was contact a local realtor. I needed to know if I could afford or even qualify for a home. The realtor assured me I could get a loan and thought it would be in my best interest to see a few houses. I told her I would like to look near Peoria, as my research discovered this area had highly rated schools. My cousin Terry's wife, Virgie, and I spent one afternoon with the realtor checking out homes. Looking at the beautiful Southwest-style houses got me super excited. Just dreaming of being able to buy a house on my own was thrilling. I was psyched.

On the drive back to Indiana, the kids and I discussed the pros and cons of moving. We talked about how much fun we had and how awesome our family of Arizona cousins is. The kids were gung-ho at the idea, but I felt they didn't grasp how serious I was or that it would ever happen. But that was not the case. I set my sights on Phoenix and crossed my fingers.

Back in Fort Wayne, I was super anxious to get on with my life. I had lots of groundwork to do, and I needed to find a job and put my nursing career in motion. With the help of my friend and neighbor, Karma, I found a full-time day shift job at Lutheran Hospital on the medical ward. I told myself it was only a year. Besides, I needed to save enough money to be able to afford to leave Indiana permanently. I wasn't even sure I would be granted permission to move out of state by the court.

Adapting to working twelve-hour shifts was hard, and I was single-parenting as best I could. Working long days meant juggling the kids between daycare, school, and after-school care. I dropped the kids at three different locations in the mornings and picked them up at two separate places after school.

The ex continued giving me grief, and on his visitation weekends he never picked the kids up when he promised. Often it was a day later, so I could never make plans, or I would have to call a babysitter at the last minute. The effort to control me prevailed. It broke my heart when the kids would ask me, "Mom, why does Dad never keep his promises?" How was I supposed to explain that he was only trying to hurt Mommy? It was clearly affecting the children.

In March of 1996, while the kids vacationed in Florida with their dad, I returned to Phoenix. I was determined to find a job and break loose from Fort Wayne. Although I hadn't worked as a nurse for quite a year, I had to build a blueprint. During my week in Arizona, I visited three additional hospitals, and all of them offered me nursing positions. I just had to decide which one I wanted.

I again met up with the realtor and looked at more houses. I needed to narrow down where I wanted to be. I still felt partial toward Peoria in the West Valley and was offered a position at nearby Boswell Hospital. I was leaning toward accepting the job and finally felt that everything was falling into place.

When I returned to Fort Wayne, I alerted my parents to the trip's success. On the one hand, they were happy for me but also sad to think about us leaving. They spent their time between Alaska and Indiana, so they understood my wanting to get out.

The next step was calling my ex-husband, and this was where I felt the most apprehension. I felt nauseous as I slowly dialed the number. "Hello, what's up?" spouted the unfriendly voice.

As courageously as I could, I replied, "I'm taking a job in Phoenix and am planning on moving there with the kids."

Here it came, so predictable. His enraged voice came across loud and clear. "NO, YOU'RE NOT!" The one thing I clearly remember is him yelling, "I don't want my kids going to school with a bunch of Mexicans." His response was nothing less than I expected.

Long story short, in May of 1996, we took our argument to court, and each of us took the stand to plead our cases to the judge. In his hand of cards, he pulled out a joker. All of the crap he had played on me over the past couple of years was laid out on the table for all to see. I played my ace, explaining to the judge how I had put myself through nursing school, landed a job, and now was trying to better my future and the future of my children. Sharing how moving to Phoenix would give us a new start and that I wasn't making a blind leap, I informed the judge how I had taken my children to Phoenix before making the decision. To make my final point, I reported I had a few job offers, looked into housing and schools, and knew a robust support system was in place; my Arizona family was there.

The court's decision arrived a month later. I was granted permission to take the kids and relocate. The words "elated," "overjoyed," and "satisfied" come to mind. My fortitude had gotten me through the lengthy ordeal.

Graduation Day May 5, 1995. Angie, me and Bonnie

Jan, Drew, Brock, me and Angie

Brock age seven, in front of rented camper

Grand Canyon June 1995. Drew, me and Jan

Stepping Out the Door

The moon is the first milestone
on the road to the stars.

~ *Arthur C. Clarke*

Pulling up stakes and relocating 2400 miles across the country with four kids, ages six to thirteen, took guts. Getting the hell out of Dodge and leaving Indiana in my rearview mirror was the second bravest thing I did. It allowed plenty of distance from my former spouse. This meant he could only harass me over the phone.

It was a hot June afternoon in the summer of 1996 when I parked the U-Haul on the street in front of my cousin Anita's patio home in Scottsdale. Having a family connection in Arizona eased some of the anxiety of moving. The kids and I were ecstatic to finish the four-day ride from Fort Wayne to our new destination.

Leaving my parents and our friends behind was not easy, but I needed a new dream to chase. I was hoping to start fresh and decided to head west. The kids were more sad than excited, and I tried to reassure them as best I could.

They were acutely aware of their dad's spiteful behavior, even though they were young at the time. Still, it is hard to explain to a thirteen-year-old that it was in Mom's best interest to be selfish and take care of her own needs for once. I knew they would despise me for a while.

Angie, at thirteen, my eldest and only daughter, was angry with me for taking her away from her friends. Drew was eleven and looked forward to living in the same city as his favorite NBA team, the Phoenix Suns. Brock had just turned eight, and he was less than happy to be moving. He was sad to leave behind his many playmates, especially his best friend, Keith. Jan was only six and didn't have a strong opinion either way. I hated myself for causing them pain, but I needed to step out that door and start a new chapter. It was time to explore the unknown and leave fear in the dust.

Having joint custody meant the kids would be spending their summers back in Indiana with their dad. This gave them the chance to catch up with old friends and spend time with family. I could only hope that their dad would pay more attention to them than he had in the past.

Relocating to Phoenix opened many doors for my kids and me. New house, new job, new friends, new schools, and a new life. We settled into our Sonoran desert life. It was stressful for everyone at first. Within a few months, the kids all adjusted to their new community. Each found their niche, and life moved forward.

Moving to Phoenix had been one of the best decisions in my life, at least up to this point. The 300-plus days of sunshine grew my soul. I fell in love with Arizona, and it had so much to offer. I've always been a fit and active person, but after coming to Arizona, I went hog wild.

My new best friend, Debbie, got me into hiking, skiing, and back into running. Deb and I met while working together at Boswell Hospital, and we were two peas in a pod. I was a runner in high school and college, but my running fell to the wayside after having kids. Debbie talked me into entering a local running event, the Whiskey Row 10K.

The race was held annually in May in the mountain community of Prescott, Arizona. Whiskey Row became well known during the late 1800s when Prescott was a rowdy cowboy town with a street full of saloons. After finishing the difficult 6.2-mile race, I was hooked. Running became my new fixation. I was born to run. My mom said I refused to walk until I was fourteen months old. Then I bypassed walking and started running everywhere. I grew to be 5'10", 80% legs, 20% everything else.

Hiking became another of my passions, thanks to Debbie. Although Phoenix was a huge metropolis, it had dozens of parks with mountainous trails within the city limits. Some days we'd head out of town to hike for the day. One of our favorites was Mt. Humphreys in Flagstaff. The trail there led up to the highest point in the state, 12,633 ft.

Most people envision a beautiful, glowing, orange sunset with the tree-like saguaro cactus in the foreground when thinking of Arizona. The desert sunsets are spectacular, but Arizona also has six National Forests and four ski resorts. Eventually, Deb decided she was sick of the hot summers and moved to Minnesota, but not before teaching me how to downhill ski. We remained good friends after she moved away and frequently visited each other for the first few years.

Our new home in Peoria, Arizona

The U-Haul and trailer I drove to Phoenix

Pursuing the Goal

A dreamer is one who can only find
her way by the moonlight.

~ *Oscar Wilde*

When I moved to Phoenix in 1996, I had been a registered nurse (RN) for only a year, and I found it to be a love-hate career. The money was good, there were plenty of jobs, and for the most part I enjoyed patient care. Every day at work was different. Some days were fulfilling, and on the flip side I sometimes found myself crying on my drive home. Being an RN is draining emotionally, mentally, physically, and spiritually. I was the type of person who got attached to my patients too easily.

After building my nursing career over the course of sixteen years and having had a multitude of work experiences, I was feeling discontent and ready to find something extraordinary. Jan, my youngest, was about to graduate high school, and with the kids all at an age where they were nearly self-sufficient, I was soon to be unattached and had a bad case of wanderlust. I ached for something wild and entertaining to stimulate my soul, mind, and spirit. It was now my time.

I was anxious to break away. I yearned for a career change, one that would trump my current list of experiences. What could be more adventurous than working as a flight nurse on a helicopter or caring for wildland firefighters in a burning ponderosa forest?

My nursing career was much like the Johnny Cash tune, "I've Been Everywhere, Man." My version goes like this: I've done everything, man, I've done everything. Medical, surgical, telemetry, emergency, ICU, cath lab, pre-op, post-op, I've done everything, man, I've done everything. Fixed-wing, rotor wing, wildland fire, I've done everything, man! A bit cliché, I know, but you get the idea. The only thing I hadn't done as a nurse was work in the operating theater, pediatric ICU, and labor and delivery.

My idea of a dream job included a far-off exotic place, maybe a tropical rainforest with deadly snakes or the African savanna with dangerous wildlife. You could say I'm a big dreamer. I was then and still am. I started searching for an adventurous career move. I wanted to follow the moon, to travel and go to some inimitable place outside of the US. I had always been fascinated by wilderness medicine and had hoped to find a job in that field. My mind was swirling with ideas. Maybe I could work for National Geographic or be medical support on an expedition. When looking closer, I discovered that these unique jobs do exist if you're a physician or if you want to volunteer your time for room and board only. I found this disappointing, but I knew I'd find something.

My search uncovered an assortment of jobs, including a company that kept flashing across my radar. Remote Medical International (RMI) looked promising, so I delved deeper into their website. I learned they were looking for adventurous medical providers to work in austere and remote areas of the world. I thought this might be a good place to start chasing after my goal.

RMI had their fingers in a few different pots. The company consisted of a training center, a topside medical support division, along with staffing paramedics, doctors, and nurses in awe-inspiring jobs around the globe. My dream job.

While scheming on how to get my foot in the door, I discovered I would need to attend one of the organization's specialized classes. The company required their medical staff to be certified in a special remote providers course prior to being hired. So my plans began. While fantasizing about working in an exotic place, I signed up for the required course. My plot played out like this. Once I finished the training, I would set up a meeting with the HR person and see if I could get an interview.

The tactic of going directly to the person doing the hiring, looking them in the eye, shaking their hand, and introducing myself had landed me numerous jobs in the past. I found this to be an effective way to sell myself. With a smile on your face, you can cunningly convince them you're the right person, and the face time allows you to get some of your own questions answered before you decide if the position is right for you.

The four-day seminar was scheduled in the middle of November 2010. Set in the Cascade Mountains of Washington State, I found the North Cascades Institute lodge nestled deep in a forest of oversized cedar trees virtually in the middle of nowhere—well, roughly seventy-five miles outside of Seattle. You might as well be in the middle of nowhere; it was amazing! The European-style resort was warm and cozy with a spectacular lounge that featured a large stone fireplace. It was heavenly sitting inside, looking through the enormous windows at the stunning views of the surrounding landscape.

Our class was a small group of thirteen, plus the three instructors. The only other people around were two or three lodge staff; otherwise, we had the place to ourselves. The workshop's objective was to educate medical folks on treating and managing ill and injured patients in remote settings, whether in the great outdoors or another isolated situation. Whether or not I would get hired by Remote International, the skills I would acquire during the training would be an asset to my career and CV.

Within our small class, we had a diverse bunch of characters, most of whom were men. There were two FBI agents from LA, a CIA agent from DC, an Australian who employed medics on oil rigs off the coast of Western Australia, and an offshore medic who worked for a UK company called FrontierMedex. The three women in the class, including myself, were employed as hospital nurses, and it seemed our work was somehow unremarkable compared to the other students.

Everyone had thrilling stories to share as we sat around the fireplace each evening drinking beer. It was clear that we were an adventurous and unique group of souls. As the Aussie opened his second, third, and fourth beer, he would raise the bottle to the rest of the group. "Cheers mate, first one for the week." I thought this was such a catchy phrase. So if you ever have a beer with me and hear me repeat the saying, you'll know this is where I stole it from.

One of our three instructors was Jordan, a local paramedic and the company's founder. He was a thirty-four-year-old entrepreneur who mixed his medical knowledge with his passion for the outdoors to build an internationally acclaimed business. The second instructor was the company's medical director, a well-known physician and a published author in the wilderness medicine field. The third instructor was Jordan's right-hand man. It was stimulating to be in the presence of these highly ranked individuals, plus this was a perfect situation to get to know a few of the company's top people. When the timing was right, I would inquire about what it took to work for Remote International.

The lectures and course material were superb, from search and rescue, heat illness, managing fractures, and reducing dislocated joints. The segment on suturing wounds intrigued me, as it was something I'd always wanted to try. It was amazing to have the opportunity to learn these advanced skills but nerve-racking thinking about performing them in some out-of-the-way place, possibly on my own.

As a flight nurse, I had managed to care for some horrifically injured patients, but I never treated them alone. I always flew with another skilled partner, either a paramedic or nurse. On top of this, we scooped them into the helicopter and speedily transported them to a hospital normally less than an hour away.

Truly the most practical thing we learned was how to improvise when you have no actual medical equipment on hand and you're hours or days from help. I learned how to make a splint out of hiking poles and what materials can be used to start a lifesaving fire. Pearls of wisdom to add to my outdoor expertise.

We spent half of our training outside practicing our newly learned skills, working in a group of three. As a group, we were handed a scenario where one of us would act as the patient, with the other two deciding how to treat and manage the victims using the skills from our lectures. Everyone had a blast, taking turns simulating being the patient and acting out an illness or injury, while the other two had to figure out what was going on.

One particular night, we went out after dark in the frigid cold to retrieve two people who had been in a simulated plane crash. We found our victims barely alive. To get our victims to safety, we had to stabilize them first. Of the many mock scenarios we carried out, this one involved clumsily navigating down a narrow, rugged trail through the forest while lugging a person's dead weight on a stretcher. It was tedious work, and as I was assisting with the carry I tripped on the wet rocks and fell. It could have just as easily been a fractured ankle, but luckily it only resulted in a bruise on my leg. During the simulation, my mind stayed busy with thoughts like: Are these scenarios from actual previous incidents? Are these the type of patients I could potentially find myself dealing with?

The following afternoon our whole class took our lunch break outside, and with the cooler temperatures a crust of ice had formed around the lake's edge. Jordan took his jacket off and suddenly jumped into the cold lake. It was an unexpected move that surprised us all, but we soon realized it was part of our training. We sprang into action, with two of the students pulling him out of the icy water. Taking the circumstance as a real danger, we stripped him out of his wet clothes down to his underwear, covered him with a jacket, and carried him a quarter-mile uphill to the lodge. In this case, he could have rapidly become hypothermic in only a few minutes. Point taken, bad things can happen anywhere, anytime, and YOU might be the one who can save the day.

The snow began to fall on our final morning at the lodge, with fresh powder blanketing the ground. The snow was coming down hard, and the forecast predicted snowfall for the remainder of the day.

The class finished early so we could safely get back over the mountains before the roads became treacherous. It seemed that no one wanted to leave, having had a memorable time with a group of strangers who left as friends. I have always treasured this unique excursion and the memories made.

One of the other nurses and I caught a ride back to Seattle with Jordan. This ended up being the perfect time to discuss working opportunities at his company. Jordan was very encouraging as he shared information on the various job postings and locations available. Everything from movie sets to jobs in Greenland—I was smitten. I was given the number with instructions to contact HR, and without hesitation I called as soon as I got back to Seattle. I had no trouble getting an appointment and was asked to stop by before flying back to Phoenix the next day. Perfect, this was my plot all along.

Lindsey, the HR manager, took the time to explain more about the company and what it would be like working for Remote International. She informed me that the company was currently accepting applications for new positions. Following our discussion, she handed me an application and instructed me to fill it out and return it along with my resume.

The company had sixteen openings; they were hiring both instructors and medical staff to fill various remote contracts worldwide. Jordan had mentioned they were the medical support for the famous TV series *Ice Road*

Truckers. He also spoke of having contracts in Greenland, the tropics, and on a variety of ships, all of which sounded enticing. Lindsey informed me that the company had already received more than four hundred applications and would be narrowing the list down to just seventy two. Next came a three-day interview, where an invitation would be extended to the lucky ones to make the shortlist. The numbers were discouraging, and the odds of being invited to the interview seemed nil. Oh well, I did have a varied work history and decided to proceed toward making the cut. I would not allow my pessimistic thoughts to slow me down. I never expected this quest to be anything but arduous.

Looking back over my shoulder at my past life, I had dealt with my fair share of grueling ordeals. Beyond the emotional toils, there had been plenty of adversity during nursing school. Even in high school, I had never been an A student and had always worked hard to achieve B's or C's. Twice I came close to getting kicked out of the nursing program. Once was when I screwed up my microbiology project. We were given an unknown organism and had to work through a process to identify what cell form we had. I somehow messed up the slide stain and was three weeks into the class when I realized something was wrong. The professor had little patience in helping me get on track, and I finished the course with a D. Another time I was in the hospital doing my clinicals and had been assigned to one of the staff nurses who would be my mentor for three weeks. I must have drawn the short straw as she was a mean and unhelpful tutor. One day, I left the floor to meet up with our instructor and the other students for the weekly post-clinical debriefing. Before leaving, I missed giving my assigned patient her noon medication and forgot to tell my mentor. I got written up and received a verbal warning.

Looking forward to the next challenge, I pondered, of the seventy selected applicants, which of them would be willing to put forth the most effort?

Making the Cut

If you strive for the moon, maybe you'll get over the fence.

~ *James Wood*

When the confirmation letter arrived with an invitation to the three-day hiring workshop at Remote International, I was shocked. After all the effort I made to attend the advanced-provider course and taking the time to chat with Lindsey, I was now seeing the fruits of my labor. What was more, I had climbed up the career ladder a few rungs higher than most, and my impressive resume validated just that. With the help of a professional resume writer, I was given the much-deserved attention. Not to brag, but I had worked extremely hard to get to this point.

In January 2011, I went back to Seattle. The location for the intense three-day interrogation was just outside Leavenworth, Washington. It was again in an outdoor setting surrounded by large pines with the addition of fresh waist-deep powder. There was a central lodge, and the ten beautiful rustic cabins were our assigned accommodations. Remote International certainly had the right idea of holding their sessions in unique remote venues.

My roommate, Genova, was from just outside London, England, where she worked as a paramedic. Like many other candidates, she was an out-doorsy, adventure-seeking soul looking to take her career to a new level. We were both feeling overwhelmed and stressed. Interviewees were under the microscope from the moment we arrived until noon on the third day, when the interview process would cease.

This was crazy. Who has ever been through a three-day interview? It was a perplexing, demanding, and intriguing ordeal. It started with introductions, and then we were placed in teams of four with the task of electing our team leader. My team chose Nell, a guy with a confident, strong personality. We had not even been there an hour when the action started, summoning us all to a mock car accident. We had no medical equipment. The scenario played out like this—there was no cell reception, we were three hours from medical aid, and we had four injured victims, two critical. Now go.

It was pretty much nonstop from there. We were awakened at 0400 the following day to search for a missing person in the forest. We hiked up a hill in the deep snow to reach our casualty, who was nonambulatory. We carried him down in the dark and then had to start an actual IV on him outside in the cold. I was assigned the task but missed my first try, a strike against my score. The frown on our team leader's face displayed his disappointment. Embarrassment overcame me, and I felt my stomach tighten. I wanted to cry but held it back.

The most insane scenario we had to manage involved an individual who had fallen over a cliff. You could hear him yelling for help from where we were, but you could not get to him or get a visual. We were required to assess the patient via a verbal discussion with him, which revealed that the person had sustained a punctured lung from the fall, a critical injury. Using verbal communication, I instructed the patient to find an item in his backpack and guided him to self-decompress a pneumothorax, that is, air in the chest cavity. The injured person was panic-stricken and argued that he couldn't do what I asked him to do.

To succeed at this skill station, you have to not only convince him to do as directed but also to shove a sharp object, like an ink pen, between his ribs to release the air causing the collapsed lung. Unfortunately, Aron Ralston wasn't my victim (*Between a Rock and a Hard Place*). If you remember the story, Aron cut off his own arm to save his life. I passed the ridiculous challenge.

Remote International put a great deal of thought into gauging our abilities through nonstop testing and scenarios. We were scored individually in some of the challenges, and in some we were marked as a team. We were thrown everything from cardiac arrest, antibiotic recognition, managing and setting up transport for a suicidal person via the radio, to personal interviews. When noon came on the third day, I felt more confused and unsure than I did on day one. They sent us home and said they would notify us of the results in a couple of weeks.

I felt good about some things and knew I performed weakly in others. I presume everyone must have felt the same. No matter the outcome, this course forced me to think unconventionally, and I gained an immense amount of knowledge. More than just an interview, we also would receive continuing education credit and something unique to add to the resume.

The notification came via email that I had not made the final cut. I was sorely disappointed. I did not know it at the time but later realized it was a blessing in disguise. Nell, my team's leader, was one of the few who made it but was still waiting for a job assignment six months later. By this time, he was contacting me asking about other job opportunities.

I Am Good Enough!

Follow your inner moonlight.
Don't hide your madness.

I highly suggest as you go through life to secretly have at least a Plan B and, even more wisely, a Plan C stashed in your pocket. My Plan B went like this. While I was at the advanced-provider class in November, I spoke in-depth to the offshore medic about his company and job. FrontierMedex was headquartered in the UK. The medic had shared with me the contact information and company details. This time I was not going to be able to walk into their office and directly inquire about a position.

My previous failure left me feeling somewhat uncertain. In reality, this was an irrational notion, and it was foolish to allow this one rejection to get in my head. I needed to keep my eye on the ball in other words to remain focused on my goal. No excuses, period.

After further researching the company, I decided to inquire if they could use me as one of their remote nurses, having no idea where in the world it might lead. I contacted them and learned that I needed to first forward my *curriculum vitae*, otherwise known in the United States as a resume. For the record, everywhere else in the world asks for your CV, not a resume.

Several days went by, and I'm not exactly a patient person. Finally, the HR person got in touch and requested that I fill out more paperwork and let me know that, yes, Frontier would like to talk to me. I was ecstatic. WOW, could this really be happening? A hundred what-ifs filled my mind. What if they hired me, where might I go, what about leaving my family, etc.

A few days later, Adriana called and informed me that Frontier was interested but wanted to make sure they shared details of how they operated and what to expect if they hired me. She explained that the next step would be for the organization's medical director to call me to have a discussion. The interview with Dr. Wilson went well. I was nervous, but he didn't ask anything I couldn't answer. After being quizzed on some basic emergency medical questions, he inquired about my work experience. His voice assured me he was pleased with my answers. I knew on the spot that I had made the cut this time.

Making it to this point took commitment and drive. I continually got back up after falling down countless times. It had taken years of preparation. My moment had come, and I had earned it.

Now what? It was February 2011. The next steps included more paperwork and documents to be completed then sitting back and waiting for Frontier to find me a position. At the time of my hiring, Frontier did not have any openings for me. They assured me that something would come up but did warn me it could be a few months.

In the meantime, Adriana planned to accompany her husband to Las Vegas as he had a business trip there. She asked if I would mind traveling to Vegas to meet with her. She said it would be a good time to learn more about each other and an opportunity for me to get any additional questions or concerns answered.

I made the short jaunt over to Vegas the night before our scheduled meeting. Getting together with Adriana was pleasant and worthwhile. One of the main reasons she wanted to talk with me was to assess my mental frame of mind. Could I handle traveling, working, and being in a far-off location? It ended up being a talk of "do we fit?" Frontier was making an investment in hiring me. If I couldn't cope with working in an austere environment for some reason, it would be costly for the company.

After hearing about some of my many adventures, she said she worried I might actually be bored working for Frontier. I could not imagine that happening, and I was definitely willing to take a chance. I expressed that I highly doubted working in a foreign land would be overly dull. This meetup was productive for both parties, and I had a better understanding of Frontier while Adriana learned more about who I was on a professional and personal level.

So, what about this company, FrontierMedex? Who are they anyhow? Adriana enlightened me. Frontier, for short, is a thirty-year-old company that puts medical professionals in remote locations around the world. A vast majority of their contracts are in the oil and gas sector with offshore and onshore projects.

I wondered how long it would take them to find me a job. Would it be weeks or months? How long a notice would I get? What might the conditions be like? Would I be sorry I decided to try this?

During this same time, I worked per diem as a registry nurse for the Abrazo hospitals in Phoenix. The position allowed me to control when and for the most part where I worked a shift. There was no shortage of nursing shifts available, and during the summers I was also going out and working as a medic on wildfires all around the southwest United States.

It was May, and I had not heard anything from Frontier since April. Then one day, my phone rang as I was working a shift at Baptist Hospital in the ICU ward. It was an international number, so I stepped into an empty patient room and answered the call. I heard a distinct English accent. "Jonea, we have a position we hope you might consider." The woman came across timid and hesitant but continued, "Frontier has a need for a female medic in Iraq." There was a pause. "And it's for a land project for BP."

I felt she was waiting for me to respond with a "No, thank you," but she went on to give me a few other details, mentioning that they felt the camp could use a female's influence. They thought I might be a good fit and asked if I would please think about it for a couple of days, then let them know my answer.

Now, I did not expect Iraq! There had just been a war there, and the media was continuously reporting about terrible things still happening over there. Iraq! It's not exactly an exotic tropical island, and I presumed it would be a rugged environment, but it sounded pretty exciting. After thinking about it for about two minutes, I knew I wanted to go. I knew my parents would be less than excited to hear I was going to agree to work in the Middle East.

Later that evening, I called my son Drew and said, "Hey, Frontier called me. Guess where they asked me to go?"

He guessed, "Africa."

"No."

"China?"

"No, Iraq!"

His voice betrayed worry as he quizzed me for details. I shared the news with the rest of my kids, family, and friends, and as I suspected my parents were less than thrilled. Telling my family my plan was comparable to a seventeen-year-old telling his mother he had just joined the marines.

My daughter, Angie, was skeptical and alarmed about me going off to Iraq. She was pregnant with her first child and was counting on me being there when the baby arrived. When I accepted the job, I mentioned this to Frontier. They assured me they could arrange for me to be stateside for the birth of my first grandchild.

Brock was just finishing his degree at Arizona State University and was in the process of joining the Navy. At first, he raised his eyebrows at my decision, but knowing his mom's crazy passion for adventure and my prior history of being a daredevil, he knew I had found my next enthralling odyssey.

Jan was on his own path. He had decided that college wasn't in his stars and had moved back to Indiana to live with my parents on the family farm. My new career move did not come as a surprise to my eighteen-year-old son. He was excited for me and was aware this was a big milestone in my life.

People's thoughts were so varied; some thought I was totally crazy, and others believed it would be an adventure of a lifetime. Everyone who knew me well was aware of my love of adventure. Living on the edge enticed me, and over the years I had become a bit of a thrill seeker, especially if it involved a physical challenge. I have always attributed my daredevil spirit to my father—a not-so-common farmer who had his own small plane, took his family a hundred miles into the Canadian wilderness for vacations, and purchased a trading post in a small village in Alaska. I had for sure inherited his DNA.

Iraq was still in the news almost daily, and although things had started to settle somewhat, there were still bombings, IED explosions, and rockets being fired at the remaining US troops. People were still dying. Iraq wasn't exactly a vacation spot.

The following day I called and let Frontier know I would accept their offer. Adriana voiced how pleased she was that I had agreed to step up to the task. I could tell they were relieved I had accepted the position. What woman in her right mind would offer to go to Iraq?

The big house, as we referred to it

The kids and I at the big house, Drew, Jan, Angie, Brock and me

Travel Chaos

*Don't tell me the sky's the limit. There
are footprints on the moon!*

~ Dorothy Parker

The next few weeks involved more paperwork. I
was required to have a thorough medical exam,
then apply for an Iraqi visa, and obtain a Letter of
Invitation (LOI), which is part of getting approval to enter
the country. The LOI would allow me to come there to work
and stay for the approved period. I was told that sometimes
the Iraqi papers could get approval in twenty days, and then
other times it could take three months. There was no telling
when the approval would come through. Frontier was hoping to get me in the country sometime in mid-July.

Every imaginable thought was pumping through my head,
from feeling proud that I was achieving my goal to being scared shitless.
Despite being proud and happy for me, my parents wished I could have been
heading to some more pleasant locale. I didn't want anyone to worry about
me. I felt that it had to be somewhat secure or BP wouldn't be allowing their
people to work and travel there.

Life started getting hectic. I was making ready to embark on a new career and life adventure while another part of my past was closing. I had lost
my beautiful dream home to the bank. In the US housing crisis, over six
million homes went into foreclosure, and I was just one of the millions of
Americans who had to walk away. Losing the battle and having to walk away

from something you poured your guts into is absolutely heartbreaking. I had worked as many as five jobs at one time to support my kids and give them a beautiful and stable home to live in. Then, when the economy fell apart, there was little work available, and I couldn't even find a single full-time job. I was digging my financial grave by trying to hang onto the house, and when it came down to the wire I turned my back on the impossible situation and headed in a different direction.

When I was trying to get organized to leave for the Middle East, I was in the process of moving out of what my family called "the big house." It was huge, with five bedrooms, and my family had made so many memories in that great big house. It seemed surreal as I made one last trip between my old and new address with my belongings.

In early July, I was still waiting for my Letter of Invitation to come through, and Frontier was trying to arrange for me to attend the mandatory Hostile Environmental Training (HET). I remember thinking, *Wow, this sounds cool and entertaining!* All the expats working on this contract for BP had to attend a two-day course in the UK, just outside of Liverpool. Frontier struggled to get everything to line up time-wise so they could get me into Iraq and asked how much notice I needed before deploying. I requested a week, minimum, but would take whatever I got. The plan was to fly to the UK, attend the class, and then go by rail down to Mitcheldean for a project briefing in Frontier's head office before continuing onward to Iraq for my first rotation.

One thing that crossed my mind as I was preparing the numerous forms and information they requested was that I hoped that FrontierMedex was a reputable organization. What did I really know about them? I did not want to find myself in a situation in Iraq, hoping that the company would have my back if something went awry. I started feeling more comfortable as more of the paperwork seemed to cover every detail. I knew this was the real deal when I started filling out the proof of life document! Essentially proof of life is a way for your family to ID you and contains confidential information that they would use to confirm whether a person is still alive in case of kidnapping, abduction, or detention. My head was whirling. What was I getting myself into?

Things were falling into place. My Letter of Invitation came through, and Frontier had booked flights, purchased train tickets, and confirmed my seat in the HET course.

On Saturday evening, the ninth of July 2011, I boarded a massive 777 British Airways jet. I was psyched! Once on board, I found my window seat in the back section of the airplane and organized my things: a book, water bottle, and jacket. Unlike domestic flights, international flights start boarding one hour before departure, so I had time to settle in for the nine-hour journey. People kept pouring in, and it became apparent that this would be a full flight.

My anticipation grew, having never visited Europe before. Of course, I had experiences in foreign travel, crossing a few places off my bucket list. My memorable adventures included Africa (twice), Mexico (of course), Costa Rica, and who could forget Canada? For the first time in my career, I was being paid to travel and was tickled pink that I wasn't paying for this trip.

From my seat, I noticed that a seasonal monsoon was building southeast of the airport. With its colorful lightning, the storm was slowly working its way into Phoenix. In the back of my mind, I was hoping that we would get out before the storm reached the city.

The plane jerked back from the jet bridge and stopped. Several minutes went by, and the passengers began to grow restless as the temperature in the aircraft increased. We continued to wait for what seemed like forever when finally the pilot's voice crackled through the intercom. "Hi, folks, apologies for the delay. We have had a mechanical issue that has caused a slight delay. Since we have already pushed back from the gate, we aren't able to connect to the ground air conditioning system."

It was July in Phoenix, and we were stuck in a giant metal tube on the tarmac. Not cool, literally! People started undressing their kids, and the flight attendants ran out of water to give out. We were there for no less than one and a half hours. I was so glad that I had brought two large bottles of water with me and that I lived in the hot desert and had a high tolerance for the heat. I felt terrible for those suffering; little old women were fanning themselves, while others were pouring sweat. Then at long last, the pilot told us we were nearly ready, and the air conditioning had at least now started re-cooling the plane.

Gazing out the window, I realized the storm had rolled into Phoenix, and the wind was twirling dust through the night air, lightning sliced the low, dark clouds like a mad warrior defending his clan. I knew enough about flying to know what the next announcement would be. "Ladies and gentlemen, sorry, but we need to hold up till this storm passes, maybe another twenty minutes or so."

Three hours and twenty minutes late, the Boeing Triple Seven pushed out onto the tarmac and proceeded to taxi. We lined up with the dozens of other delayed aircraft trying to leave Phoenix. Thirty minutes later, "Good evening once again from the cockpit. Sorry folks, but we have now burned too much fuel and will need to return to the gate to take on additional fuel." Were we ever going to get out of here?

The long delay in Phoenix was only the start of the headaches yet to come on this journey. Arriving late into London caused me to miss my connecting flight up to Liverpool. It was Sunday afternoon, and Frontier's office was closed. I was instructed to call the on-call duty officer if any issues arose over the weekend or after office hours.

I had made few, if any, international calls from outside the United States, and honestly international phone numbers confused the dickens out of me. Trying to figure them out gave me anxiety.

There is nothing like learning on the fly. I now had no choice but to figure out how to contact the duty officer and get some advice on my current situation. First, I found a phone booth, and yes some places like Heathrow Airport still have phone booths. Standing there, I stared at the unfamiliar number I held in my hand. Confused, I asked myself, "Do I need to dial 011 to place this call? Oh, wait!" It suddenly dawned on me that I needed to get some local change for the P-A-Y phone. I returned with the correct change and plugged the British coins into the pay phone. With the amount of quid needed for a phone call, I crossed my fingers and carefully dialed the number, leaving off the 011. Boy, was I pleased to hear the familiar ringtone on the line. After a deep inhale, I prepared to give my explanation, but guess what? No answer. The call went to voicemail, so all I could do was leave my name and report my situation. Feeling perturbed, I quietly thought, *Wait, isn't this supposed to be the emergency call number? And what if it was a real emergency?* Actually, it felt like it was!

Minus the assistance of Frontier, I would have to figure this out on my own. Somehow, I needed to find my way to the town of Whitchurch, located more than one and a half hour's drive outside of Liverpool. For the record, HET class started at 0830 the following morning. Grateful that I was at least in an English-speaking country, I headed for the British Airways customer service counter, where a friendly gray-haired gentleman greeted me. The service agent informed me that the next flight to Liverpool did not leave until early morning. Feeling frazzled, I accepted the fact that traveling by airplane was not going to work.

The kind man told me to wait a minute, and thirty seconds later returned with the train schedule. He confirmed that if I got a move on, I could get there that night by train as he proceeded to write down the steps I needed to follow. Agreeing to the plan, he next called the baggage department and instructed them to retrieve my bags so I could claim them for my journey by train. I repeatedly thanked the kind man as I rushed away from the desk.

Heathrow is a massive and complex airport, and being there for the first time increased my anxiety. When I got down to baggage claim, my bags had yet to be found, so I paced around, watching the time and looking for someone to ask for assistance. After spotting the baggage claim office, I got in line with half a dozen others. My blood pressure started climbing as I nervously waited my turn. The clock was ticking, and I had forty-five minutes to get from Heathrow to Euston Station, twenty minutes away. My goal was to get there in time to catch the last train of the day to Whitchurch. "Crap, hurry up, would ya! I can't miss that train," I whispered under my breath.

Frontier had a difficult time getting me a spot in THIS class, so I felt compelled to do everything in my power to get there. If I failed, who knew when there would be another opening. Besides, I was unsure how this would go over. After all, I was working for a new company. At last it was my turn, and I hoped the woman behind the counter could help. After listening to my explanation, the woman picked up the phone, and a minute later, she said, "You can go wait by the carousel."

I raced back up two levels toward the airport storage desk with my luggage in hand. In the additional ten minutes at the airport, I had decided that leaving one of my large suitcases behind would undoubtedly save me time plus lessen my struggle and frustration. At least I had been smart enough while packing to divide up what I needed for traveling to the UK and what I didn't.

Many people in Europe and around the world travel by train on a daily basis. It's the norm, but for us Americans...not so much. I must confess my knowledge of train travel wasn't so great.

Having secured a ticket for the seventeen-minute ride to the Euston station, I felt hugely relieved knowing I had conquered this first obstacle. I collapsed into a seat next to the window, immediately closed my eyes, and mouthed a "thank you," not sure who I was really thanking.

Once I exited Euston station, my instructions were to walk two blocks to a different station to catch the northbound train. Looking around, I had no clue which direction to go, so I started to ask a few people passing by. "Can you please tell me where Paddington Underground station is?" I finally realized the majority of the people rushing down the street were heading to the same station.

With only eight minutes between trains, I quickly queued up, as the Europeans say, to buy another ticket to my destination. Looking down at my watch with four minutes to spare, I was relieved that I was going to make it. Smiling as I approached the ticket counter, the ticket agent greeted me with, "You're cutting it pretty close, young lady."

I could only think, *Dude, if you only knew!*

Now able to breathe easy, I started to unwind, knowing things were coming together. The past twelve hours of chaos left me exhausted. The butterflies in my stomach now were replaced with grumbles of hunger. Luckily, there was a food stand next to the platform where I was about to board the incoming train, so I quickly ordered some unknown fried food item and two bottles of water. As I was stuffing my dinner into my backpack, the train squealed to a stop. Hot damn, so far, so good.

Unsure how the boarding process worked, I followed the impatient passengers in front of me while trying to manipulate my awkward belongings— one large forty-pound bag, a roller bag, and my backpack. Why'd I bring so much stuff? At this moment, I realized how smart it had been to have left the other hefty bag at Heathrow.

I felt my blood pressure rising again as those behind me acted annoyed that they had to wait twenty-two seconds as I manhandled my luggage. I wondered if everyone in England was always short on patience and unfriendly. In the two and a half hours I'd been in the country, I had met only one helpful, kind soul.

After securing my bags in the luggage rack, I sat my exhausted body down on a nice comfortable seat in a quiet car. The train lunged forward, and we were on our way north. After enduring a two-hour and fifty-minute ride, it would be late when I arrived at the Whitchurch station. My next thoughts turned to how I would get to the hotel. I didn't know how to call a taxi using my cell phone.

Opening my backpack, I took out the mysterious food item I had recently purchased, unwrapped it, and took a bite of warm fried crust—yum. The inside had some kind of meat substance filling, like a meat pie thingy. I wolfed it down like a poorly behaved dog and settled into my seat for the long ride to my next destination.

Several minutes into the ride, I started thinking, *Hey, anyone could hop on and ride the train without paying.* In the next second, the smartly dressed conductor appeared, just like in the movies, approached me and asked for my ticket.

"Ma'am." I hate being addressed as ma'am.

"Yes, sir?"

"You can't sit here. There's an extra charge for this car," he said and turned and walked away. Without more of an explanation, I had no idea where I should be sitting.

I called after the conductor to get his attention. "Where do I need to go?" He never looked back and continued to the next car. "Nice," I said aloud.

A distant-looking woman peered over her book and said, "You need to move up there a couple of cars," as she motioned toward the forward car by rolling her face in that direction.

The funny thing was I'd never really felt like a second-class citizen until I started traveling internationally. Collecting my bags from the stowage, I proceeded to drag them down the impossibly narrow aisle, realigning them every five feet. I had always been an independent woman, but at that moment I was questioning what had happened to chivalry. Was it, in fact, dead? It would have been a welcoming gesture to have a hand here, as my long travel day was getting longer. I made my way to the cheapo seats in a forward section of the train. Hard, cold, and uncomfortable, the seats seemed to be part of a punishment, but I was not alone.

The train made dozens of stops along the route, and as we got closer to my destination, I started worrying about the taxi situation. How would I manage to call a cab when I arrived at Whitchurch station? Hoping to find some answers, I started a conversation with a friendly young lady sitting behind me. When I mentioned my dilemma, she told me not to worry and that there were always taxis at the stations, but if not, just wait a little bit, and one would show up.

Finally, at 12:20 a.m., the train slowed into Whitchurch. I made my way through the station and stepped out into the street. Greeted by the damp night air, I shivered from the sudden chill, and a new sense of excitement spread down my spine.

"Wow, I'm in England!" Walking toward the signposted taxi, I spied one lone cab parked ahead of me and simultaneously noticed a man dressed in business attire walking around to the car's other side and getting in. The car zoomed off before I could reach the driver to ask if there might be another cab soon. Surveying my surroundings, I realized there was virtually nothing there but a quiet, dark street in some kind of tiny village: no stores, businesses, or other passengers in sight. I had no clue where I was. It wasn't long before I turned, looked over my right shoulder, and much to my relief saw a familiar yellow car slowly approaching.

An ancient male removed himself from the right front seat and met me at the cab's rear. We lifted my annoying luggage into the boot. I started to follow him to the front seat when I remembered that the driver sits on the right in this country. I handed him the piece of wrinkled paper that contained the name but no specific address, MacDonald Hills Valley Hotel and Golf. "Mmmm, I think I know where this place is." Crap, I hope so. He asked me where I was from and what I was doing wandering around in the middle of the night. The thought did cross my skull that this was a dark and lonely place, and no one really even knew where I was.

We headed down the road driving for about fifteen minutes, when the cabbie pulled over and asked to see the hotel's name again. He turned the car around and after another ten minutes turned down a narrow lane, and then we saw the small, faded sign. Within five minutes, I was standing in the lobby of a beautiful little resort. The staff were so kind. "We have been waiting for you." The woman at the check-in gave me instructions for my pickup for the morning, and the bellhop assisted me to my room.

I was excited and proud of myself. Woo hoo! I pulled this fiasco off, and I had succeeded in figuring out my travel drama. It was hard to sleep even though I was drained and could now unwind. This was my first trip to this part of the world, and I could not wait 'til the sun came up so I could see where I was.

Don't Cry Wolf

There are nights when the wolves are
silent and only the moon howls.

~ *George Carlin*

After a seemingly short night, I was up when the sun peeked out. I jumped out of bed and scanned my surroundings, trying to see through the low-lying fog in the distance. The sun quickly burned off the haze, and I could view the beautiful garden and grounds surrounding the resort. MacDonald Hill Valley Hotel was in a rural setting on a lush golf course lined with mature fir trees on the greenest greens I've ever seen.

The resort was in such a quiet, quaint setting. The hotel consisted of a single building, only two stories tall, with thirty rooms. It included a spa, indoor pool, and a lovely little restaurant that served the typical English fare, including a traditional English breakfast.

The famous British breakfast contains sausages, baked beans, stewed tomatoes, eggs made to order, mushrooms, English muffins, and tea or coffee. Then there's the black pudding. Black pudding is not a pudding at all but a sausage made from pig's blood, onions, herbs, spices, oatmeal, or barley. Yummy . . . not really. As the saying goes, try everything once, and I did. I tasted it but found it to be nasty stuff.

Sitting down to enjoy my plentiful breakfast, I felt the sensation of the underlying tiredness pulling at my core. Anticipating an exciting but long day, I hoped the three cups of coffee I drank would sustain me for at least a few hours. While waiting in the lobby, I noticed four other men lingering nearby, and after asking I learned they were also taking the Hostile Environmental Training course. Soon after, our transportation arrived, and the cordial driver ushered us to a van to take us to the site of our program. Inviting me to take a seat in the front beside him, I immediately thought, *It pays to be the sole woman in the mix of a male-dominated vocation.* Pleased to have a premium seat, I buckled in and took in the beautiful countryside I had missed in the dark a few hours earlier.

Our driver introduced himself and gave us details of our schedule for the next two days. He forewarned us that the material covered in training would be highly intensive, and we would be working through lunch. The hotel would be providing us with a sack lunch each day.

After discussing the programming, our driver shifted the conversation to the history of the training site. The lowdown was that the grounds sat on the edge of the historic Combermere Abbey, founded in 1133. A former Cistercian monastery, the building was later converted into a country house, and I wondered how a building could remain intact for more than 875 years.

The thirty-minute ride brought us to our destination, and our driver promised he would show us around Combermere Abbey later, but now we needed to get our training started. The Abbey was perched on a hill several hundred yards away from our classroom, and I was in awe of the view.

The training class required my full attention, and I immersed myself in the coursework. With a specific focus on Iraq, we delved into topics like what to expect while working in the Middle East, cultural sensitivity, personal security measures, and how to conduct oneself in hostile territory. Learning about anti-hostage techniques was captivating and terrifying at the same time. The instructors talked about who our enemies were and the protocol for traveling safely in unsafe countries.

Barely perched on the edge of my seat, I'm sure my wide-eyed stare was noticeable as the lecturer described some of the dangers of the terrain. Improvised explosive devices (IEDs) and unexploded ordnance (UXO) were just a few of the risks we needed to be aware of, as there were hundreds of thousands of landmines leftover from the war.

The training site even had a simulated minefield set up as a visual aid for identifying various explosive devices. During the two-day training, we worked through role-playing scenarios, and the drills were as realistic as they could make them. If we were ever in a bad situation, these survival techniques would give us the best advantage possible. We donned a bullet-resistant vest and a helmet and set out on our first exercise. I hadn't anticipated the weight of the gear, and maneuvering in the field was immediately cumbersome. It was something I'd have to get used to if I was going to succeed in the trenches. First, we were bombed and had injured personnel to deal with. Next, our armored vehicle became disabled during an attack, so we had to transfer to another vehicle safely. The security men literally pulled us out of the stalled truck, threw us into the back of another SUV, and took off. The protective gear made it harder to move quickly during the transfer, but the adrenaline rush certainly helped.

During the training, our instructors stressed that the number one thing to remember out in the field was to follow the protocols given to us by our security teams. It was their responsibility to watch out for our safety, but our responsibility was to minimize risk by following their directions.

At the conclusion of the day, I felt the need to let down my hair and unwind. Upon returning to the hotel, I grabbed my running shoes and headed outdoors. I intended to explore the picturesque surroundings while jogging a lap around the fairway while I still had some daylight. Running had always been my way to escape and decompress. Besides, the past few days I had been confined to sitting, and my legs needed a stretch. As dusk overtook the day, the last of the golfers headed toward the pub, where they were no doubt enjoying a round of cocktails while comparing their successful day of play. When it became too cold to continue, I retreated to the warmth of the resort.

Showered and dressed for dinner, I wandered down to the lounge, taking the last seat at the bar. To my left, a gentleman gulped down the last of his pint of beer, turned in my direction, and smiled. He politely welcomed me with, "Good evening." So I returned an equally polite but quick hello. Averting my eyes to the variety of brews displayed on tap, I only recognized Guinness and Heineken. The three other choices were unfamiliar and were more than likely regional beverages. Struggling to decide, my new acquaintance piped up and suggested that I try the cider.

"OK, I'll give it a go. So cider it is," I instructed the attractive bartender who was patiently waiting to take my order.

Within moments he served up a pint of the golden fizzy beverage. "A mug of Magners for ya, mum."

"Cheers," I replied as I tipped my mug's rim to my barmate. Raising the cold cider to my lips, the smell of sweet, crisp apples met my senses. "Mmmm, nice," I said. Refreshed after several gulps of cider, I ordered up another and found a table where I could enjoy my evening meal.

Once back in my room, I settled in for a quiet and peaceful evening with the gentle country breeze drifting through my open windows. The sun had left the sky, which signaled my last day at the resort. Setting out my suitcase on the bed, I leisurely folded my clothes and gently returned them to the same state they had arrived. Simultaneously, my mind raced with imaginative thoughts and premature images of the next few days and weeks ahead of me.

A chilling cry pierced the evening's silence, echoing outside my window. With my thoughts suddenly disrupted, I sprinted to the window and leaned my head out to investigate. Silence filled the darkness as I tried to eavesdrop on the bewailing. I waited. A moment later, a high-pitched *"ewyeww"* shattered the silence. Dismissing the clamor for what I thought was a couple of cats, I turned away from the window and returned to packing my suitcase. It was mere seconds until a distinctive female voice cried out, "Stop it! Please stop." Startled by the sound of the panicked cry, I peered into the darkness, only able to see a few yards out into the lawn. The night had returned to silence once again.

Did I imagine the voice? I listened to make sure, and then I heard a loud moan, seemingly coming from a line of trees off in the distance. I stood there helpless, wondering what I should do. I called out, "Hey, what's going on?" I waited for a response, then shouted, "Are you OK?" Still no reply. When the victim's cries and moans continued, I realized I had to find someone to help this poor person. I was so shocked that someone was being tortured and needed to be rescued, right here on the resort! I raced over to the phone, pressed the button to contact the front desk, and a young male answered the phone in his posh and pronounced English accent. I tried explaining to him the situation going on outside my window. He was slow to understand my urgency. "Sir, someone is being attacked and needs help."

"Madame, I'll send someone out to check."

A male figure appeared moments later, and I watched as he scouted the area below my window. Finding no apparent evidence, the man looked up at me and called out, asking me from which direction I had heard the cries. "Over there," I exclaimed as I pointed to the trees several yards out. From his unenthusiastic tone, he seemed slightly annoyed and perhaps thought I was overreacting. I had undoubtedly disrupted his calm evening. On the other hand, I'm thinking, *Dude, you want to find a body on the golf course in the morning?*

Suddenly the desperate whimpers again filled the cool evening air, louder and stronger than ever. The distressed woman's tone then changed without warning, sounding less like a cry for help. Hearing this, the investigator called out to me as he pointed to the window below mine. "Oh! She is . . . in there . . . Madame, it's coming from there. She's OK." My face instantly flushed with embarrassment, and I quickly retreated from the window as I realized my misjudgment. In the heat of the moment, the pair of passionate lovers hadn't bothered to close their window. I finished packing and climbed into bed, annoyed that the couple below had seemingly cried wolf and made me look foolish to the staff.

At breakfast the following day, I eyed all the couples and wondered who the guilty party was. The people-watching was as entertaining as the assumptions in my mind, although there was no clear culprit in sight. Time was ticking, so I gulped down my breakfast, retreated to my room, and put the thoughts behind me.

It was bittersweet to be leaving my lovely accommodations, and I wished I had more time to explore the area and nearby castles. It would have to wait for another time. Staying at the resort had been like a mini-holiday, but in reality I was actually on the clock, and with this in mind I still planned on enjoying my free time as best I could.

With the HET course now complete, it was time for me to focus on the next leg of my journey. That morning, I set off for more training at Frontier's head office, boarded yet another train, and trusted that my future travels would be less challenging than they had been thus far.

Kidnapping incident folder

Me at HET course with armored gear on

Simulated mine field

Please Don't Wake Me

Stay wild, moon child.

~ Riitta Klint

The southbound train ground to a halt at my next destination; I had arrived in Gloucester. Collecting my gear, I disembarked and made my way to the parking lot, where I met my driver, a middle-aged man wearing a black suit and driving a black sedan. To me, it was an impressive look, and having a driver in such a stylish get-up as my private escort made me feel important. As he led me to the car and placed my luggage in the boot, the gentleman introduced himself as Harrison. Once in the car, Harrison questioned where I was from and asked if this was my first trip to the United Kingdom.

"Yes, sir, it is."

Harrison was eager to share his knowledge of Gloucester and the surrounding area. "Ms. Mounsey, did you happen to see the tall spirals of Gloucester Cathedral as your train approached the city?" Harrison quizzed.

"Yes, I did see them. It made me curious about the huge church."

Harrison replied, "We have a few minutes to spare if you'd like to have a quick look."

"That would be awesome," I answered.

My chauffeur pulled into the lot next to the cathedral and quickly stepped out, rushing to open my door. His promptness was his way of being a courteous fellow, and I discovered that I liked being treated like a lady. "Please

45

take only five minutes," he requested as he pointed to the side entrance of the historic jewel.

With 1300 years of history behind it, the spectacular church had many stories to tell. I admired the medieval church's architecture and noticed several hair-raising gargoyles perched high overhead. These mythical creatures with evil faces, horns, and wings amused me as I wondered why a church would display these uninviting stone carvings on the roof. Harrison explained that these beasts have a purpose. First of all, the mouth with its tongue hanging out serves as a rain spout. Secondly, most medieval Europeans were illiterate, and the priest needed a visual reminder of the horrors of hell to drive people into the church. The installation of gargoyles on the building's exterior supported the idea that evil dwelled outside the church while salvation dwelled within

I was intrigued to learn that several famous films had scenes shot at the enormous cathedral, including *Sherlock, Dr. Who, Hollow Crown,* and Harry Potter. The massive house of God was an impressive sight. I wished I had more time to explore this landmark, but I had to keep to my schedule. I hoped to be back in the area one day and spend more time there.

Following a quick lunch at my hotel, Harrison drove me to Frontier's office in the village of Mitcheldean. Feeling nervous and tense, I pushed the elevator button for the third floor. When the doors opened, I found myself standing at the company's reception desk. I introduced myself to the soft-spoken lady sitting on the other side of the counter. "Please sign in and take a seat. I will let them know you have arrived."

A few minutes later, a stylishly dressed woman approached me. "Hello, I'm Ann. Nice to meet you finally. How was your trip?" I was led through the many departments while being introduced as the new hire for the BP project. Our stroll ended up in a small conference room where I joined another new employee. Nicky stood, shook my hand, and gave me a quick hug. Nicky would be what they called my back-to-back (btb) for the BP Iraq project, covering the opposite rotation when I went on leave and vice versa.

Nicky was a local nurse who lived only a short distance from Frontier's office. Although this was our first in-person meeting, Nicky had sent me an email a few weeks earlier, inviting me to her home for dinner following our office session. Grateful for the offer, I looked forward to a home-cooked meal and the chance to get to know Nicky on a more personal level.

Ann stepped out of the room, leaving us to chat while waiting for another staff member to come and start our briefing. We were both obviously excited. Nicky began by asking, "Have you ever contracted before?"

I responded, "No, have you?"

"Neither have I," she replied. Our chatter ended when Melinda entered and proceeded to familiarize us with the ground operations of the Rumaila Oil Operation's (ROO) project.

Melinda explained that Frontier had the medical contract for the Rumaila project and already had four people in place. The newly built Rumaila clinic, run by two operational leads (Ops) and two physicians, now needed additional medical support to serve the growing number of Iraqi and expat employees. The increasing need was why they hired Nicky and me, and with the title of remote medic our jobs would entail being the medical coverage for the north side of the oil field.

It surprised me when Melinda informed us, "You will be single-handedly crewing an armored ambulance each day, managing any injuries or illnesses outside the main camp." Pushing myself up in my seat, I swallowed hard and glanced at Nicky, wide-eyed. Her expression mirrored mine, and I was relieved to find that I wasn't the only one who felt out of my comfort zone.

Seeing our disturbed expression, Melinda tried to reassure us, saying, "You won't be alone. You'll have your ambulance driver, although he will probably only have minimal medical knowledge."

"Geez," I whispered. Discussing it further, neither of us had worked alone, and the thought of working solo was overwhelming, adding a whole new level to my already-growing anxiety.

Melinda went on to talk about the work schedule. Frontier's employees would be on a twenty-eight-day duty rotation. Twenty-eight days on base followed by twenty-eight days leave, which included our travel time to and from our home location. We would receive a daily wage for the twenty-eight days in Iraq and our travel time. If we needed to change our schedule for some reason, we would have to work it out between ourselves as a back-to-back team. BP booked and paid for our travel, and we would be entitled to business class seats. The wages weren't too shabby already and included hazard pay, so these perks were icing on the cake! I was getting more excited by the minute.

Crammed into the afternoon was an overload of information. Onboarding new employees included the briefing from Melinda plus countless forms that needed to be signed, acknowledgment of company procedures and protocols, and watching presentations highlighting other important information. I was delighted when the medical director, Dr. Wilson, made a brief appearance. Dr. Wilson had been the one who interviewed me and gave Frontier the thumbs-up to offer me a position. He welcomed us both and encouraged us to contact him anytime we had a question or concern.

With our brains saturated, we made one last stop before it was time to call it a day. Ann instructed us to help ourselves to the array of clothing in the uniform closet. Piled high were countless pairs of tan pants, gray polos, and cotton button-down shirts, both long and short-sleeved, all tagged with the FrontierMedex logo. "Please don't forget to grab a jacket. You'll need one when it starts to cool off." Finding space in my stuffed luggage for more was going to be complicated. I hadn't planned to acquire this many extra items. I'd have to find a way, even if it meant carrying them in my hands.

We were exhausted and headed to the door, informing Ann that Nicky would be driving me back to my hotel as we planned to have dinner together. It was a quick drive to Nicky's beautiful and cozy single-story cottage where she and her partner lived. Colorful flowers overflowed from the garden, and as we strolled around the property the sweet fragrance of lavender filled the air. Nicky pointed out several varieties of plants, some I recognized and some I didn't. Soon we were summoned to the kitchen and instructed to take a seat at the ornate table. Nicky's partner served a delicious home-cooked meal paired with wine and engaging conversation. Over dinner, we shared stories of our unique pasts, debated the details of the day, and shared many laughs. The evening flew by, and soon the vino started to take my head over; it was time to call it a day.

As planned, Nicky returned me to The Kings Head Inn, and I immediately felt that it had already been a long few days. Feeling knackered, I found my bed as soon as I entered my room and anticipated the word "tired" would become my middle name for the next few weeks.

The following day, Harrison picked me up on time and returned me to Frontier's office, where I finished the rest of the training. With an encouraging farewell from the head office, they sent me off to catch the afternoon train back to London's Heathrow International Airport.

As the train moved along the tracks, I gazed at the green fields and cityscapes that slipped by my window, collecting my thoughts of the past seven days. They had come and gone like a child anticipating Christmas Day, and I wondered how it would feel when I awoke from this dream. I expected disappointment to set into my soul, for I knew in my heart these kinds of opportunities didn't exist for the common sort. Could the moon ease my woe? Surely, I must be dreaming. Please don't wake me.

Gloucester Cathedral

The medieval Gloucester Cathedral

Touchdown in the Middle East

Follow Your Inner Moonlight

Heathrow was reportedly the second-busiest airport globally, which was likely why I found it frustrating to navigate. Thankfully, I had allowed myself more than enough time to retrieve my stored bag, check in, and take a few moments to sit and enjoy a glass of merlot before boarding my British Airways flight to Kuwait City.

Soon after we took off and leveled out, the flight attendants got busy and proceeded to serve our meal. With a few international flights under my belt, I was starting to notice this was the usual routine. Passengers are fed as quickly as possible, allowing them to settle in and relax during the rest of their flight. But this was not the case for me. During the six-hour flight, I was unable to unwind; I was anxious and nervous. It had been emphasized to me the importance of keeping track of my passport at all times. I must have gotten up every hour to check that no one had taken my passport out of my backpack, which was located in the overhead bin. My mind was heavy with other apprehensions; I worried about meeting up with the agent at the Kuwait airport. What would I do if I got left behind? But actually my biggest fear was working alone in the ambulance. I had never heard of such a thing. It sounded unsafe to have only one medically trained person manning an emergency vehicle. Thinking about it terrified me.

We touched down in Kuwait, and my sense of excitement instantly replaced my anxiety. I was in awe to officially be in the Middle East. My instructions were to go to the Pearl Lounge and wait for the agent to come find me. After taking the elevator up to the lounge, a beautiful young woman greeted me from behind the reception desk.

"Welcome! Passport, please." She checked me off the list and motioned me past the desk into the lounge. "Ms. Munziay, please have a seat. You're on the 9:30 flight to Basra, and someone will get your luggage and call your name when it's time."

This was my first experience being allowed into an airport lounge, but it would be far from my last. The brightly lit lounge was busy and filled with Westerners and Middle Easterners coming and going, so I found a quiet seat in the corner.

Sitting in the Pearl Lounge, it dawned on me how naive I was about Muslims and their culture as I timidly looked around the room. Until this moment, I hadn't given much thought to how to interact with this intriguing society. Suddenly, my curiosity awakened, and I became immersed in a world with people much different than myself.

Back in the United States and during my other world travels, I had seen a few Muslims, although I had never felt out of place until now. However, while sitting there I unexpectedly became very self-conscious. I felt naked among the well-covered locals, and it was apparent I was a white Christian woman in a foreign land. I felt like I stuck out like a sore thumb.

Culturally, everything was a learning experience for me. Most Muslim men wore the traditional white tunic called dishdasha or thoub with a checkered headscarf—a keffiyeh—and the women sported long black robes called abayas, their hair covered with a hijab. A few women wore a niqab, a face veil with only their black eyes peering out of the headdress. In contrast, the children were dressed in clothes very close to what Western kids would wear.

Seeing the men and women in the lounge with their long robes and head covering caused my heart to skip a beat as my mind revived a fond memory from my childhood. When I was nine years old, I saw an Arabian horse show with my aunt and uncle, who also bred and showed these superior animals. My favorite part of this event was the mounted Native Costume class. The rider's attire was a native Bedouin type, colorful, flowing cape, headdress, and scarf. The horse also wore decorated breast collars, tassels, and blankets. From a young age, I had known that my best-loved breed of horses, the Arabians, had originated in the Middle East. Sitting in the Pearl Lounge among these Middle Easterners, I hoped one day I would become more self-assured while traveling in their territory.

The lounge included a complimentary hot food buffet, non-alcoholic drinks (Kuwait is a dry country), a smoking room, and a prayer room. Feeling drained, I thought a couple of coffees would be the best way to pick up my energy levels. While grazing from the buffet, I eyed the many travelers, wondering who might be heading to Basra. The instruction sheet stated that I'd be escorted from the lounge to a charter jet for the next leg of the journey.

At 0850, a gentleman appeared and called out a list of names, none of which were even close to mine. Upon hearing their name, each person rose out of their seat, gathered their belongings, and exited the lounge. After reading the last name, the man disappeared as quickly as he arrived. Worried, I approached the reception desk to inquire if I had been left behind. The receptionist reassured me that there would be another group and that they would call my name shortly. I returned to my seat and waited.

In the meantime, a tall tanned Arab in his white thoub took the seat next to me. He greeted me with a quick hello and asked where I was going. After opening the door to conversation, he peppered me with questions.

Unsure how much information I should be sharing with this stranger, I gave little detail beyond the basics. When he found out I was a nurse, he told me I should come to work in Saudi Arabia and that I could get a well-paying job working at the hospital his brother ran. Perhaps he thought I would quit my current job and go to Saudi Arabia or was just curious about the foreigners that passed through here.

Finally, the escort returned to call out three more names, and I was relieved that one was mine. As the gentleman introduced himself, we collected our belongings, and he informed us that our checked luggage was waiting for us. We followed him downstairs to the customs booth, where he handed our passports to the immigration officers. We were cleared immediately without going through the long lines queued behind the Kuwaiti immigration desks.

Next, the escort ushered us to a waiting van that would drive us through the congested airport traffic. We only went a short distance to the far side of the tarmac and were assisted into a small building where they scanned all of our bags. Once inside, the other two gentlemen in my group introduced themselves.

"Hello, I'm Mark!"

"And I'm Russell. You must be the new medic."

Soon we were boarding the aircraft, a Hawker 400. The sleek private jet was designed for comfort, only allowing eight souls to fly in the cabin in oversized plush leather seats and classy polished wood decor.

With another experience to add to my quickly growing list of firsts, I was excited to have this unique opportunity to fly on a private Lear jet. The only comparison I had was when I toured the private plane that was flying Vice President Dan Quayle's mother from the airport in Wickenburg, Arizona.

The copilot was a very friendly American named Ron, and as he stored our luggage I found myself apologizing for my two large bags. He shrugged it off as I told him my bags were likely over the thirty-pound limit. Ron politely replied that it wasn't a problem this time as there were only three passengers on this flight. Can you imagine living in a remote camp for a month with only thirty pounds of belongings? Heck, I probably had twenty pounds in Frontier uniforms alone.

As I climbed the four steps and entered the jet, I felt a rush of adrenaline flood my body. I can only compare my mood to having a runner's high, that rare feeling when endorphins fill your veins and you reach a magical state of euphoria. Being just an ordinary woman, who would have ever thought I'd be awarded such an opportunity? Feeling like a celebrity, I chose a seat and buckled in.

Ron handed us each a cold water bottle, and as he took his seat in the cockpit he informed us that our flight would be ninety-two miles and take only twenty-five minutes. Due to the short distance, the plane remained at a lower altitude than a commercial jet would fly. Being closer to the ground gave me a fantastic view of the foreign land out my window. The landscape was an arid blanket of sand dotted with glowing sky-scraping towers, unmistakably the domain of oil production.

It felt surreal that I had finally landed in Iraq, and I could hardly believe it. After the long journey, it still felt like I was wandering, lost in a dream deep in my head. The jet landed, taxied off the runway, and shut the engines off near the terminal. As we exited the aircraft onto the tarmac, the airport transport approached, and Ron handed out our luggage. Not knowing how this worked, I followed the lead of the two other passengers. The bus carried us what seemed like only a hundred feet to the terminal. It would have been just as easy to walk the short distance. With our gear in tow, we walked up a set of stairs where we entered the airport. I was so thankful when one of the guys stopped to assist me with my suitcases up the narrow steps. Boy, I was so done with lugging my bags around and was looking forward to finally unpacking.

Upon entering the Basra airport, my instructions were to first proceed to the visa counter and hand over my passport and US$202 in crisp, new bills. I watched my associates head to the customs line, leaving me to figure out the following steps on my own. Without anyone to guide me as I approached the visa staging area, the sense of anxiety again returned. Suddenly I was overrun with two hundred people who just disembarked from a Turkish Air flight, aggressively pushing their way past me to queue up for the visa counter. No one cared that I had been there first, and I remember thinking, *How rude!* My thoughts then went straight to the people waiting for me and my desire not to make a bad first impression on the security team.

It did take a while, but one of the Iraqi agents saw me waiting and rescued me, bringing me to the front of the line. After the visa processing, I was one step closer to being done. Next was to line up to clear customs into the country, and I wondered what I would do if I was denied entry. With drops of sweat running down my back, I stepped up, offering my passport. A straight-faced, brown-eyed Iraqi reached out and quickly snatched the book away. Scanning through the book until finding the freshly pasted visa, he nodded his head at me to place my fingers onto the scanner sitting directly in front of me. It took me a few tries before getting the green light. Stamp, stamp came the approval as my passport received its blessing. "Welcome to Iraq," the agent said and gave a warm smile.

Wa-hoo! They let me in, and I was instantly relieved. Step three: find my meet-and-greet escort. Until now, I had never been one of those people you see greeted in the airport by someone meandering through the crowd holding up a sign. I glanced over a flock of bystanders searching for a placard with the BP logo. Before making my way into the waiting area, a guy leaned over the railing out of nowhere and said, "Hey, are you Jonee Mousee?"

Despite the incorrect pronunciation, I was more than happy to accept. "Yes, I am!"

"Well, follow me."

He led me to where a small group of people gathered, and I instantly recognized the two men from my flight.

Soon I was noticed as a new face, and everyone in the group welcomed me and introduced themselves. Shortly after assembling, we were escorted out of the airport and to the parking lot, where we donned our flak jackets and helmets then got into our designated vehicles.

The flak jacket is a sleeveless outer garment made of heavy fabric reinforced with metal or Kevlar plates and is worn as protection against bullets and shrapnel. It weighs around eight pounds and fits snuggly on all shapes and sizes with adjustable Velcro. The ballistic Kevlar helmet weighs 3.5 pounds, and the weight of the gear instantly brought me back to our HET training days. Wearing the gear was protocol to protect our skull if the unthinkable should happen, "just in case."

Within the first five minutes of having these essentials on, I discovered how awkward they were. The protective gear was hot and heavy and smelled of horrendous body odor. Along with the stench of old sweat, the helmet was so large that I had to hold it in place to see out from underneath it. In an emergency, no way would I be able to see my way out of the vehicle if I had to.

On the other hand, it was an adrenaline rush to be geared up and traveling in an armored convoy through a recent war zone. Every vehicle in the convoy had an armed guard riding shotgun and an armed driver. Of course, anyone with military experience would not think anything of this, but I felt like the big cheese.

If my previous coworkers could only see me now!

Honestly, it was a bit overwhelming to be in one of the most feared countries in the world, at least from an American's viewpoint.

Within a few kilometers of the airport, we pulled off into a dirt parking area known to many as the Dust Bowl. We transferred into a different armored convoy for the fifty-minute drive to the oil field's main camp, Rumaila. Traveling to Rumaila's camp was eye-opening as we drove along a two-lane freeway. There were no road lines on the pavement, no road signs of any type, no speed limit, mileage information, or highway markings. Vehicles passed us like they were racing in the Indy 500. The local drivers seemed impatient, and they would overtake us on the dirt shoulder when we were already in the far-right lane. It was total craziness, and I then understood another reason for the helmets . . . to protect our heads from road crashes.

The freeways weren't heavily traveled, used mainly by ancient-looking semis and heavy trucks pulling one or two trailers. These lorries looked unsafe and likely unmaintained. Bald tires seemed to be the norm, and the cargo was heaped high above the top of the trailers. Often, I saw trailers hauling huge rocks piled so high they looked like they would slide off onto the road at any second, and occasionally you would see loads dumped across the roadway. So much for weight limits or driving regulations! I wondered what the statistics of deaths and injuries from traffic accidents were beyond the regular roadside bombings.

Flare stacks off in the distance grew closer, and I knew we were nearing our destination. Burn stacks were common on oil fields, with bright orange fire and atrocious black fumes rolling out into the sky. I didn't know much then, but I later educated myself about oil fields to understand the hazards of working in this unfamiliar place. I learned that the function of continually burning flares was to burn off the natural gas that separated from the petroleum as they extracted it from the earth. Because the gas is highly combustible, they burn it off to prevent it from exploding, thus the burning flares.

After an hour of having the oversized helmet sliding back and forth, stressing my neck, I already had a headache. Arriving at the main gate of Rumaila Oil Operations, I took a deep inhale and breathed out a sigh of relief. Yet at that exact moment I also questioned whether I was prepared for what lay ahead.

As we approached the camp, my first thought was, *Whoa! What is this place?* It looked nothing like I imagined it would. From the front gate, all you could see was a large area surrounded by drab, boring concrete barriers. My first impression was that this place appeared to be very confined and dull. How was I going to survive here?

We were cleared through the gate as security checked our badges. Since they hadn't issued my credentials, I thought I might run into problems at the gate, but they checked my name off their list like I was a VIP entering a party. The airport caravan pulled into the camp, and we passed by the tennis courts. Seeing the grounds had been decorated with trees, grass, and flowers quickly changed my opinion. Things were starting to look more positive; maybe it would be alright. My first step outside the van took my breath away instantly. The air was thick and dense, making it laborious to suck enough oxygen into my lungs. I had experienced extreme heat before, but not like this. The temperature was more than 120°F, and it wasn't even noon yet. Imagine standing behind a Greyhound bus in Phoenix in July and inhaling the engine exhaust. That is the best explanation to describe the sensation.

The incoming gang dispersed with their luggage as quickly as they could. I looked up, wondering what I was supposed to do. A scrawny middle-aged man greeted me. He extended his hand and gave me a firm handshake. "Welcome to ROO. I'm Joc," he mumbled as he used his lips to squeeze the cigarette in the corner of his mouth. Joc made no effort to remove his cancer stick but instead grabbed my gear.

"Let's take your bags to your room." After Joc led me to my living quarters, he left me to freshen up and orient myself to my accommodations, instructing me to find my way over to the hospital. He pointed in a vague direction and vanished, leaving me to my own devices.

The living quarters looked like shipping containers, with three equal-sized cabins in each module. The prefabricated trailers were arranged in several rows, divided by sidewalks. It was a sea of off-white blocks, and the only differentiator was color-coded trim of red, yellow, blue, and green. These trailers made up the housing sections spread around the Rumaila Oil Operation's (ROO's) camp, and each expat had a cabin, which they shared with their back-to-back shift partner.

My cabin was located on the end of a yellow-colored unit and was surprisingly delightful and rather quaint. It was a simple room furnished with a single/twin bed, bedside nightstand, a desk, a chair, TV, telephone, kettle, a double-sided wall closet for stashing belongings, a private bathroom with a shower, and a mini-refrigerator supplied with bottled water, chocolate bars, soda, and juice packs. Everything was clean and seemed pretty new. Perhaps this was not going to be a bad gig after all.

I was too anxious to see the hospital to bother showering, so I dug out a clean outfit, changed, and wandered in the direction of the hospital. I must have seemed lost when I bumped into a friendly gentleman who offered to show me to the clinic's front door.

As I walked into the hospital, a staff member met me at the entrance. Jean had gray hair and was a well-tenured French physician who preferred to be called JP. Joc joined us from an adjacent room and offered to give me a grand tour of the hospital. The facility had two large patient treatment rooms, a smaller patient care room, two good-sized rooms for storage, two lavatories, and a small office that Joc claimed. The hospital had high ceilings and several tall windows that allowed the sunlight to flood the rooms. It was awe-inspiring for being essentially in the middle of nowhere. I was thrilled to become a part of the operation.

JP was one of two Western-trained doctors who worked at the clinic, and the other, Leon, was currently out on leave. Joc was an American medic and one of two clinical leads or clinic managers. Besides managerial duties, the clinical lead also treated patients under the supervision of the doctors. Joc had been the first health care provider on the ROO several months before the addition of the doctors.

Joc escorted me to the security office, leaving me with the staff to go through the process of getting my official credentials. Two gentlemen were sitting behind the desk. Mr. Kennedy looked up at me with a giant smile and started with friendly banter. I can't recall the exact words, but the tone seemed flirtatious, and I remember blushing at Mr. Kennedy's comments. Next to David Kennedy was a handsome red-headed man who introduced himself as Ginge.

My thoughts wandered. *This job might be entertaining with so many attractive men around.* David had my ID badge finished in no time, and I effortlessly found my way back to the baby-blue-colored hospital.

ROO's main headquarters consisted of a multitude of buildings. Besides the housing cubicle, located in the center of the camp, was a supersized DFAC, slang for dining hall. There was a small Iraqi DFAC, a few offices on the base, including the security building, a power supply center, a fuel station, and a giant warehouse. The facilities I used the most were the educational and meeting halls, two tennis courts, a tiny little shop, which I referred to as the mall, and most importantly the three workout gyms.

There was much to discover during my time on base, and I was just getting started.

Hawker 400 Lear

Iraqi Hwy, no markings, no traffic signs, no worries

Flares burning off the natural gas

My cabin on Rumaila

Soft-skinned (non-armored) ambulances lined up at ROO

Bunker, a protective hard cover shelter in case of artillery attacks

Why Are We Here

Full moon shining bright
Let your light cleanse my sight
Attract new beginning to my life
                              ~ Laura Weigel

B efore getting hired as a subcontractor to work in the oil field, I knew little about the industry. So when my son, Drew, started asking dozens of questions I couldn't answer, I figured I had better educate myself. "Mom, how big is the field? How long has it been in production? How many barrels are they pumping?"

The information I received during the project briefing was rather basic. I yearned to understand more about both Rumaila and Iraq. I learned oil in Iraq was first discovered in October 1927 near Kirkuk, 140 miles north of Baghdad. Each piece of information I gathered helped me further understand Iraq's long and complicated struggle as it slowly developed into one of the world's leading oil producers.

Exploring further, I discovered that Rumaila had contributed to Iraq's production for fifty-seven years and was the country's largest oil reserve. The more I read, the more absorbed I became. By the late '70s, production had peaked at 1.75 MILLION barrels per DAY! Yes, per day! I found this number unbelievable, but what did I know about the oil business anyway? My curious brain sought more answers.

During the oil crisis in the 1980s, I was in my twenties, and I remember it being in the headlines on the news. I became sick of hearing about the ongoing tension. But the one thing I learned way back then was how vital oil was and how it affected world politics and economics. I could never have imagined, thirty years later, that I would be so closely involved with the industry.

Iraq fell into harsh times of conflict starting in the 1980s. Production began dropping. The Iraq Oil Company worked painstakingly to keep the operation running. If two decades of strife from outside of Iraq weren't enough, in 2005 Iraq started feuding within its borders on ownership of the oil reserves. At the same time, a new law was being drafted, the Federal Oil and Hydrocarbon Act, to be specific. For the first time since nationalization, this new order would allow foreign investors to become part of Iraq's future oil and gas industry development.

As you may have guessed, the law was written to allow Iraq to reach out. Once the regulation was in place, the Iraqi Ministry of Oil decided that it would be in Rumaila's best interest to involve outside leadership, namely BP and China National Petroleum Corporation (CNPC). Until this point, Iraq and her oil had encountered many barriers. Rumaila's original company, the Southern Oil Company (SOC), would now be joined by the two new players. All three companies would reap significant financial rewards for working in the field.

Joining the ROO team meant that I would be involved in the care of members from all three companies. The three players came from three contrasting regions, bringing their varied work ethics and culture which I would come to decipher during my employment in Iraq.

BP had already been a part of Rumaila for eighteen months when I arrived. The partners had set a goal to boost Rumaila's capacity from the current 1.1 million barrels to 2.85 million barrels a day in the first six-year period. In addition, the worn and outdated fifty-year-old technology and equipment were about to get an overhaul.

The knowledge I gathered had me feeling a bit smug. When people back home quizzed me about my job, I would proudly boast about working on the largest oil field in Iraq. Rumaila is recognized as being quite unique, I'd say. She is blessed with being one of the world's supergiant oil fields containing over a billion barrels of recoverable black gold.

At the time of writing, seventeen billion barrels were still beneath Rumaila's 1,600 square kilometers, an area 80 km long by 20 km wide (50 miles x 12.5 miles).

I Choose the Moon

The new contenders had their work cut out for them. The list was long and only becoming increasingly complicated as the project got underway and more unforeseen perplexities started to surface. Miles of pipe needed to be replaced. Old well heads required maintenance, and dozens of new wells would have to be drilled. Degassing stations were out of date and deemed to need facelifts. Finally, they needed to figure out how to build a water injection system, and a big question was where the scarce liquid water would come from.

The arid desert presented numerous difficulties, with temperatures often reaching over 50°C or 122°F. On top of the heat, the flat landscape allowed high winds to blow up sandstorms that could last for days, which not only stopped the movement of vehicles but affected the work processes. I remember being stuck in camp a few times waiting for the wind to settle.

Besides the natural elements, the field had been strewn with thousands of landmines and unexploded ordnances (UXO) left from the past wars. Seeing the telltale warning signs around Rumaila was sobering. Red sandbags were used to signal that an area was unsafe and contained UXOs. Rumaila was littered with thousands of silent killers left over from Saddam's era. White sandbags indicated the area had been deemed safe and was clear of danger.

Digging deeper, I discovered that Iraq possessed 25 million pieces of ordnance, remnants left behind from the Gulf War and the Iraq/Iran war. In addition, there were estimated to be 50 million cluster bombs dispersed throughout the country. I can't imagine living in fear of my children accidentally stepping on an UXO.

Both Iraq and the US were responsible for using landmines during the Gulf War. Iraq used them to defend the border with Kuwait, and the US used them in both Kuwait and Iraq. I had to wonder if these soldiers gave any thought to the aftermath and a country left bestrewed with hidden explosives. Because landmines are buried nearly three meters or about ten feet in the soil, they are tough to see and find. After being underground for decades, they are virtually impossible to remove and need to be detonated where they lay once discovered.

As for the mines on and around Rumaila, Saddam Hussein's army placed most of these to prevent Iran from destroying Iraq's vital oil infrastructure. As an employee on the oil field, it was scary to think about driving or accidentally stepping on a deadly bomb. For this reason, all ROO workers had been told not to walk or drive in uncleared areas. I always hoped the Quick

Response Team, QRF, our security detail, knew what was and wasn't safe, as the ambulance followed them many times down dirt paths throughout the field. Occasionally, driving along, I would look out the window and see a line of red sandbags marked with a skull and crossbones, the universal danger sign. Knowing these were probably placed under the direction of Saddam sent a shudder up my spine. My mind entertained thoughts of how many had suffered the ramifications of these weapons. My question was answered when I learned the United Nations Development Program reported that mines had caused 14,000 casualties in Iraq between 1991 and 2007. Half of them died from their wounds.

Having a better understanding of the country's past, along with its trials and tribulations, would no doubt help me to connect with the people and my work. Every fact I learned was a step toward seeing the big picture.

Degassing station on the Rumaila oil field

Miles and miles of pipeline

Rumaila written in Arabic

Sandstorm on Rumaila

The Art of Using a Squat Toilet

She liked the moon, because, like herself, it shined the brightest when no one was around to see.

Joc was a straight-to-the-point kind of guy. I figured out quickly he wasn't going to cut me any slack. Either he planned to break me or decided to see if I could cut the mustard. I was not given any time to adjust to my new environment. There was no actual orientation. It was basically: there's the ambulance...now go figure it out. On the other hand, he would soon learn that I was bred as a bring-it-on person. I accepted the challenge and refused to leave as a DNF participant. DNF, did not finish, was a term from my adventure racing days. You don't quit unless you are close to dying or have run over the time limit. . .period!

Joc's experience had been working primarily with male colleagues in military settings. Maybe he thought if I broke a nail, I'd decide not to return on my next rotation. This wasn't the kind of job or place an average person would consider, let alone a woman. Whatever he had in his head, I was out to prove I could hold my own. I hadn't gotten this far to wimp out. It had taken a lot of blood, sweat, and tears to land my ideal job. One hard-nosed man wasn't about to break me. I was too tough to let that happen.

I was surprised when Joc told me I was scheduled to start traveling with the ambulance the following morning. He lined out the list of my expected duties, and they began immediately! Along with crewing the armored ambulance, I was scheduled to start teaching Iraqi nurses Western medicine fundamentals with the help of an interpreter. In addition, each evening I was to help Joc in the clinic until ten or eleven p.m. Plus, I'd be on call to cover the clinic after hours a few nights a week. On top of this, if the ambulance were called out at night, I would be the one to respond. My duties sounded overwhelming. When was I going to get to sleep?

As a remote medic, the main focus of my job was to provide medical support to the expats who worked on the north side of the oil field. I would be the solitary medical provider, traveling daily from ROO's main camp up to a location known as Lion. Lion was just a codename for an office complex where I would stage during the day. The post was located 22 miles or 35 klicks, slang for kilometers, from Rumaila's HQ. I traveled in an armored ambulance driven by a guy from the personal security detail team. My ambulance driver was not armed, but the ambulance would always be escorted by two additional security vehicles that did provide armed security. These two vehicles made up the Quick Response Team or the QRF. Three of the four security men were Iraqi nationals. The other was the team leader (TL), a UK ex-military guy.

So my new career began. It would be immeasurably different from anything I'd previously done as a nurse. I was nervous as heck, expecting it would be stressful not having another medical person helping me care for patients. Not wanting Joc to jump to conclusions about my capabilities, I never shared my fears with him. My drivers were not trained as medical support; they were security dudes and could assist with the basics, which was all I could expect. I wondered if I could handle this. The closest I came to handling emergencies in an isolated setting was while I worked as a flight nurse and as a medic on wildfires. But in these situations I had a highly skilled partner to assist me. I was starting a new role on the oil field, so no one could say for sure if I'd be busy or not. Of course, Joc told me I would be, and I presumed he knew.

My imagination went wild. Suppose that I encountered a badly hurt patient. My thoughts drifted to one of the worst-injured patients I had ever cared for. A seventeen-year-old kid with a gunshot to the chest, an often-fatal injury. I was a flight nurse working out of a base in Florence, Arizona at the time. Our flight team was dispatched to a GSW (gunshot wound), a twelve-minute flight from our base. On scene, we found an alert and oriented seventeen-year-old struggling to breathe and writhing in pain. I vividly remember the paramedic from the ground ambulance looking at me and asking, "You're going to have to put in a chest tube, huh?" Flight crews were trained in advanced procedures in cadaver labs. You were always kind of hoping you'd get a chance one day to be a hero and hopefully not mess it up. On this particular cold night, I got my opportunity. I gave the young Hispanic male a cocktail of drugs that sedated and paralyzed him. Thirty seconds later, my partner placed a 7.5 mm endotracheal tube into his trachea so that we could breathe for him. Next, we pulled the stretcher out of the well-lit ambulance into the poorly lit parking lot. After another dose of medication to keep him sedated and pain-free, I cut away his bloody shirt and prepped his chest. My heart was racing to beat the band.

Inside my brain, a battle was happening. One side of my consciousness said "fukarama" (my version of the f-word), and the other side was stoked. While my brain was playing tug of war, the flight medic and I agreed upon the insertion site where the flexible hollow tube needed to be placed. We counted the ribs under the patient's right armpit to find the fifth intercostal space. I was then handed a scalpel and immediately made a two-inch cut at the agreed-upon site. Next, I pushed the beveled end of the tube into the patient's pleural cavity using forceps. As I punched through the thick tissue wall, I felt the pop, a sign I was doing it correctly. Blood came shooting out the other end of the tube, just like it was supposed to. Thus, the reason we had removed the patient from the ambulance…the ground medic didn't want three pints of blood left to clean up. That night, I saved the kid's life from the deadly hemothorax (blood leaking into the chest cavity) caused by the bullet.

Thinking about the what-ifs could drive me insane if I weren't careful. I could only do what I could as a medic working alone. So I pretty much crossed my fingers every day.

My daily routine went like this: each morning, I met my driver at the camp's hospital fifteen minutes before we needed to leave. The driver assigned for the day gave the ambulance a quick check-over. He kicked the tires, checked the oil level, and visually inspected the truck, making sure it was good to go. While the driver was looking after the ambulance, I showed up and loaded up my required medical gear, a large emergency crash bag weighing 50 lb /23 kg, a drug box, and the Lifepak monitor. Before locking up the hospital, I retrieved the portable cooler and my pre-packed lunch. Everything was put in the back of the rig and secured in place. After gearing up with our infamous armored vest and helmets, we then climbed into our seats, where we waited patiently for the QRF to give the signal to move.

There was a pool of four to five different drivers, and occasionally I would get a fill-in or temp driver. I was pleased to learn that two of the guys were David and Ginge, the men I had first met in the badging office on day one. Red-headed Ginge was my escort (driver) during my first week at ROO. Davy (David) rotated in after that. These guys were awesome, and they gave me more of an orientation than Joc ever did. Davy always had the biggest grin on his handsome face. But when he spoke, I struggled to understand his thick-tongued, Northern Irish accent. For example, "Davy, how air you chew-day?"

Or, "See ya Tuh-Sa," (See you Thursday) or "Sure is *haht*" for hot.

A few weeks later, Mark and Seth showed up. These two were from the UK and talked funny too. Months after working with them, I found myself adopting British words, many of which I still use—boot, rubbish, air con, etc. Throughout my time on ROO, I would spend a great deal of time with these people, riding to and from work and staging in the same building for hours each day. I learned about their families, life history, and their hardships. They became my mates.

Lion was a two-story office building located on the north side of the field. The main building, a giant pearl-white brick structure, must have been pretty impressive when it was new. The interior was just as remarkable. The center corridor was a large open area with a vast high ceiling. A hallway could be found on either side. Each of the two halls had several individual offices. One side had a large conference room with a humongous, beautiful, dark-wood table. There was, of course, a male and female bathroom at the end of one of the hallways. The second story had more offices, which were scarcely used, plus storage space. The flat roof was easily accessed by a set of stairs and was an excellent location to look out over the desert for miles in any direction.

The facility showed its age and looked to have been built in the 1970s. The carpets, curtains, and furniture were very outdated and needed to be replaced badly. In addition, it was not the most comfortable place; it was hot in the summer, cold and drafty in the winter. The air conditioners hardly worked, oozing condensation down the walls.

During my first few weeks at Lion, I had to share an office with one of the Iraqi field managers, making me uncomfortable. He would often ask me to step out so he could meet in private with various people. I was relieved when I was finally given an office of my own, and at the same time the QRF (Quick Response Team) commander was also given an office next to mine. Sadly, the Iraqi security men were expected to stay in the parking lot with our vehicles. I hated thinking these guys were sitting out in the trucks all day, even if the vehicles were left running and the air con was on. The ambulance driver would either sit in my office or the team lead's office.

Lion's complex was surrounded by the famous T-walls, which were found everywhere there were buildings and people lived or worked. The T-walls are twelve feet tall and made of steel-reinforced concrete; they are blast walls to deflect and withstand the detonation of IEDs and other explosive devices. T-walls look like upside-down T's, with broad bases with the wall extending upward.

However, the best part—NOT—was the toilet. The door to the bathroom displayed the letters WC and a picture of a male or female figure. I can only guess that WC meant a water closet. It was indeed the Middle East with squat toilets and all, no resting your bum on a seat. A squat toilet is made of porcelain, and it sits flat on the floor. To use, you place your feet on each side of the oblong hole, squat, and hope for the best. There is a learning curve to figuring out how to squat and not miss. If you pee on the side and miss the hole, you end up splattering your shoes and pants. But, guys, you have it made; at least you can see where you're aiming. The art of pooping—OK, you have to squat and make sure you're lined up. If you miss . . . holy shit! Lookout. Oh, and by the way, toilet paper is a Western thing. In this part of the world, the way locals are accustomed to cleaning down there is, well, I'm not sure. Each toilet had a bucket of water sitting next to it, along with a scoop, plus there is also a spray hose hanging out of the wall. The idea of a squat toilet is they are supposed to be more hygienic! But luckily, there was toilet paper available, and you quickly learn baby wipes aren't just for babies. It makes you wonder how Muslim women do the squatting toilet thing while wearing an abaya—the full-length cloak covering a Muslim woman from head to foot.

My day at Lion ended when all of the expats were finished working each afternoon. The security lead would give us the thumbs-up that we could head back to camp. The process was virtually the reverse of the morning. Once back in camp, the driver parked the ambulance next to the hospital, leaving it as it was found that morning. I would unload my gear and then regroup with the other Frontier staff in the clinic.

Start and finishing times varied day to day depending on what was happening around the field. Because I traveled with the Quick Response security detail, we were the first out in the morning and the sweep coming back to headquarters each evening. It was cool to be a part of this vital group, except this required working long hours.

Each evening at the main camp, a meeting was held for all the expats. This gathering was referred to as prayers, but it had nothing to do with religion. Prayers was another codename; as best as I could tell, even the security guys couldn't answer how it became named. All employees were expected to attend this informative assembly that included daily security news from around the country, oil field reports, and other relevant information. In addition, we were always given an update on any hostile events happening in Iraq, current production numbers, and any setbacks. I liked attending prayers; it was a time when I could socialize with people from the other departments within ROO. I thought it was awesome that BP kept everyone in the loop, not just the admin and the engineers. It provided a sense of being a part of the ROO project.

Lion complex

T-walls at the lion complex

Lobby at Lion

My office at Lion

Seth standing with the armored ambulance

Wearing the required flak vest and helmet

Squat toilet at Lion

Ramadan

*Comparing the sun with the moon is similar to
those who try to compare God with the devil.*
~ *Mwanandeke Kindembo*

I'm not sure if I had ever even heard of Ramadan, let
alone knew what it was until I took a job working in
the Middle East. But this quickly changed. Within
two weeks of arriving in Iraq, the Ramadan holiday began. At first, I had no idea how significant this religious
period was, but being surrounded by and working with
Muslims, I was about to learn.

Ramadan takes place in the ninth month of the Muslim
lunar calendar. Unlike Christmas, the dates change slightly
each year, and the holiday lasts for a full thirty days. It seemed
surreal that this event could linger for a month, especially once I
learned of the stipulations. During this spiritual time, healthy adults are to
refrain from eating, drinking, sex, anger, and other immoral acts, from dawn
until dusk. I couldn't imagine anyone going all day without drinking at least
some water. On top of this, they are expected to worship, pray, and read the
Quran. Also, acts of charity are encouraged.

This particular year, 2011, Ramadan started on August 1. I felt privileged
to experience and learn about this holy month. At the same time, this was the
hottest place I'd ever experienced. Temperatures reached more than 50°C or
120°F. It was stunning to watch as these hardy souls followed their cultural

rituals in one of the harshest environments there is. I had never met another culture as devoted to their beliefs as these people are.

I found out that Muslims routinely get up early and eat a pre-dawn meal called *suhoor*. After that, they are to refrain from eating and drinking until they break their fast, after sunset, with a meal known as *iftar*.

The whole idea of Ramadan is to practice self-restraint and engage in self-reflection. Fasting is valued as a way to cleanse one's soul and empathize with those in the world who are less privileged. Muslims continue to work, go to school, and participate in their usual activities, minus those mentioned above. I daresay trying to function at work on an empty stomach and while being dehydrated would be unachievable in my view. I don't think I could survive a day.

Muslims who have reached puberty and are in good health are obligated to fast. The sick and elderly, along with travelers, pregnant women, and those who are nursing, are exempt. Those who are healthy enough are supposed to make up for the missed fast days at some point in the future or help feed the poor.

I was told that girls start at age ten and boys start at age fourteen. I found this interesting and wondered why. Upon researching this further, I learned children are to participate in Ramadan once they reach puberty. However, girls get there sooner than boys.

As healthcare workers on ROO, we needed to respect the cultural ways of the local people. It was easy for medical personnel to get frustrated with our patients when they made bad choices and put their health at risk. But this was a time we had to put aside our Western mentality and our judgmental thoughts.

Some Islamic workers would consume water but not eat during their workday. I can say not much work got done during this religious period of time. People had no energy; they acted exhausted between not eating and the high heat. The workdays were made even shorter than usual. Most locals were on their way back home by noon or sooner. You knew they were dedicated to their religion when smokers went from a pack and a half of cigarettes daily to none from sunrise to sunset.

We treated several patients with dehydration and heat exhaustion. Most of these people took our advice when we told them they needed to consume fluids. Heck, in this part of the world, everyone was probably a quart low without even fasting.

When Ramadan finishes, the Muslims have a grand party known as *Eid al-Fitr*, the Feast of Fast-Breaking. Unfortunately, I was home on leave when the fasting broke that first year. However, the following year I got to experience the three-day celebration of *Eid*, enjoying local cuisines prepared in our DFAC. For Muslims, *Eid al-Fitr* is a time for special prayers and having meals with family and friends. The celebration of *Eid* is to show gratitude toward God after the month of reflection. This holiday serves as a reminder for Muslims to be grateful for what they have and to share with those who are less fortunate.

The Team

In the presence of the moon, nobody sees stars.
~ Amit Kalantri

Joc was my supervisor and the person I reported to; Lilith was our overall boss. Lilith was a striking European woman with an enchanting personality. However, she was not a Frontier employee but the corporate manager who told Frontier how things were to be. In addition, Lilith was the overseer of our medical team, the go-between for BP and the medical support.

I was introduced to Lilith upon my arrival on ROO. She had been the one requesting Frontier to add a couple of females to the medical team. I learned quickly she was a person of status. Behind her back, Joc did not hesitate to share his dislike for the woman. He reported she was sly and scheming and lacking the skills to manage a medical department. Being the newest team member, I had no clue who to believe. Joc, so far, hadn't impressed me with his leadership abilities. It seemed a competition over control; each thought they should be the top dog. I planned to stay out of their way and not take sides. Time would tell who would dominate.

Lilith had big plans in place for the medical department. More staff were being processed to join our roster, and the list included ambulance managers, trainers, and additional physicians, both expats and local nationals.

Nicky served as my reliever, mirroring my position, as I mentioned earlier. Our nursing backgrounds were very dissimilar. Nicky had been a nurse in the British army yet had little hospital experience. Furthermore, she was intelligent, wise, witty, had a passion for education, and was experienced as a trainer and instructor. We were fortunate to have her as part of our team.

Joc's reliever was an American nurse by the name of Doug. Doug was much more easygoing than Joc. I got on well with Doug, who was helpful and friendly. He had been out on leave when I first arrived in Iraq. We shared a common interest in the great outdoors. We shared stories of backpacking and spending time in the wilderness when time allowed. Because everyone's schedule was staggered, I usually worked part of each rotation with both Ops leads, Joc and Doug. Working with Doug, I always felt respected and knew he had my back.

Nicky and I were soon followed by the arrival of Vic and Lee. These two were hired to manage and train the new Iraqi soft-skinned ambulance drivers. Vic, an American paramedic, had a long history of working remotely and was a solid, smart guy. He reminded me of my eldest son; both have photographic memories and are walking dictionaries full of knowledge.

Lee, a British lad, came about the same time Vic had. Lee's background included having worked in the UK as a flight paramedic and a quick-response car medic. He had excellent medical skills and was a splendid asset to the team. Lee was entertaining to hang out with and was always making me laugh. Occasionally, we would cross paths when out walking in the evening, stopping to chat, and the next thing you know, an hour had passed. I loved sharing war stories from our flying careers. We both would get so excited telling each other about some gory accident we had tended to. It was awesome to have someone who could relate to this line of work.

Four months after I had started working in Iraq, Joc and JP were let go. Frontier and Lilith felt they weren't a good fit with the local nationals. Honestly, I wasn't disappointed to see Joc move on. He was challenging to work for. Joc routinely put me in situations to test my capabilities, to see if I would fold. For instance, he made me start teaching Iraqis after being in the country for only two days. With no time to prepare the lesson or become familiar with the culture, I was to educate a group of local male nurses on Western medical skills. He must have known I had no skills in teaching Middle Easterners. I felt sure this was a setup for failure—a woman telling Iraqi men how to do their job.

Vic soon moved into Joc's position as the Ops lead. Vic fit the role well. He was quick to learn the ropes and took his cues from Lilith. I remember Vic loved being organized and was passionate about keeping count of supplies; I got stuck doing inventory at least eight times. Doing inventory meant counting every single item, medications, equipment, needles, Q-tips, Band-Aids, you get my drift. I hated doing inventory, a tedious and frustrating job. Thinking about this still makes me cringe.

Dr. Johannes, a German physician, was hired to replace JP. Johannes was a quiet, gentle, laid-back guy. He had worked on other international contracts, including working on cruise ships. One of the things I liked best about him was his outstanding bedside manner; in other words, he was good with the patients, showing courtesy and kindness to all nationalities.

Galvin, an ex-military nurse, came to fill Vic's original spot as a trainer. Galvin was a super cool guy with an extraordinary history, including being an officer in the Royal Navy. He had a mile-long list of experience and credentials. Galvin was a first-rate trainer and got on well with the team. I admired the man a lot.

Although Stan wasn't a Frontier employee, our team interacted a lot with him. Unlike the medical team, Stan was a BP employee. As ROO's industrial hygienist, he was responsible for protecting the employee's health by reducing physical, environmental, and chemical risks. Stan was a busy guy and worked closely with Lilith. Part of his job entailed creating new safety policies and procedures throughout the oilfield. He started coming by the clinic every evening before the camp meeting, and then he would join us for dinner. He became a good friend. This gang had become my Middle East family, and I was blessed to know them.

With the number of Iraqi employees working on the field, BP and Frontier felt it would be good to add local, national physicians to our medical team. Unfortunately, between the language and cultural barriers, the locals were not being serviced as well as they should. Dr. Hadi and Dr. Adel were the first Iraqi doctors to come on board; hiring these men worked out well. They each rotated shifts in ROO's clinic, treating and caring for the LN employees. This freed up the Western providers, allowing them to focus on doctoring the expats. Both Dr. Hadi and Dr. Adel were skilled physicians and spoke English. It was an honor to work with and get to know these kind individuals.

Once Joc was gone, life was good; I enjoyed my coworkers and felt we had a strong team. They were all good people with interesting backgrounds and fun to be around. I only saw Nicky in passing when coming and going. I got along with everyone, including Lilith. Things seemed to be sailing smoothly. There was always oilfield drama, but not so much within our group. In the beginning, anyway.

Tane

*I always look up at the moon and see it as the
single most romantic place within the cosmos.*
                                    ~ Tom Hanks

It was September when I returned to ROO for round
two. I had survived my first rotation and truly enjoyed the experience minus Joc's insensitive nature.
Besides, I spent my days away from ROO's main camp
and only had to contend with the managers in the evenings.
At least most of this hitch, Joc would be home on leave. It
was a relief to have Doug on duty as the Ops lead when I
arrived, knowing he would be easier on me than Joc had
been. Hopefully, I wouldn't be expected to work in the clinic
until ten o'clock every night as I had during my first rotation.

Soon I began settling into the daily routine and life as a remote
medic. To clarify, I am an RN, a nurse, and have never had a paramedic license. Therefore, being hired as a medic (paramedic) had more to do with my
duties than my licensure, although my flight nurse skills did cross over with
paramedic qualifications. These competencies led me to be hired to work on
wildland fire detail, the most fun and entertaining job I had ever encountered.
Believe it or not, this even trumped working as a flight nurse on a helicopter.

I actually left my original dream as a flight nurse to go work with
Wilderness Medics. When I joined them, the company's main focus was
providing medical support for wildland fires around the United States. When
a forest fire starts burning and grows to Level 3, additional resources are

mobilized, including medical aid. This is where Wilderness Medics came into play.

Several requirements had to be met before being considered for employment with the company. First, you needed to be a licensed EMT or paramedic. Because I had flight nurse experience, the company's owner grandfathered me in based on my medical skills. Next, to work on any fire, you had to attend a wildland fire training course and lastly pass the arduous physical pack test by walking three miles while carrying a forty-five-pound pack and finish in less than forty-five minutes, more challenging than it sounds.

Unfortunately, working wildfires is a seasonal job. Some years are busy, and you get plenty of work; other years are slow. Essentially you have to wait around until you get the call to go. Then they usually want you to leave the same day if possible and be gone for minimally two weeks and preferably three. Tricky if you're working full-time. Working wildland necessitates owning or renting a 4-wheel drive vehicle and having camping gear; you will be sleeping in a tent and camping out during your stint.

Honestly, being the outdoor woman I am, I loved working wildland; there was always something exciting happening. Of course, it is a dangerous job, wildfires are very unpredictable, and they have injured and killed many wildland crews. On the other hand, what's not to love about getting paid good money to sleep in your tent, take care of the hotshot crew who refuse to be sick, injured, or ill, along with having delicious catered picnics in the burning woods? Golden.

One day halfway through my second rotation, I showed up at the hospital expecting nothing out of the ordinary. Instead, I was surprised to find a fill-in driver prepping the ambo, a man I had never seen or met before. The unannounced change was baffling since I had not been notified of the switch. With a confused expression on my face, I approached the unfamiliar male. "Hello, sir, I'm Jonea or Jo for short." My eyes met his as he turned to introduce himself and offered me a firm handshake.

"Hello, I'm Tane. I'll be your driver for a few days. Seth is working in the badging office this week."

I remarked, "Oh, OK, cool, I'll grab my gear and be ready in a few minutes."

When I returned, Tane was sitting in the driver's seat, engine running, air con blasting on high in an attempt to cool down the inside of the truck. Heck, it was six a.m. and already over 95°.

Tane asked me questions about our standard operating procedure and what to expect on a typical day. It was his first time as a temporary driver and the first time he had ever driven an ambulance. I verbalized the details.

Much like the other drivers, I quizzed Tane, asking things like, how long have you worked in Iraq, where are you from, do you have a family, and so on. I'm a curious person and like to investigate different people I'm around.

Quickly I learned Tane was quite a character. He was a fascinating guy with an amusing personality. Over the course of the week, I kept trying to dig deeper and learn more about the handsome yet quiet man. For whatever reason, I desired to know more about the man behind those eyes of coal. I'm happy to say this wasn't his last time being my driver. Tane became a regular fill-in. Sometimes, he would turn up for a day or two, and other times he would cover for the week.

Soon after meeting him, I became captivated by the guy. I think it happened that first day our eyes met; I found this man intriguing.

On the outside, hair black, lips full, stature minus six-foot, expression smileless. Skin the tint of a Pacific Islander, eyes as dark as a moonless night. I held an infatuation for males who possess mysterious sable eyes and a unique dialect; he filled the role—someone I was destined to flirt with.

The deadly Iron Complex fire I worked in California 2008

I worked as a flight nurse with LifeNet for 5 years

HQ Responsibilities

*If the Sun and Moon should ever
doubt, they'd immediately go out.*

~ *William Blake*

Most evenings, upon my return to ROO HQ, I would walk into the clinic to find the rest of the Frontier staff gathered for the daily medical team meeting. Unfortunately, Lilith was too inflexible to hold out a few extra minutes until I arrived. Being excluded from the discussions left me feeling like an outsider. Showing up in the middle of the conversation, I had little or no clue what they were talking about. However, this kept me out of most of the office drama, which was slowly building. The one thing I was conscious of was that as the number of staff increased so did the number of dilemmas.

Once the hospital meeting wrapped up, we would make our way over to the building where the five-thirty security brief took place. With the daily business affairs finished, it was off to the chow hall to feed our rumbling stomachs. I was always hungry by mealtime; my cold box lunch of bread and dried-out chicken did little to satisfy my appetite. My coworkers enjoyed a potpourri of hot choices for their lunch, unlike those of us working remotely.

Occasionally someone would have to remain in the clinic to provide care for any lingering patients. Routinely I ended up staying behind to cover, in which case I would go to dinner late and by myself. The thought was, I spent the least amount of time in the clinic of anyone, so I was asked if I minded watching the patients.

Having extra staff lessened the number of times we each had to take night calls. The nurses and paramedics filled this role, and each took turns providing after-hours coverage if someone required medical care.

Being on call meant you had to be available from six p.m. until eight a.m., seeing any person requesting medical attention during these hours. Most callouts were lame, and the person could have easily waited until morning. However, periodically someone truly ill or injured would show up, in which case one of the doctors would have to be awakened to help manage the patient.

I was dispatched to the hospital to evaluate an injured patient during one such time. Jumping out of my cozy bed, dressing as quickly as I could, heart pounding, I raced over to unlock the clinic door and waited for the wounded man to arrive. Minutes later, an Iraqi oil field policeman came in yelling and holding his left thigh, *alm, alm* (pain); he claimed his leg was broken. Once I examined him, I knew he was overreacting and probably faking it. There were no signs of an injury, no bruising, swelling, or deformity of any kind. He didn't have a mark on him, yet I had to call Leon to come and check him out. The man did not have any fractures or injuries but was looking to get out of work; this, unfortunately, was a common practice we saw.

On average, there would be five or six callouts a week. Of course, you always hoped it wasn't on your night. The worst thing for me was I had to be up early every day to travel north. Some nights, I got little or no sleep.

Being on call also interfered with my gym time. Once in a while, I was exercising when I had to respond to the hospital. Seeing patients while wearing gym shorts made me feel uncomfortable, especially if it was an Iraqi patient. I usually tried to run to my cabin and change into long pants. We were expected to respond within ten minutes, which meant I had to run.

It was hard to sleep soundly on the nights I took call. It was like when I was a flight nurse working a twenty-four-hour shift. I slept with one eye open and one foot on the floor, ready to respond.

One night I was awakened by my phone ringing. It was after midnight, and I was directed to the room of an ill person reportedly too sick to walk over to the hospital. Worried the patient might be having a heart attack, I rushed to his room. No one answered the door when I knocked, so I let myself in. Instantly I recognized the pale-faced man as one of the company's executives.

At the same time, I started asking him what was wrong. I was overcome with the stench of vomit. The smell was so intense I could hardly breathe. Glancing into the bathroom, I noticed his sink was full of puke. The poor guy was lying on his bed wearing only boxer shorts. The fifty-year-old male stated he was too dizzy to stand and had been throwing up for the past three hours. After checking him over and getting a set of vitals, I needed to figure out how to get him to the hospital for treatment. I decided my best bet was to call Lee to come help me. We managed to get him into one of the soft-skinned (non-armored) ambulances and over to the hospital. Using all our strength, we had to drag him onto a stretcher, and then again, we lifted his dead weight onto a hospital bed. In reality, the man was not that sick. Dizzy, yes, but he could have at least tried to help us help him. Lee went back to bed, and I treated the patient with two liters of IV fluid and anti-nausea medication. At three a.m., I put the man back in a wheelchair and pushed him back to the rank-smelling room across campus. I didn't envy the cleaners the next day.

Besides our on-call responsibilities, Lilith decided to put Nicky and me in charge of doing the Health and Hygiene inspections of the DFACs on the main camp. When I first started doing the assessments, there were two DFAC facilities. One was known as Phase Zero; this was where the local nationals and security guys ate. The larger DFAC was where the rest of us expats dined.

Even though I had no formal training in these types of audits, the management team didn't care. I was encouraged to do my best and sent off to complete the ninety-three question-checklist for each cafeteria. Some of the answers were straightforward; others stumped me. Completing the thirteen-page form required me to do both a visual inspection and interrogate the canteen's manager, which sounds simple enough.

The audit form is broken into several different categories. General: is the air conditioner 100% working, and is it serviced regularly? Is there adequate ventilation, and are the doors and windows correctly screened and insects controlled? Do the staff wear uniforms and use appropriate PPE? Are the uniforms regularly laundered separately from the standard service?

Electrical and safety questions: are there working smoke detectors and a fire blanket? Questions about the kitchen staff: are the worker's health records up to date, and do they come to work when they're ill? Plus, the common questions about cleanliness and food storage.

Some items on the audit I had a hard time figuring out. Are sink and wastewater drains provided with traps to prevent sewer gas intrusion? "Umm, I don't know." Are the appliances anchored correctly? "I guess so." I had to rely on the manager to be truthful when I asked him questions I couldn't figure out. The managers were always busy and frustrated with all my inquiries. Sometimes they would request that I return at a different time, which didn't go over well with my bosses. I would get sent back and told to finish the paperwork.

The only good thing about doing these inspections was roaming around the camp and killing some time. Although I felt I wasn't knowledgeable enough to decide if the DFAC was up to standard, no one died of food poisoning while I was there; it must have been OK.

A Case of Zoochosis

*You can be the moon and still
be jealous of the stars.*

~ Gary Allan

Within the oilfield boundaries were two Iraqi health centers. The north clinic was in the village of Al Khora, located only a few minutes from the Lion complex. The south clinic was a few kilometers from ROO's headquarters. Although these facilities were not officially part of the oilfield, the clinics provided medical services for the local Iraqis living and working nearby. BP, with the support of Lilith, had determined that these care centers would benefit from an overhaul. The objective was to remodel the buildings, supply new and improved equipment, and teach the current Iraqi staff Western medical skills, all of which would be funded by British Petroleum. BP felt this was a positive way to improve a crucial community resource.

I had been appointed the task of educating the local clinic nurses. The daily lessons started on my second day at ROO but didn't last long. After only two weeks, the plug on my training workshops got pulled. I'm not sure how much they learned from me, but I unearthed an invaluable amount of knowledge from them. These individuals were, in fact, the first Iraqis I interacted with on a personal basis. Our discussions had me asking all kinds of questions. Before I could do any actual teaching, I needed to identify who these people were. I needed to become acquainted with them as individuals and not only with their medical comprehension.

I credit these local caregivers with introducing me to Iraq's ways of life. Early on, I came to understand the importance of religion within this Muslim nation. After Allah (God), family means everything to these conservative people. It was insightful to hear about local customs for dating and marriage. I was shocked to learn one of the nurses had gotten married at age eight to a twelve-year-old girl; the couple's parents had arranged the union. Puzzled, I had to ask, do an eight-year-old and a twelve-year-old know how to be married. I was reassured they did not and were not expected to share a bed.

Spending time with the Iraqi nurses, who were all males by the way, ended up being a rewarding experience. First, I was astonished by how many could speak English; this made communicating with the class much simpler, even though I did have the help of a translator. Secondly, I was impressed by their nursing abilities, and they knew more than I thought they might. However, one of the major drawbacks was the lack of modern equipment and medication shortage.

When the training sessions ended, I was left with countless hours of downtime. My days at Lion were filled with monotony and boredom. Every day was mostly "same-same." I made up a routine that I repeated each morning to make the time pass upon arriving at Lion.

Step one: unload the ambulance. During the hotter months (April-September), I lugged the valuable medical equipment indoors to avoid being damaged by the extreme heat. The inside of the armored ambulance must have been hot enough to bake bread by mid-morning. My driver for the day and the Iraqi security guys politely helped to carry my burdensome gear—fifty-pound crash bag and the twenty-six-pound Lifepak monitor—into the compound. Once everything was situated in my office, the next step was to complete the daily equipment checks and fill in the paperwork. Then, morning chores completed, it was time to enjoy a cup of coffee while sorting through emails.

Weekday mornings, Lion was a bustling place. The hallways were crowded and noisy, with expats coming and going like popcorn in a skillet. The complex was a center for daily meetings and a post for several of the Iraqi oil field administrators. In passing, my cohorts would stop by and greet me with a handshake and a "How do you do?"

Afternoons and on weekends, Lion became quiet and empty. Friday and Saturday, in Iraq, are observed as the weekend. These days the Iraqis didn't work. In fact, during the week, most of the locals left to go home by one p.m. Not the usual Western standard of eight or ten-hour workdays. The expats struggled with this. They wanted to get as much done during the day as possible. The more work done, the sooner the financial gains would show up. So many things had to rely on the LN's input and resources before most tasks could move forward; BP found it a slow process.

Lifeless afternoons brought a sense of slothfulness for those of us left at the desolate hangout. Although the tranquility made the clock move slowly, we were pretty much free to chill once all the offices cleared out. The security team leader and ambulance driver often occupied themselves by watching a movie. As for myself, I hated sitting still for too long. Being idle caused me to feel enervated and made me stir crazy. To prevent this, I walked laps around the courtyard; even in the hot summer heat, I paced around the compound like a tiger with zoochosis. Zoochosis - unhealthy captive animal behaviors including pacing, circling, bar-biting, head-bobbing, and self-mutilation. Don't worry; I didn't do any self-mutilation.

Sometimes I'd up the challenge by wearing my fifty-pound medical backpack or my armor-plated vest. This type of exercise was beneficial if I was training for some physical event, which I was ninety percent of the time. For the rest of the afternoon, I could likely be found sitting in a grungy plastic chair upon the dust-ridden roof, reading a book.

Haider and Mohammed were Lion's hard-working IT guys. I was in their office asking them to help me figure out some computer issue every other day. I was pretty much a tech idiot. Because I was unfamiliar with the data and programs used by Frontier, I struggled to learn the systems. My IT mates were patient and helped me to overcome these frustrating obstacles. Able to fix everyone's computers, software, and Wi-Fi dilemmas, they were probably the two busiest and most popular guys at Lion.

These two men had good English skills and were super resourceful. We became good friends within a few weeks, and I was *saeid alhazi* to have Haider and Mohammed as my *sadiq*.

My IT companions started walking with me in the courtyard during their breaks. Haider decided we should pick up the pace, so we jogged a few laps. The guys were engaging to talk with and made me laugh. They had studied at the University of Basrah, where they earned a degree in computer science. Like my Iraqi girlfriends, they educated me on their way of life and answered questions my curious mind thought of.

I liked asking them about how it was to live in Basra and what they do on their days off. Haider explained that Basra was a large city, home to two million people. He said it was noisy and congested with lots of traffic. Information shared during prayers often included details about terrorist attacks that had taken place in Basra City; these were mainly explosions. Haider went on to say Basra's past was better than its current status. This wasn't the first time locals had told me this. Basra was once a beautiful place. Haider asked me, "Did you know the city was once called the Venice of the East?"

"No," I replied, "but I did see some recent pictures, and it looks a bit disheveled."

Mohammed chimed in, "The local people don't ever go out after dark; it's not safe." With each story the Iraqis shared, my respect for them grew.

For every holiday celebrated, there was always exceptional food associated with it. Haider was so kind to include me in these cultural feasts. I remember the *dolma*—spiced rice wrapped in grape leaves and *biryani*—rice, spices, vegetables, and lamb. My favorite and yet a simple item was *samoon*, Iraqi stone bread, super delicious when served warm.

While staging out in my office at Lion, I started having a regular male visitor. The stout—and I do mean stout—LN enjoyed coming by my office and looking around. He was an assistant to one of the supervisors down the hall. The round-faced man would randomly wander into my room with a huge grin on his face. He always wore black jeans four sizes too small. His belly drooped over the top of his pants, and his crack peeked out in the back. The buttons on his shirt were stretched beyond capacity, exposing his brown skin. He looked so uncomfortable being squeezed into his clothes that my stomach hurt looking at him. I would literally stand up, suck my stomach in and pull up my own pants, thinking we'd both feel better. Seth started teasing me and called him my Iraqi boyfriend. As he browsed the room and my desk, he would see some item he desired and then ask me if I would let him have it. No, you can't have a box of Band-Aids, no, you can't have my lunch, or ink pen, etc. Although he had his own wire-rimmed shades, he became infatuated with my sunglasses. He desired my white Nike sunnies. He would pick them up and try them on. It would have been hysterical to see him walking around with my girly white glasses if I weren't so attached to them.

Anwar and Sofia

The moon is a loyal companion.
It never leaves. It's always there, watching,
steadfast, knowing us in our light and dark
moments, changing forever just as we do.
Every day it's a different version of itself.
Sometimes weak and wan, sometimes
strong and full of light. The moon
understands what it means to be human.
Uncertain. Alone. Cratered by imperfections.
~ Tahereh Mafi, Shatter Me

Most afternoons, I could be found hanging out on the flat roof of Lion. From my perch three stories up, I amused myself by watching the people on the ground come and go. Rarely did anyone ever look up and see me spying on them from high above. For some odd reason observing these subjects unnoticed gave me a sense of power. I couldn't help but wonder if my targets ever felt like they were being watched.

A caravan of Iraqi soldiers would occasionally cruise past the compound in their Humvees, looking all important and cool, with a couple of guardsmen manning the machine gun on top. I envisioned being a movie hero, but I did not have any armament.

Like the others, the soldiers never glanced up or knew that they could be the subject of someone else's crosshair.

The dirt-covered zone became my Iraqi happy place. My mind would wander, daydream, reminisce, plot, and plan. It was my escape. Scarcely did anyone bother to come to the rooftop. I liked it this way, for I had claimed it as MY space. It wasn't any kind of paradise; in fact, it was pretty dingy. Like many things in this country, the elements of heat, sun, and dust took their toll on everything man-made. Furthermore, good housekeeping or keeping things tidy seemed to be lacking. The roof was cluttered with rusty TV antennas, broken chairs, and various other forgotten debris; everything was always covered in dust.

My number one favorite thing to do was visit my Iraqi friend Ms. Anwar. I remember well the first day we met. One day during my second rotation, Ms. Anwar noticed me as she strolled by my office. Curious about who I was, Anwar stopped at the door. Looking up from my computer and seeing a middle-aged Iraqi woman, I stood to greet her. "Come in," I encouraged the round-faced lady. "Hello, I'm Jonea," and I extended my right hand to shake her hand. I was the newest white chick to arrive, and many of the local workers had made observations of my presence.

After introductions, I invited Anwar in, offered her a seat, and then explained my role on ROO. Anwar quizzed me, "Ms. Joe Nia, where are you from?"

I swallowed hard and held my breath. I had planned on lying and tried to answer Canada, but that's not what came out. "I'm . . . I'm uhhh, American," I spoke timidly.

I had always heard or been made to believe that the Iraqi people and most Middle Easterners hated and despised Americans, and why wouldn't they? We had invaded their land with our powerful military troops during the various wars over time. During the most recent conflict, many people lost their lives, not only the bad guys but also many others. Just like in the Western world, Iraqis had been influenced by their local media and made to believe Americans were untrustworthy.

I waited and watched for a cynical reaction. I even think I cowered back a bit, or at least my ego thought I did. "Oh, good, you are much warmer than that cold British lady." Relieved, I shook her hand and relished the warm welcome. Our friendship grew from that day forward.

Anwar was employed as a senior engineer; it was uncommon for an Iraqi woman to achieve such status. She had fifty men who worked under her guidance. Anwar's English was excellent, although she always disagreed and was constantly apologizing for her language skills.

Ms. Anwar stopped in to visit whenever she had a chance, once a week or so. Her office was across the road in one of the prefab office modules. The structure was similar to our accommodation cabins but significantly larger. Anwar was a very busy lady, and when we did get a chance to chat, it was usually only for a few short minutes. Soon she started asking if I could come over to her office, which for her, was more convenient.

Each visit with my friend required having a member of our security team escort me to the gate of her building. However, it was a short distance from our secured entrance to the guard shack of her complex, and it seemed unnecessary to need a chaperone. If my driver wasn't busy making badges, he could serve as my protector for the two-minute walk.

If possible, I would have loved to visit her every day, but in reality it was unworkable. Anwar was the key player in her department, so she had little free time. On the other hand, I stressed that I would have to run back to the office, grab my gear, and race to the ambulance if we got a call out.

Davy and Ginge also liked going with me to see Ms. Anwar, who warmly welcomed them too. The Iraqis are a very hospitable people, so on every visit to see Anwar, we were offered tea or coffee and some type of biscuits that were similar to an American shortbread cookie.

When time allowed during our get-togethers, Anwar and I engrossed ourselves in a session on improving our knowledge of each other's language. It sometimes became a game of Pictionary, Anwar would draw a picture of something she didn't know the word for, and I'd try and figure out what word she was searching for. Thank goodness she was a decent artist. Sometimes I was at a loss of what the picture was; we would giggle as I made random guesses.

Soon Anwar and I became greatly connected. First, we were the same age; only five months separated us. As single mothers, we could relate to the challenges of working and raising kids. Both of us were elated to have a unique acquaintance with the other. Each was honored to share our backgrounds and delighted in educating the other on our cultural differences. Obviously, the two of us were more venturesome, bold, and motivated than the average woman, be they Iraqi or American. Our personalities just plain clicked.

I recall having a serious conversation one particular day when Ms. Anwar said to me, "Ms. Joe Nia (her mispronunciation), if ever you need my help or were in a precarious situation, I would sell my house to save you, sister. I would give my life to save yours." These words are tattooed in my soul. I knew she meant it. This is the kind of love a parent has for their children. So let me ask you, are you willing to give everything you own up to help your best friend? Everything?

Many would say I'm a fool, but I would have trusted my life with my generous *solicitous* friend. Cultures, color, language, or religious differences did not prevent us from developing our sisterhood. We never judged each other, and we shared our darkest secrets knowing they were safe with each other.

Many of her stories were shocking. Once she had her car stolen, and she knew who the guilty party was. Even though this thug had threatened to take her life, she pursued him until she recovered her vehicle and the man was arrested. Remember, a good portion of the country and its agencies are corrupt. Women have little power when it comes to receiving a fair deal. I loved Anwar's spirit and admired her bravery.

Anwar had successfully divorced her unfaithful husband. While Anwar was the breadwinner, her unemployed husband was enjoying himself. Since leaving him, Anwar had fallen in love with a handsome man who had a fire in his heart for her. They wanted to marry, but Anwar needed permission from her male guardian, who happened to be her uncle. As it has been explained to me, it is an Islamic custom for women to have a male guardian or protector (*wali*). This person is normally a relative whose role is to protect the woman's future interests. Although this role should not be abused, it sometimes is. In Anwar's case, her uncle repeatedly denied her permission.

Anwar, in confidence, shared with me particulars of the man she longed for. She knew of my attraction to Tane. She was the only person in Iraq I had confessed my feelings to. Our secrets linked us even more. Anwar explained that Islamic women in Iraq aren't allowed to sign a contract without permission from their guardian either. They are limited in the time they can interact with men outside their families. This is why public buildings, parks, and means of transportation are segregated by sex or have been in the past.

Interestingly enough, in court, the testimony from one man equals that of two women. Things are starting to slowly change for these women in some parts of the world. At the time of this story, these laws were still in place.

As I tried to understand this particular law, it reminded me of when I was a teenager. My father would deny me certain privileges—going camping with a boyfriend or staying out past a specific time. But, of course, he was only trying to protect me. Five years later, Ms. Anwar was still single. She had given up the hope of marrying the man she wanted.

In the office next to mine was a fully covered Islamic lady who introduced herself as Sofia. Sofia was the secretary of the Iraqi general manager of the oil field. Sofia donned a black hijab, including a black veil and gloves; only her beautiful black eyes were exposed. She had a sweet, soft, and gentle voice. I remember how Sofia loved perfume. Her office always smelled of roses.

Sofia was so welcoming to me. Every morning, she invited me to her office for a chai and a sweet or a biscuit. These women were going to cause my waistline to increase if I wasn't careful. Like Anwar, she was excited to have another female in her workplace. Nearly every week, she would bring me a gift from the markets of Basra, sweets, perfume, a paperweight, PJs, and flowered serviettes. One time she brought me a beautiful maroon and pink flowered scarf that smelled of fragrant flowers.

She took me into the WC, and she showed me how to wear the scarf, covering my hair like a local *alnisa*. When I returned to my office decorated in my new *keffiyeh* or scarf, Dr. Adel was so pleased his face lit up with approval. Everyone wanted to get a picture with me in my scarf.

Sofia and I too became great friends. She explained that she remained fully covered because she was mourning the death of her father. He had been dead for five years, and Sofia missed him immensely. She told me she would continue the practice until her heart told her it was OK to unveil. Sofia was unwed, which was surprising as I could tell from her dark eyes that she was a beautiful lady.

Whenever anyone had a question or needed something, Sofia was a pantomath; she was the one person who either knew the answer or would find it for you. I learned quickly to be careful asking for some things from her, because she would never ever say, "Sorry, I don't know." She did the same for everyone.

I learned not to give too many compliments, "Oh, what a lovely cup you have." It would immediately become mine. Not accepting a gift offered to you was considered an insult. I must say, I have a splendid collection of articles from my Iraqi friends, such as a cup and saucer, a tea set complete with miniature spoons, a flower vase, a pen holder, and other previously mentioned gifts. I treasure these unique gifts as I do the friends who gave from their hearts.

I tried to bring each of the ladies something back from Arizona, a coffee mug, a wind chime, or a handkerchief. It became impossible to keep up, so I quit trying. ROO management had a rule that we were only to accept small gifts of minimal value. If they only knew the stash I had received.

Sofia shared how important her father had been in her life. She reported that he was a kind, gentle, and affectionate person that she had adored. Her heart was crushed to pieces when he passed. It had been years, and she was still feeling the pain as though it was yesterday.

I disclosed to Sofia that my own father was ill and dueled with cancer. At this point, his treatments were not keeping up with the evil jinn that had overtaken his flesh. Sofia started becoming infatuated with my father. She asked me almost daily how he was and if I called him. Although I did call my parents twice a week, Sofia felt I should call daily. She would ask me to tell my dad that she was praying for him and thinking of him. Repeating the following *du'a* seven times: *Asalu Allah al Azim rabbil arshil azim an yashifika* (I ask Allah, the Mighty, the Lord of the Mighty Throne, to cure you), a prayer used to heal the sick. It was as if she now had a second father to worry about and care for.

At first, my dad felt a bit weird about some unknown Iraqi woman taking an interest in him. Once I showed him a picture of Sofa in her niqab, which covered her entire body except for her eyes; his expression was a big "huh." My father had been a farmer all of his life and had not been exposed to many other cultures. Living in rural Indiana didn't offer the opportunity to meet Islamic people. His only international travel was to the neighboring country of Canada.

Dad would ask me dozens of questions about living and working in the Middle East. He was sincerely captivated by the information I fed him. He lived my experiences vicariously through my narrations.

Sofia offered me gifts of money to help pay for my dad's medical treatments. She would reply she knew good medical care was expensive and wanted to give my father every possible chance to recover. What I couldn't explain was that no amount of cash would make this illness vanish.

My dad couldn't fathom why someone he had never met would care so much about his well-being. The two of them built this odd bond in spite of living half a world apart and having radically different cultural backgrounds.

Both of these women, Anwar and Sofia, lost their mothers while I was stationed at Lion, eight months apart. I became both a resource for their countless medical questions and a support person for their emotional stress. I witnessed that impending *mawt* (death) is never acceptable in this culture. Muslims do not give up hope for ill patients. They believe God has the power to keep life going, which is a fair thought. On the other hand, death is imminent at some point, and Christian culture seems more open-minded to being emotionally prepared to deal with the dying process.

My Iraqi friends both became desperate to find a medical solution to save their mothers. Unfortunately, I didn't have the answers for them. I could only try and explain the disease process. Medical treatment in this part of the world was poor and difficult to obtain.

Before the 1990s, Iraq had a decent health care system with highly trained doctors and specialists. However, by 2014 more than half of the physicians had fled to safer countries to work. During the recent war, Iraq's multiple infrastructures were hit hard, including hospitals.

By the time the American soldiers left Iraq in December 2011, doctors in Baghdad were being killed at a rate of 47.6 per 1000 professionals. During this period, nearly 5,400 doctors emigrated annually. It wasn't safe to be a medical provider in this country.

ROO's Iraqi doctors had explained how the hospitals weren't able to give quality care and how overwhelmed the system was. They remarked that people would show up early in the morning, wait in line all day to be seen, and then be told there wasn't any medication available.

Not only was there a shortage of doctors and nurses, but Iraq also suffered from a drug shortage. Many of the medications they do get their hands on are expired or come from questionable safety standards. Dr. Hadi (another local physician) told me that Iraqi citizens all want to be given an injection no matter what their ailment. They seem to believe getting a jab can cure anything.

Iraq's healthcare crisis has led to a breakdown in trust between doctors and patients. It's common for a patient's tribe to assail a physician if anything goes wrong during treatment. Some physicians even purchase medications for their patients out-of-pocket, whether it be out of moral obligation or fear of attack. This practice is illegal, as drugs given in hospitals need to come from the hospital store. If caught, this practice comes with potential jail time.

If a family member is hospitalized, the family will be responsible for feeding the person, cleaning them, and doing their laundry. Nurses don't provide this type of care, nor do hospitals offer inpatient meals.

If a family can afford to, they will travel to another country to obtain advanced medical care. As a result, they sometimes spend their life savings, only to return to Iraq to find that maintenance therapies are unavailable.

The health of Iraqis is not a priority, and the numbers show this. Basra is the economic center of Iraq, and it exports enough oil to account for 90% of state revenues. For example, in 2019, a year of truce, the government allocated just 2.5% of the state's $106.5 billion budget to its health ministry, a fraction of spending seen elsewhere in the Middle East. On the other hand, security forces received 18% and the oil ministry 13.5%.

Posing with Anwar

View from the roof of Lion

Wearing the scarf Sofia gave to me

Saving Lives

It is a beautiful and delightful sight
to behold the body of the Moon.

~ *Galileo Galilei*

J oc had been wrong; the north field medic did not
become busy as predicted. Instead, most of my patients at Lion stopped in to have their blood pres-
sures checked, a chronic condition among the locals. But
in reality, these men could care less what their blood pressure readings were and only wanted a few minutes of the
American woman's attention. Sometimes being nice comes
with a price. I had been told by Lilith not to accommodate
these people, as they would continue to take advantage of us.
But I didn't have the heart to turn them away, so I continued
checking their vital signs when requested.

One particular morning an elderly LN was brought into my office. He
looked quite ill and was holding his hands over his chest. I recognized this
gentleman, as he was often sitting out in the foyer. I never knew why he hung
around. I thought he must have been too old to be an employee, but he was
there almost every day. I had smiled and greeted him many times, and he
would grin back, placing his right hand over his heart, slightly bowing his
head and mouth *assalamu alaikum* (peace be upon you).

Today he was not here to share a greeting with me; he was seriously ill.
The man spoke no English, and someone translated that he was having pain
in his chest. Concerned he might have had a heart attack, I closed the door

and had the pale man remove his *thawb*. I motioned to him to lie on the floor, for no gurney or stretcher was available in my office. In principle, a female nurse would not typically care for an Islamic male, but because this was an emergency and there were no male doctors around, I proceeded to treat him. Quickly I placed the ten sticky electrodes on his bare chest; he laid motionless and did not protest. Then, turning on the heart monitor, I closely observed the wavy lines moving across the screen, looking for any abnormalities. I was relieved to see a normal tracing and was thankful the feeble patient didn't need to be zapped. However, he still needed to be transferred to the hospital in Basra for a complete workup.

A few days later, he was back, still inhaling the smoke of an addictive death stick. He came to thank me dozens of times, "Thank you, doctor." I was told he thought I'd saved his life.

All the Iraqis from the beginning had called me doctor. I got tired of saying, "No, I'm a nurse," so I just let them have their way and learned that this meant they respected me.

Although most days passed slowly, a few were over the top with excitement. September 20, 2011 was one such day. I answered my mobile to hear Vic's adrenalized voice on the other end. Immediately I knew something serious was happening by the urgent tone in my manager's words. "Jo, you need to respond to the compression gas facility at the southside of the oil field. There's been an explosion."

Led by the QRF, we raced as fast as the bulky ambo would move, lights and sirens engaged. Apprehension pumped through my veins during the thirty-minute drive to the degassing station. Half of me was thrilled to be a part of this exciting event, but the other half was nervous, wondering what I would find at the scene.

A massive plume of black smoke could be seen miles away. As we drew closer to the location, orange flames shooting hundreds of feet into the air came into view. Seth and I looked at each other in astonishment; neither expected to find such a massive fire. We encountered dozens of vehicles, including fire trucks, parked along the road, a mile and a half from the actual fire, as we approached the scene. Following the QRF, we drove past several vehicles trying to get nearer to the accident but were stopped by the incident commander and told it was not safe to get any closer. Seth turned off the ambulance, and I stepped out to get a full report and check if there were any patients. Instantly my breath was taken away by the immense heat. My face felt like it would melt. I joined the swarm of men standing along the road glaring at the flames. No one was going to be able to approach that fire until it calmed down. It was a sobering sight.

The Iraqi workers were emotionally distraught, yelling and moaning in loud voices, some kneeling on the ground, fearing the worst for their coworkers. Honestly, I couldn't imagine anyone surviving the explosion or the fire if they had been close by when the accident occurred.

Amazingly, I only received one Iraqi patient from the incident. My patient was distressed and in emotional shock, making it difficult to examine him thoroughly. Compassionately, I took the man's hands in mine and looked into his wet brown eyes. Once I had his attention, I encouraged him to take deep, slow breaths, first by demonstrating with my own exaggerated movements. I had no translator, so I had to improvise as best I could. Following my direction, he finally started to calm himself. I was then able to do a proper exam. I found no major injuries, just a small superficial abrasion to the side of his head. Wanting to get him away from the scene's drama, I decided to transport him to the clinic.

Later I learned three others had been taken to the HQ clinic before I had arrived at the scene. These few patients were treated for minor burns and throat irritation. Although the local news reported nine people injured and no deaths, we heard otherwise. The inside story had seven missing; the truth is probably only known by Allah.

The cause of the accident was supposed that SOC had a maintenance team changing equipment on a gas compressor when the explosion happened. It was hard to imagine how anyone standing near the blast could have survived. Sometimes it was hard to know what was the truth and what was rumor.

BP's goal was to teach safety to a culture that was mindless on the topic. While working in this highly dangerous vocation, knowledge of personnel welfare and life preservation skills was lacking. It seemed that the consequences of poor judgment never crossed their brains. If you pass a vehicle at a high rate of speed and there is oncoming traffic, no problem. I saw this type of behavior every day while out on the roads. I was glad to have had the safety of a heavily armored vehicle to protect me.

Traffic accidents topped the list as the number one thing I responded to. A few of these incidents come to mind. One afternoon I was dispatched to a crash near Lion. A sedan with four off-duty Iraqi oil field policemen had pulled out onto the road in front of one of Rumaila's armored security SUVs. The sedan took the impact on the rear passenger's side door, leaving a one-foot-deep intrusion into the occupant compartment. It was clear that the police officer driving was at fault. Unfortunately, the unbelted policeman sitting in the backseat of the police car was DOS, dead-on-scene.

Not only had someone died in the crash, but the Iraqi driver of the private security vehicle was also wounded. Knowing I could not fix the dead man, I turned my attention to the injured driver. Approaching the truck, I found my patient still sitting in the driver's seat, dazed and staring off into space, his face covered in blood. My trauma training had taught me I should be worried. The victim could have severe head, spine, or internal injuries. Doing a quick assessment, I found the cause of the bleeding to be a deep laceration on the side of his head from striking the side window on impact. Ruling out any immediate life-threatening injuries, I bandaged the driver's bleeding head.

Although the patient's condition wasn't critical, he still needed to be treated and have a further evaluation at a hospital. The traumatic event was devastating for the troubled driver. He displayed signs of being in emotional shock—pale, sweaty, and trembling, and he was nervous as hell.

What unfolded next stunned the crap of me. While waiting for Dr. Adel (ROO's Iraqi physician) to come and transport the injured Iraqi to the hospital in Basra, I was approached by a security team member. "Hey, Jo, you should know that the off-duty police captain is telling us the patient is being taken to jail and isn't allowed to go to the hospital."

"What? Are you kidding me? He needs his head sewn closed and a CT scan. I don't understand. Why are they taking him to jail? He needs the hospital."

"Sorry, Jo, I guess they are charging the driver with killing the passenger."

"That's bullshit," I exclaimed in anger.

Without thinking, I turned and walked over to where a group of men stood, having a heated discussion. ROO's security guys were trying to explain that the driver was not at fault. Four on-duty officers now joined the off-duty policemen. Stepping forward and to the center of the crowd, my appearance surprised the men who grew quiet. Standing there two feet in front of the captain, a bolt of panic electrocuted my body, and my head suddenly felt heavy. The weak side of my conscience was screaming, what are you doing? Did you forget where you are? "Sir," my voice remained calm but firm, "the driver needs to go to the hospital because he is injured. Please, sir."

The irritated officer shook his head. "No, no, he must go to jail."

Woman or not, it was my job to advocate for my patient.

I had not always been this bold in the presence of domineering men. Having spent fourteen years living under the same roof as an oppressor had been more than enough time of being belittled. No more.

My days of being afraid to stand up against controlling men had been entombed sixteen years earlier, along with my dancing shoes: a funny but true story. I did bury a pair of my shoes. It was the same summer day I left Fort Wayne to move to Phoenix in 1996. My good friend Karma and I decided to commemorate our friendship by digging a hole in the flower bed that separated our properties and putting our worn dancing shoes to rest. We cried, laughed, and reminisced as we stood in the rain, planting our scuffed pumps in the dirt, rushing to finish before the earth turned to mud. I was sad to be leaving my confidante and ally, but freeing myself from my past and finding self-confidence had empowered me. Maybe the ceremony of leaving those shoes in the ground seems silly, but burying the ability to let anyone ever dominate me again was rational.

I was so relieved when Dr. Adel arrived, so I rushed to meet him and explain the whole scenario. Then, crossing my fingers, I hoped Adel could convince the police to change their minds and let the patient be treated and not locked up.

First, Dr. Adel checked over the patient, asking him questions that I had been unable to do because of the language barrier. Initially, I tried to get my Iraqi patient to act more ill than he was and then attempted coaxing him to get into the ambulance. I failed at both. The man was too stressed to listen to me, and he had no clue of my objective to protect him.

In Arabic, Dr. Adel did his best to persuade the authorities to let the patient be transported to the hospital for treatment. But unfortunately, the police officers didn't care. Instead, they wanted justice for the death, unfair justice.

At least Dr. Adel had done a better job influencing the authorities and was finally granted permission to take the patient to the clinic at Al Khora village, where his head wound was sutured. However, the ruling was that the injured man would be handed over to the police directly following his treatment.

In the meantime, BP's safety rep Mr. Greggory showed up to write up the investigation. Those of us involved filled him in on the story. Greggory, in return, discussed the incident with the oilfield police officers trying to change their minds about convicting the crimeless man. Mr. Greggory's efforts were also fruitless, even after conveying that BP would take responsibility and pay for the damaged vehicle. When Dr. Adel returned with the patient, he was taken away to jail. My heart was saddened, and I finished the day feeling defeated.

Dr. Adel later explained what truly had happened here. The deceased policeman belonged to a specific local *eahira* (tribe), and the driver was a different *eahira*. This was a matter of tribal conflict.

I needed to understand precisely how the Iraqi tribal society worked to make more sense of this. Ms. Anwar had never mentioned local tribes before. We had only spoken about three groups of Muslims: Shiites, Sunni, and Kurds.

I was surprised to find out tribal structure has existed in Iraq since Mesopotamia, 5000-3500 BC. They have survived through centuries of ruling by empires, monarchies, multicultural powers, and national governments. Throughout time the tribes have been extremely crucial to Iraqi society. The tribal leader, a sheik, is responsible for protecting his clan. This tribal society precedes the advent of Islam. In modern clans, traditional ways still exist. Justice rules and laws are much unchanged. This includes blood feuds or tribal war, which is basically a longstanding conflict and involves protecting family or a clan's honor. So this is why the driver was being punished. It was a matter of vengeance, which is highly important. I learned male members are under an obligation to avenge the death of another tribe member. Sometimes this would be done by taking the life of one of the enemy tribe members for the murder of one of their own, but nowadays, it's more common to seek financial compensation for the death.

Dr. Adel said it was most likely what would happen to the poor Iraqi driver; his tribe would have to pay a few thousand dollars to the opposing tribe. No court of law would be involved, just ancestral politics.

One morning I stepped out of my cabin to find a cloud of fog covering the camp. As I made my way to the clinic to pack up the ambulance for the day, I wondered if we would be delayed. I started reminiscing about my childhood when we would have school postponed or sometimes canceled due to heavy fog. It would be such a treat to go back to bed for an extra couple of hours.

The QRF arrived, as usual, to lead us north for our daily routine. The team leader radioed us and told us to be cautious and that we would be traveling at a reduced speed today. The fog became so thick on the road that we couldn't see ten feet in front of us. Seth verbalized how crazy this was. After driving several kilometers, Seth got on the radio and shared his thoughts with the TL, who luckily agreed. If we were the only ones on the road, it would have been one thing, but with the erratic Iraqi drivers, it was hazardous to be sharing the road in these conditions. We pulled off the road into a large lot near a railroad track and degassing station to wait it out. Seth had his window down, and we could hear the occasional vehicle whizzing past. We both said someone is going to crash out there. It wasn't even ten minutes later when the tumultuous sound of metal smashing metal and glass shattering echoed through the thick air. "Crap," I feared the worst!

Seth boasted, "What'd I tell ya?"

A Toyota Hilux and a large work truck had hit head-on. The small truck had four or five passengers; of course, two guys had been riding in the back, standard practice. No one wears their seat belt even though there are signs all over ROO saying to.

Luckily, nobody was dead. The two guys in the truck's bed had been thrown out and had head injuries with lacerations. I was busy working on these guys when the soft-skinned ambulance arrived to transport them to the hospital in Basra. This was why we had trained and hired these men to be the ambulance crew. My role was to be there for the expats and not to be focusing on the locals unless they were critically ill, and then I could only transport them as far as our clinic at the main camp.

Callouts were always exciting, especially when we were sitting around Lion watching the minute hand on the clock pass ever so slowly. Many of our calls out were for the QRF to go and investigate some unexpected situation. We never knew what we would find waiting when we showed up.

One particular day, the QRF was called to check out some suspicious object lying out in the desert north of Lion. First of all, the directions given to the site had confused the TL, but after several wrong turns, we made our way to the location. It had been reported that someone found a missile from the recent war. This turned out not to be the case, but instead, some rusty old pipe sticking up out of the ground.

We often received emergency calls to respond to vehicle crashes, but after driving all around we would never find anything. Getting detailed directions never happened, as the expats had specific names for the road, and the locals knew them by something else. On top of that, there were no mile markers, and everything seemed to be just a guess. The QRF would get frustrated, but I didn't mind, as I loved getting to be out looking around the fascinating landscape.

Whenever the Quick Response Team (QRF) had an emergency call, the armored ambo was required to tag along. However, some team leaders disliked waiting on the slow, slothful ambulance, as our top speed was about 55 mph.

On one occasion, when Tane was filling in as my driver, we had an emergency call for an injured person out on the oil field. Our ambulance had been having carbonator issues and would, on occasion, choke and sputter and then lose power. So, it decided to act up as the QRF led the way to the scene. I remember Tane cursing and being embarrassed that he couldn't keep up. It must have seemed that we were lollygagging around. The QRF had to pull over and let traffic go around while they waited on us to keep up. I remember them calling us on the radio and inquiring what the heck we were doing. I, of course, had to tell them the ambo was misbehaving. It was annoying to be riding in an emergency vehicle with red lights flashing as traffic passed by us. So much for rushing to the accident.

Eventually, we got to the scene where I found an Iraqi oilfield worker with a hand wrapped in a shirt. He had squashed his hand when a heavy pipe was dropped on it. The poor guy was pale and screaming with pain. Placing a tourniquet around his arm on the opposite side of the injured hand, I located a vein to cannulate. His skin was nearly black with oil and dust residue, and it was impossible to get his skin clean. I must have used ten alcohol swabs and then gave up. Palpating a large vessel, I pushed an 18-gauge IV needle into his leathery skin. Bingo, a flash of red rushed into the flashback channel. I focused on my task even though I could feel the eyes of a small audience observing, including Tane. I loved showing off my skills; maybe I'd even impress someone. I opened the drug bag and drew up the morphine. With my patient more settled, I could then attend to his bloody hand. I could tell he was going to need some suturing and an X-ray. I washed off the wound and wrapped it with a clean dressing for transport to the medical center. Another life saved!

Boring or exciting, I was enraptured by being a remote medic in this extraordinary habitat, meeting and interacting with many different people. My dream job was far from what I pictured it might be like, but I was not disappointed. I would not be one of those who look back on their lives and say I wish I had. Forging ahead and taking the risk, the word "regret" will never roll off my tongue.

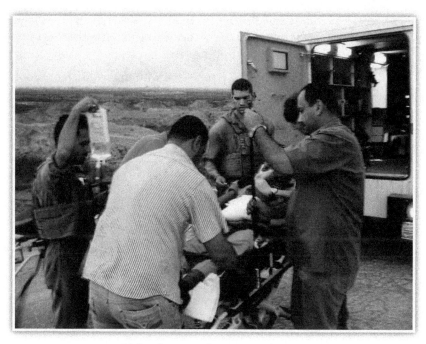

Adel and I caring for an injured patient

Head-on collision on Rumaila

Explosion on the oil field

Ready for action

A Target for a Good Kidnapping

*The moon's an arrant thief, and her pale
fire she snatches from the sun.*
                              ~ William Shakespeare

O ne hot August morning, the QRF team was sent to a lorry (heavy truck) accident. We arrived to find that a trailer filled with sand had overturned and was blocking part of the roadway. The QRF's duty was to secure the scene and control traffic until a cleanup crew arrived. Seth and I had nothing to do but sit inside the air-conditioned ambulance and patiently wait; security had instructed me to stay in the truck. Jokingly I asked Seth, "What do they think I'm going to do, go for a run in the 120° heat?"

Noon came and went, and still no one showed up to remove the sand. Seth and Chase, the security TL, were getting impatient and grumpy, and everyone was getting hungry. We had rushed off and left our lunches at Lion, thinking we'd be back by now. Thankfully, we had plenty of tepid water to drink. There were always a couple of cases of bottled water in the ambulance for this type of situation. Some hours into our stage-out, I had to pee, and soon I had to pee badly. Being the kind man he was, Seth got out of the ambulance and lit up a cigarette. I crawled into the back and peed into the wash bucket, as there was nowhere outside to pee without having eight men watching. Surveying to see that the guys were distracted, I jumped out the back door and emptied the bucket behind the ambo. Sometimes being a woman in a man's world means improvising. Finally, the cleanup crew arrived with a front-end loader and took over the situation. Thank the stars, they arrived before I needed to pee again.

Sandstorms are a common phenomenon in the Iraqi desert, arising more frequently during the summer months. These blinding storms can last for days. Sandstorms occur when the winds strengthen and lift grains of sand off the ground, blowing it through the air, causing decreased visibility and a brownout! Sand can get into your eyes, nose, mouth, and lungs if you are caught outside. Along with physical harm, blowing dust and sand can be similar to driving in snow. Sand can pile up on the roadway, as we found out the hard way on ROO.

It was always exhilarating when a sandstorm moved through, unless you were heading out on leave and your travel plans were affected. Luckily, I managed to escape any travel delays due to these nasty storms, but many expats were not so blessed.

Sandstorms were occasionally bad enough to halt operations on the oil-field. But since the QRF was the responsible party for evaluating hazards around the field, we still went out when other moves were stopped. The overpass we drove across en route to Lion always collected sand during these storms, which added to the excitement. The bridge had a very short guard-rail and was arched in the center; below was a four-lane highway leading to Baghdad.

I remember several times the sand piling up knee-deep on the bridge. If the driver didn't get up enough speed, the hefty ambo would sink in and come to a halt. On the other hand, speeding into the sand drift was death-defying. The armored ambo would slip and slide all over the road as if there was a sheet of ice on the bridge. Gripping my seat, I was petrified of falling over the edge onto the motorway below. My mind envisioned our truck sliding halfway off the bridge and coming to a stop, rocking back and forth like some wild Hollywood movie scene. I imagined my driver would probably open the door and jump to safety, and I would end up tumbling off the bridge along with the ambo. Sounds like a nightmare, huh?

We did get stuck a few times and had to shovel sand to get out. Soon we started avoiding the bridge when it was covered in brown grit by going down to the motorway below the bridge and coming back up the exit ramp on the other side. Finally, the QRF guys decided they had had enough shoveling sand.

There were permanently placed security posts throughout the oil field known as checkpoints. These stations were operated by armed Iraqi police personnel. Their job was to help keep the oil field safe by monitoring those vehicles traveling through the reserve, stopping any unregistered or suspicious vehicle, and doing a visual search where deemed appropriate.

I was appalled at the condition of these shacks. The quarters consisted of a scrappy small, half-fallen-down box that hardly kept the sun off the men working in these posts. No air con or heat source was provided. Each location also had a rusty container for the guards to hang out in when they weren't on duty. It looked like a miserable job.

Each day going and coming from Lion, we passed through two of these checkpoints. Neither CPs ever gave us any grief, and I can't ever remember them searching our vehicles. Instead, they became familiar with us as we passed through at least twice a day. At one particular CP, the guards would shyly flirt with me. Sheepishly they would hold their hands to their hearts, looking at me through the ambulance window, while bowing their heads and extending their arms in my direction, a gesture of respect. One young man started blowing me kisses, and I would blush and wave back, appeasing my admirer. Sometimes Seth would do a quick stop while moving through the gate and hand the guys some extra bottled water. It was Seth's way of showing respect to these men who stood out in the 125° heat all day.

Just north of Lion was a checkpoint I will refer to as Zebra (not its real name). This particular post was unreceptive to our caravan nearly every time we tried to pass through. In fact, I had strict instructions not to talk to these men if they stopped us. If I spoke, my nationality would be disclosed. Being American increased my risk and made me a target for a good kidnapping. There was so much corruption in this country I was told to trust no one.

I never figured out how the other CPs were more relaxed than Zebra, where we were harassed by the guards quite often. The QRF detested passing through this station. It was also crucial that I carry my passport or at least a copy of it. Only once did I have to show my documents to the Zebra guards, and once satisfied they waved us through. Funny thing, this wasn't a concern for Nicky as she was a Brit.

Security told me to lock my door and never allow the guys at this post to open it. But on two different occasions, they attempted to enter the ambulance uninvited. Each of these times, the QRF lead became angry and questioned why they needed to be in the ambulance. Next, an argument broke out over the issue. Listening from my secured seat as the shouting took place, I didn't know whether to feel guilty or privileged. I rather liked the idea of men fighting for my safety. I have to say I never really felt threatened, nor was I ever really fearful of traveling through this post. My guys were armed, and I doubt that the Iraqi offenders truly wanted big trouble, although I could have been wrong. Besides, I was not really of any significant value if kidnapped. I had no prestigious status, and it's not routine for major companies like BP to pay ransom anyway.

Living in the United States, being abducted rarely, if ever, crossed my mind. It's hard to fathom residing in a vicinity prone to hijackings. Yet, thinking about it gave me goosebumps. We had talked in great detail during the HET course about kidnappings in Iraq and parts of the Middle East. The facts were riveting; in 2004, members of the Iraqi insurgency began taking foreign hostages. More than 200 foreigners and thousands of Iraqis have been taken since this time. Some were killed, and others were released. The executions were sometimes filmed, which included beheadings. The motives included ransom money, prisoner exchange, discouraging travel to Iraq, and influencing foreign governments to withdraw troops or swaying foreign companies to remove workers.

I tried to imagine how horrible it would be to become a hostage. While working on ROO, I met several LN who shared stories of their friends or family being captured. For example, one of the Iraqi QRF drivers shared with me that the insurgency stole his fourteen-month-old son when he lived in Baghdad. The family had to pay $1800 US before the baby was returned. The same acquaintance said his father, a security supervisor, had also been taken. Instead of asking for a payment, he was assassinated because of his position; the rest of the family had also received death threats. The man relocated his family south to Basra to get away from this dire situation.

During my time in Iraq, I heard endless similar stories from the local people. It seemed everyone had been touched by the country's troublesome times. As I listened intently, my soul became inundated first with empathy, and my heart went out to this population. But beyond this, I was guilt-ridden.

No, it was not my fault, and I hadn't personally done anything to cause their suffering, but I was from a country whose actions brought on much of this retaliation.

In March 2003, US forces invaded Iraq, intending to destroy Iraq's weapons of mass destruction and put an end to the dictatorial rule of Saddam Hussein. Instead, a violent insurgency arose when no weapons were found, and the war lost its public support.

The insurgency started soon after the US invasion and lasted throughout the Iraq War (2003-2011). During this era, I had repeatedly heard the media talking about the insurgency, not knowing what the hell an insurgent was. I didn't care; I was a world away at that time. An insurgency is when a group forms to fight or rebels against authority, namely one's own government. In the beginning, the insurgency was focused on the multinational forces, which during the Iraq War were the United States, United Kingdom, Australia, Spain, and Poland. Then later, Iraqi security forces became the target, including law enforcement and the military. Even after the US troops left in December 2011, the mutiny continued. Now referred to as the Iraq Crisis, the violence escalated. Sectarian issues arose among Iraq's religious groups. The Shia held the majority of power in the central government, so the Sunni fought against them for control.

Understanding the country's trials and tribulations would help me connect with the people and my work. Every fact I learned was a step in seeing the big picture and deciphering their affliction.

Mark and I posing with AK-47's

Remnants from the Iraq war scattered on the oil field

A Secret Crush Coming to a Heart Near You

*She's lost under the spell of the moon
again and doesn't want to be found.*
~ *Daniel Mercury*

Have you ever stopped to think about what attracted you to your spouse, partner, or companion? Allurement is an unintelligible phenomenon. Some people know what draws them in, and others have no clue. Is it biological, psychological, or experience-based? What causes us to grow fond of someone to the point we can't stop thinking about him/her?

When we are young and naive, our emotions are all irrational. If a cute classmate gives you a smile, you might tumble over in love with that person. When I was a teenager, I wanted a boyfriend. All my friends had boyfriends, and, not wanting to be left out, I wanted one too. Desperate, I started hanging with a nerdy new kid. For two weeks, we walked around school holding hands. "Look at me. I have a boyfriend too!" The problem was I didn't even like the guy.

When I started dating my husband, I was still young and impressionable. I was seventeen, and he was five years older. I'm not sure why my parents allowed it, probably because they married young. Also, they knew his family.

Humorously, I broke up with him to date his younger brother. Then sadly the brother I was dating died in a truck accident a few days after we went to prom together. Mark had been my first love, or at least I thought so.

Mark asked me out while I was still dating the older brother. Because I was more attracted to Mark, I said yes. Sneaking out under the radar was stirring but also caused me anxiety. It was mean and disrespectful, plus Mark and I both knew we would soon get caught, so I ended it with the brother.

Dating Mark was an adventure. We were both seniors in high school but attended different schools. He lived in one county and I in another. Mark would come to my school's basketball game on Friday nights as I played trumpet in the pep band. On Saturday nights, we often went cruising around Huntington, the town he lived near. After a few laps around the city, we would stop by a liquor store, and somehow Mark walked out with a six-pack of beer. We were both eighteen and under the legal drinking age of twenty-one. With beer in hand, we would drive to some dark lot and park or go "parking," as we called it. One time we were making out when a cop car pulled up next to us. The officer proceeded to get out of his car and walked over while shining a flashlight in our faces. The policeman motioned Mark to roll down his window. I was literally shaking with fear by then. We were asked if we had been drinking.

"No, officer."

"Well, you can't park here now. Leave." Mark had remained calm and collected. I was relieved we were scolded and let go. My concern had been getting caught drinking and my parents being called. I would have been mortified.

Mark and I continued to date throughout the spring and were each other's dates for senior prom. I was crazy about this guy and planned to continue seeing him after graduation. If Mark had lived, I would have no doubt lost my virginity to him that summer. But life is not fair, and his life was taken away too soon.

After graduation, Mark and his brother headed west to deliver three semi-trucks to a buyer in Southern California. They had driven all night and planned to pull off at the next rest area once they crossed over into California. The sun was just breaking the horizon as they passed the "Welcome to California" sign. Mark didn't make it to the rest area before he fell asleep at the wheel and drove off the road, rolling the truck down a steep embankment. The semi burst into flames, and Mark died at the scene.

I'll never forget the morning when my mom, who was sobbing, sat me down at the kitchen table. She seemed so distressed, and I had no clue why she was upset and tried comforting her. "Mom, it's going to be OK."

My mother hugged me tightly, her face red as tears fell from her cheeks. Her reply to me was, "You're not going to think so. Mark was killed yesterday!"

My mom was right. I wasn't OK. Mark's funeral was incredibly painful. It was the most emotionally difficult day I had felt in the eighteen years of my life. I spent most of that summer being sad.

Soon Mark's older brother and I started hanging out, and we each felt the void of losing someone we cared for. As time passed, we became attached. Slowly our hearts healed. We had no choice but to move on.

As the story goes, I married the older brother and had four children with him. He was not the right person for me. I married for all the wrong reasons. I was impressed that he was older, had his own business, drove cool vehicles, and could afford to take me on vacations. The reason we got together was due to our emotional stress over losing Mark. We mourned together and ended up getting married. I dropped out of college and started working as a secretary for his company.

Two weeks after returning from our three-week-long honeymoon in Colorado, my new husband started letting me know who the boss was. An argument broke out when I asked if I could go to a truck auction in Nebraska with him and his business partner. While we were dating, he often took me with him on these trips. To this day, I can still hear him say, "No, you're not going. You have to stay home and run the office. Remember, I'm your boss, and I'm always right." I clearly remember being shocked by those words; I cried and wondered if this was what I had to look forward to for the rest of my life.

When I got married, I truly believed it would be "til death do us part." My parents set the standard; they loved and cherished each other. Sometimes they got angry with each other, but more often they were happy. As a child, I would walk into the kitchen and find my dad in his dirty farm coveralls, arms around my mother, kissing her. I would blush and leave the room. They married very young; my mother was only seventeen, and my dad was nineteen. They had managed to stick it out through thick and thin until death did part them.

Those who know me best would not have paired me up with Tane. First of all, I'm taller, built like a runner, and am outgoing and a wee bit rambunctious. Tane is masculine, assembled like a warrior, placid and restrained. I've been told opposites sometimes do attract.

I had this suspicious feeling that a tough guy was hidden under that tranquil personality, someone who would be able to deal with any situation at hand—an attractive trait, in my opinion.

On those days I was fortunate to be escorted by Mr. T. I methodically tried to gather facts about the person hidden behind those enticing eyes. What's this guy's story? I did learn he got his beautiful complexion through his family's native bloodline. He had fathered two offspring but denied being married. When I asked why he didn't marry, he just shrugged his shoulders, "I don't know." Tane didn't seem open to discussing the topic. Maybe it was a sensitive issue or he didn't think it was any of my business. His flat affect led me to sense he wasn't one to share his emotions. Honestly, my experience has always been that most men isolate their sensitive feelings, especially tough guys.

I hoped I wasn't being too annoying. "Sorry if I'm asking too many questions."

Tane's reply, "No, it's OK. How about you? Are you married?"

I blurted out loudly, "No, been there, done that."

I became preoccupied with a strange feeling I always had when I was around this engaging man. I felt a deep sense of security. Honestly, it was kinda weird, and I can't exactly explain it. My inner being experienced a wave that filled me with contentment and bliss. All I know is I liked feeling this way. I'm not calling it love, but it did warm my core. However, this did play an essential role in the allurement. If he were a library book, I'd check him out.

What do you do when you want him to know? Since my fixation started, I had been too insecure to figure out how to capture Tane's attention. We discussed his home country, and Tane told me I should come to visit sometime. I should have said, "I would love to. Can I get your email address?" Instead, he asked me to give him mine. Excited, I thought this might be my way in. Two weeks later, he finally emailed me, sharing his address. Super excited, I emailed him back, but by this time Tane was out on leave. Time went by, and I never heard from him. My infatuation had been going on for nearly a year by now. I had initially thought this might be the way to start something, but he told me later he rarely checks his personal email. Outside of him driving the ambo, I rarely got a chance to interact with him, and when I did, we were often in mixed company. On the occasions we were alone for the thirty-minute drive coming and going to Lion, I was at a loss about how to be both professional and impish.

When Tane and I were together for the short drive to and from Lion, I did my best to strike up playful conversations or ask him questions, hoping he would see my curiosity. Because he was focusing on the road, I never got the chance to look him in the eyes and give him that hinting glimpse. Nor was I ever in a position to get physically close enough to "accidentally on purpose" brush up against him. I laughed at his jokes and teased him occasionally when I felt it fit the scene. Outside the ambulance, I only saw him from a distance, and when I did, I didn't want to seem obvious around others.

Tane's driving started becoming less frequent. I was envious when Nicky was blessed with his presence and I was not. Sometimes it would be weeks between getting to see him. During prayers, my eyes would scan the room, and even when I did spy him, he would often vanish before I could say a quick hello. He seemed to be as sly as a fox. Maybe this was just a hopeless crush.

Mom and Dad's wedding day November 3, 1956

Sarah and Jerry Tucker (my parents) 50th wedding anniversary

Mark and I at the Southern Wells High School prom May 1979. One week before Mark was tragically killed

The Long Road Home

*Blessed is the moon; it goes but
it comes back again.*

~ Samoan Proverb

It is a long and complicated process to travel home.
The distance from the oil field to Basra International
Airport is more than one hour. The travel to and
from the airport was always considered our highest risk.
Although southern Iraq was much safer than the north, it
was still Iraq. People were still being murdered nearly every
day somewhere around the country. To travel to the airport
or anywhere, we were required to wear our bullet-resistant
vests and helmet. One size fits NO one, especially me. Our
transportation was armored vans with armed guards and
armed escort vehicles. We drove in a caravan of four to five vehicles staying close together.

Prior to arriving at the airport, the caravan would pull into a dusty
trash-ridden parking lot, the Dust Bowl. Here we would get into another
vehicle and proceed without armed guards, as they weren't allowed to have
weapons within a certain distance of the airport.

Having all this protective gear and equipment makes it sound like we
expected a major incident. So far, there had not been any hostile acts against
BP's employees working at Rumaila, but there was always a possibility that
could change. Anytime we were outside the protective walls of HQ, we became more vulnerable. After my first couple of weeks of being in Iraq, I

started to feel more at ease. But when I first arrived, I was tense and edgy. I can remember not sleeping well even though I was exhausted. My mind was filled with haunting thoughts as I lay in bed every night, wondering if this would be the night we would get rocketed. Would I even hear the alarm if we did? Luckily, my apprehension wore off, and I could settle in, except when we set out for the airport.

Border crossing stations are expected between countries, but encountering them multiple times within one country was an awakening ordeal. Working and traveling in a nation where the security was highly volatile was both engrossing and a bit unnerving. I was deeply aware that guard posts, on rare occasions, get taken over by unfriendlies wanting to harm those passing through. Therefore, I had no choice but to trust our security people, which I did. While driving in the caravan, I always tried to score the middle position in the first row behind the driver. I could see out the front window from here, and I could watch both the driver and the armed escort sitting in the passenger's seat. From this spot, I observed how seriously these men took their jobs. If they were tense, I could tell. For example, they might tell everyone in the van to please be quiet as they listened to radio traffic; other times they would mumble softly between themselves, eyes scanning the road and landscape. Yet, I never felt afraid nor worried something bad would happen. I have to say that I'm a genuinely brave woman and that my love of adventure overruled fear. Besides, Iraq is not a place for scaredy cats. Yet, stored in the corner of my mind, I held a sense of vigilance.

Between the Dust Bowl and the airport, a span of five kilometers, we passed through two different posts. The first station checked our badges and did a vehicle inspection, including using a mirror to check the undercarriage for bombs. The second made us unload our luggage so they could do a visual and a scan search of our belongings. It was always fun to be standing in line with a bunch of male expats while the Iraqis looked through my underwear for whatever illegal items I might be trying to hide.

Basra's small airport has only one terminal but boasts a very high level of security. I always wondered if having four security scanners before you actually boarded your flight was truly necessary. Women travelers were required to go to a secluded room to have our handbags checked and be given a pat-down by a female employee. I never carried a purse and only had my backpack, and I am sure they thought that I was not a very girly girl. However, they were normally friendly, and after being cleared I would be allowed to leave without speaking English. They would smile, nod their heads, and point to the door. I would nod back and thank them with a *shukran* as I exited.

When leaving Iraq, I could never really relax until I had made it through all of the airport checkpoints and the airplane was out of missile range on its way to Kuwait.

On one particular occasion, I was detained at the number three security scanner while making my way to board my flight. After I handed my passport over to the agent, he began flipping through the pages and then stopped when something of concern caught his eye. He walked over to another agent, and together they secretly discussed the issue. "Crap," I whispered to myself. "Now what?" I had just cleared two other stations without any problems. Panic set in as I was told to step aside and wait while the agent left, carrying my passport through a closed-door thirty feet away. My heart started pounding as I watched the last ROO employee vanish up the escalator. My hands now were sweating as I thought about my situation. No one but me was aware of my predicament. The security team would have already left the airport, and the other employees were out of reach. It didn't help my confidence knowing I was in a country known for corruption. Several minutes later, my passport was happily returned, and nothing was said as I continued on my way.

When I started working in Iraq, the US military was still deployed there. One of the bases the Americans occupied was at COB (Contingency Operating Base), which was only two miles from the Basra International Airport. I was a bit freaked out knowing that the insurgents were still firing rockets into the COB quite frequently while I was traveling in and out of the commercial airport nearby. I knew, good and well, that one of those rockets could easily be directed toward the crowded airport or the jets coming and going. So on the one hand it was a relief when the US pulled out in December 2011, lessening the reason for the insurgents to fire rockets, but on the other hand it had been a reassurance knowing US troops were not far away.

For the first year and a half, we traveled through Kuwait City on a chartered Lear jet that BP leased. This was because commercial flights had only just restarted flying into Basra's airport postwar (2011), and BP wasn't ready to trust having their high-dollar employees travel commercially. BP had safety concerns, and I can only presume the worry was the possibility of an explosive being snuck on board or being shot out of the sky by a rocket.

Once airborne, I always let out a big sigh as the classy aircraft headed south. It was such a satisfying feeling to know another rotation had been completed, and I had twenty-eight days to spend as I chose, minus the travel to and from Iraq. Melting into the comfy leather seat, I sat back, looked out the window, and enjoyed the splendid aerial view of the Shatt al-Arab River. Our flight path followed the river which split Iraq from Iran. The Shatt continued widening until she kissed the Persian Gulf and became one with the navy-blue sea.

This job allowed me to see places in the world that very few non-military folks have or will ever see. On the approach to Kuwait City, the country's capital, I could survey several well-known landmarks, including the Kuwait Towers and the Grand Mosque. The process was to fly along the beautiful golden shoreline, turn inland on the south side of the city just beyond the skyscrapers, landing at the airport, which was fifteen kilometers west of the town.

For most of my trips home, I would catch a commercial flight onward, leaving the same day. Coming back to work on the other hand, I always ended up overnighting in Kuwait City. It was a long trip home, more than twenty hours in the air.

Where the Bedouin Roam

Ignorance is the night of the mind,
a night without moon or star.

~ Confucius

I was pretty much always ready to return to ROO after having twenty-eight days off. Having an intriguing job in an alien land made it fun to come back to work. In reality, I only had twenty-three days off, as it took three days to travel back to the Middle East with the time difference and two days to get home. My rotation started once I arrived in Rumaila and was on vacation when I started my travel home.

From the very beginning, I had made up my mind I was going to embrace and relish everything this opportunity offered. This kicked off the minute I hesitantly gave the thumbs-up and decided to link up with Frontier. In addition, owning a positive attitude allowed me to be grateful for this precious venture.

Unlike most other ROO employees who dreaded the hour drive from the Basra airport to camp, I actually treasured the trip. Although the commute entailed a bit of danger, I found the ride exhilarating. Being fully mindful that we were susceptible to potential IED attacks didn't phase me much. I know what you must be thinking, and understandably this place is not for everyone.

While most people avoid unwarranted risks, others like me love the feeling of adrenaline. I'm unsure when this craving for adventure swept over me, but it seemed to have started building after I left my husband. Once I took a crowbar to that door, there was no stopping me. I was like a child let loose in a candy store, filling my pockets with every kind of sweet I could grab. However, I did discover not everything was as good on the inside as the wrapper led it to be. As for being an adrenaline junkie, I got a powerful high from the norepinephrine dump my body released during times of excitement. It was like an addiction. I was constantly on the prowl for a stimulating escapade.

Every trip entertained some new and fascinating sights along the route. For instance, I found it chilling when I saw Iraqi military units cruising by proudly flying their red, white, and black colored flag. My inward eye flashed visions of US troops and the Iraqi military in all-out combat only a few months before this day. I wondered if they still desired to kill Americans or if their attitudes had changed.

On one occasion, we witnessed a car driving past with a rolled-up tarp tied to the roof flapping in the wind. "Oh, looks like that family is getting a new carpet," I gestured. A chuckle broke out in front.

"Jo, that's not a carpet. That's a family taking their deceased loved one to Najaf to be buried."

"No way. You're kidding me, right?"

"Nope, it's true." They further explained that Muslims try to bury their dead within one to two days of death. When possible, the burial takes place at the Peace Valley Cemetery outside the city of Najaf. The traditional way is to lay the unembalmed body on their right side facing Mecca. *Wadi-al Salaam*, Arabic for Valley of Peace, is an Islamic cemetery covering 2.32 square miles and contains more than eight million bodies; it is the largest graveyard globally.

The desert was so barren yet so enthralling at the same time. I found the flat, dry, and dusty landscape an enticing diorama. Driving past an occasional lone building or two, where some family dwelled, the houses I saw were made of brick, concrete, or mortar, the same color as the surrounding desert sand. There are no doors and glass windows, only a simple curtain hanging in the opening. I reflected on how these hearty people survived; I felt a sense of empathy as the children would often stand by the side of the road as we drove past them. They looked dejected and seemed to have nothing to occupy their time. These children did not have a TV, let alone a Nintendo, in their homes.

Plant life is sparse in this region; the desert hosts a few shrubs and a lone gum or date palm tree. But during certain times of the year, there would actually be fields of tomatoes growing. Somehow, they irrigated the fields of sand and produced ripe red tomatoes.

My favorite sightings were the Bedouin people who migrated to the area during the rainy winter. This society of nomadic people moved with their livestock to this area so they could graze their camels, sheep, goats, and donkeys. They traveled in large trucks with all their belongings and then set up camp in the desert, living in tents and cooking over an open fire. I could never figure out what the animals grazed on. Even during the winter, the desert never turned green when it did rain. So how did one sheep find food, let alone many dozens? Whenever I saw the Bedouins, I felt like I was witnessing the shepherds of biblical times. The Bedouin children liked to run out close to the road as we drove past. They would jump up and down, trying to get us to wave back and honk our horns. This seemed to have been their greatest form of entertainment.

Somewhere deep in my soul, I always wished I could spend a day with one of these families, eating whatever they did, sleeping on the ground, hearing their stories, and seeing their way of life. But, of course, I would have needed an interpreter as they would not have been English-speaking.

Many areas of the desert around the oil field were not safe to walk or drive across, and yet these nomads would be living out there with their large herds of animals.

I wondered why they took the risk to graze in this hazardous area. The Bedouins surely were aware of the danger. The Iraqi desert was scattered with thousands of landmines and other explosives during the war. As an oil field employee, I had been repeatedly warned never to walk anywhere off either the pavement or a cement surface for this particular reason, of course, unless the area displayed white sandbags, signaling a cleared zone.

ROO employed an Explosive Ordnance Disposal team (EOD) responsible for clearing any new areas to be drilled. The UXOs would be dug up and placed in a pile, then detonated safely. This was a dangerous job, and things could go very wrong.

On October 11, 2011, while I was on leave, six employees were killed on Rumaila while defusing a pile of UXOs they had gathered and stacked in a heap. It was reported that they had attempted to detonate the pile of land-mines, but the detonation seemed to have failed. The delayed charge fired when they approached the ordnance, blowing up everything, including the EOD team standing too close.

Unfortunately, the Bedouins also got first-hand experience of what could happen. One night a group of their camels wandered away from the herd and walked into an uncleared minefield looking for some nice grass to munch on. Unfortunately, the poor camels found out the hard way the grass is not always greener. Two were killed and another wounded.

Iraqi military vehicle

Bedouin herding their livestock

Bedouin ushering his sheep on ROO

Bedouin grazing goats and sheep on the oil field

Ali Baba

*If you love, love the moon; if
you steal, steal a camel.*

~ *Egyptian Proverb*

O ne evening following our daily camp meeting, the women were asked to stay behind. We patiently waited as the men exited the building. Then, whispering among ourselves, our curiosity was ignited. It felt like we had some female-only secret to share. The phrase "girls only, please" caused my mind to flash back to when I was in the fifth grade of primary school and our school nurse Mrs. Kober gathered all the girls to discuss the birds and the bees. Sitting there next to Lilith, I mumbled, "We will probably be told we can't wear shorts in camp or something to this effect." Lilith shrugged her shoulders and didn't say anything.

When the room was clear of our male cohorts, a red-faced man stood in the front of the room. Clearing his throat, he began, "Well, ladies, this is a bit of an embarrassing subject. I'm sorry to have to tell you this, but during a search of the cleaners and laundry boy's dorm rooms," pausing, "umm, some of your personal items were found." The quiet audience now started looking around the room at each other with raised brows. Then a soft chatter broke out as the small group of women debated aloud what the speaker could possibly be talking about.

"Ladies," the man spoke, trying to take back control over the humming assembly. Continuing, the gentleman described that management had received several complaints of expats missing various electronics out of the rooms. During the search, not only were some of the missing electronics discovered but approximately forty pairs of women's panties had also been recovered. This is not what I expected to hear. I was aghast at this news, and my thoughts went straight to the gutter. There are only a couple of reasons guys would steal women's dirty underwear, gross.

Nonetheless, we were told if we wanted to come and sort through the pile, we were welcome to. But everyone was too embarrassed to go looking. Until now, I hadn't thought about it, but I was sure I had fewer knickers than when I first arrived.

One of the amenities that came with working on the oil field as an expat was that our laundry was done by young Indian and Sri Lankan room attendants. Our linen was changed once a week, and when we needed our laundry done, we were to leave our laundry bags out on the steps of our cabin. Likewise, our clean clothes were returned nicely pressed and folded later that evening, minus an occasional pair of undies.

Talk About Culture Shock

Three things cannot be long hidden—
the sun, the moon, and the truth.

~ *Buddha*

Once I secured my job with Frontier and the boun-
teous paychecks started rolling in, I decided to
pursue my ultimate dream adventure. So I signed
up to go to Nepal.

I'm unsure when I formulated a love for the mountains.
But, as I look back, I remember, at the young age of thirteen,
writing an essay on mountaineering and how dangerous it
could be. I did not grow up in a mountainous environment,
but I knew someday I would seek to experience them.

My passion grew after I moved to Arizona in 1996. Over the years that I
lived in the western United States, I got the opportunity to explore and build
my skills hiking and climbing up to elevations reaching more than 14,000
feet or 4200 meters.

I had envisioned traveling to a distant land for years. Finally, in 2006, I
found the courage to step out of the comfort of my backyard. With tremen-
dous preparation, my wish at long last came true. I traveled to Africa and
summited Mount Kilimanjaro. This adventure is a story I will save for the
next book.

I figured I had lived through the Mount Kilimanjaro journey, and I was ready to step up the challenge and head to the Himalayas, where the highest and most famous mountain of all is located.

For years, I subscribed to *Outside* magazine, an American-published journal covering travel, sports, gear, and fitness topics. Reading stories about people's great adventures and travels inspired me to want my own experiences, but my dreams got put aside with four kids to raise.

Then finally my time had come, both personally and financially. With self-sufficient children standing on their own, I started spreading my wings. Being on the mailing list and receiving beautifully colored and alluring brochures from Wilderness Medical Society, I started getting serious about joining a trip.

Wilderness Medical Society (WMS) is an international association for professionals who are enticed with providing medical care in forbidding outdoor environments. The organization hosts adventure trips in unique locations worldwide while teaching wilderness medicine sessions. They focus on educating medical providers on managing illness, injuries, and emergencies in unconventional situations in outdoor settings. This training was much the same as the course I had attended in Washington back in November of 2010.

Deciding to go to Everest was easy. Getting prepared physically, mentally, and logistically became the tricky part. I signed up seven months in advance, which allowed me time to plan. Since working in Iraq, I had minimal exposure to altitude training; basically, I got in shape running on a treadmill at sea level. Then, when I was home on leave, I hiked in the mountains as time allowed.

The dates lined up perfectly where I would be able to spend my twenty-eight-day leave in Nepal, hiking up to Everest's Base Camp. WMS's Everest program offered three different levels to choose from. The first option was trekking to Base Camp (BC). The second pick included staying an extra five days and climbing higher up on Everest to Camp 2, and the third was an attempt to reach Camp 4.

You would think I would have been content to have trekked the 38.5 miles/62 km from Lukla to BC and back. But of course not. I wanted the challenge of going higher than Base Camp and decided reaching Camp 2 would be my goal.

My African undertaking to Kilimanjaro had also been organized by WMS, which had proven to be a great experience. I expected nothing less than another fabulous excursion with like-minded companions and one more box checked off of my ever-growing list.

From the day I registered for the trip to BC, I started bracing myself for the challenges I knew I would undoubtedly face. I wasn't as worried about my physical fitness but more about my mental toughness. The mind is our strongest muscle and yet our worst enemy. To succeed, I would have to find the mental capacity to deal with exhaustion, cold, shortness of breath, nausea, and fear—fear of the terrifying Khumbu Icefall. Thus began the many nights in which I tossed and turned. Anticipatory anxiety settled in my brain, causing me to awaken at 0300, envisioning rows of aluminum ladders laid across the endless black crevasses strung throughout the Khumbu. In the quietness of the night, I started second-guessing my ability. But once the sun was awake, I regained my confidence and was totally stoked.

During my flight to Nepal, I was overpowered with emotions. Feeling everything from excitement, disbelief, anxiety, and pride, my heart was smiling all the way up to my face. I hoped I was ready to take on the Himalayas; I'd find out soon enough. An hour before landing in Kathmandu, my eyes started scanning the horizon from my window seat. I had my fingers crossed that her majesty would honor me with a sighting. Suddenly in the distance, the jagged snow-covered peaks came into view. My eyes widened, and my heart pounded with joy. There she was, standing lordly and altitudinous. I cried, not just a tear or two. I cried uncontrollably, overcome with bliss and sentiment. It came out of nowhere. Even now, when I reflect on my first glimpse of Mount Everest, I still get teary.

I arrived in Nepal's capital city of Kathmandu on the twenty-third of April 2012, a day ahead of all the others. After obtaining a tourist visa and clearing customs, I found my bags and exited Tribhuvan Airport.

I was greeted by a designated driver waiting to deliver me to my hotel.

Stepping outside, I was unprepared for the sultry conditions; sweat beads immediately formed on my face as I pushed my way through the massive crowd of travelers while dragging a cart piled with my luggage. Looking around, I felt helpless as to where I should go to find my ride.

My tension lifted when I finally spotted the Peak Promotion sign. Approaching the small dark-skinned man, I introduced myself. "Hello, I'm Jonea. I'm with the Wilderness Medicine group."

"Namaste, welcome to Nepal, home of the Himalayan Mountains. Are you here to climb?" I could sense the local man's pride in his country.

"Yes, sir, I'm attempting to reach Camp 2." Without explaining, the driver knew I was talking about Camp 2 on Everest.

"Ma'am, I will be taking you to the Yak and Yeti Hotel. Is this correct? It is one of Kathmandu's finest hotels."

"Yes, sir, that's the place."

The ride through the maze of noisy and congested streets to the hotel was a grand inauguration to the spellbinding city. I had experienced many fast-paced metropolises before, but nothing compared to this. The roads were narrow and lined with decaying architecture, beeping motorbikes, bicycle tuk-tuks, cows, chickens, and goats, then add in hundreds of pedestrians. It was a frantic, exotic atmosphere, both charming and chaotic in the same breath.

After checking into the Yak and Yeti, I dropped my bags and freshened up, then headed out. First, I stopped by the front desk to exchange some American dollars for Nepalese rupees and retrieved a city map. "Ma'am, could you please recommend a restaurant nearby?" I questioned the beautiful round-faced desk clerk.

"Yes, there is a popular place just across the street if you would care to try the local cuisine."

"Nah-muh-stay (namaste)," I carefully pronounced the Hindi greeting as I turned toward the exit.

Exploring has become customary whenever I arrive in a new place; it was no different here. Eager to get lost in the culture, I headed out in the intimidating mayhem, hoping I could find my way back before dark.

With a population of over 2.5 million people, this city was buzzing with activity. It was truly sensory overload. Traffic jammed alleys with smog-producing rickety old cars, this was my first experience seeing rickshaws. My nose was filled with the stale odor of filth and fumes, cow dung mixed with fragrant incense, aromatic spices, and the pleasing smell of restaurants stewing curry dishes. The streets were very narrow alley lanes with shop after shop selling everything imaginable: unrefrigerated hanging meats, copper wear, textiles, housewares, clothing, spices, vegetables, souvenirs, hiking and outdoor wear, books. You name it, it must have been there somewhere.

Meandering through the jungle of alleyways, I deliberated on choosing a place to dine. Keeping in mind the eatery across from the Yak and Yeti, I planned on visiting it the following day. There was no shortage of eating establishments, but I found it hard to feel comfortable choosing one as the outsides looked suspiciously unappealing, warranting concerns about food safety. This was especially true after witnessing the fly-covered meat hanging in the local markets. I had seen some eye-opening things in Africa, but that didn't compare to the streets of Kathmandu. I hoped I could avoid meeting up with the well-known Montezuma's revenge that this part of the world had to offer. Finally deciding to pull the ripcord, I landed at a lovely Asian/Nepali café. The food was delightful and cheap, and I didn't get sick either.

Over the next two days, the rest of our group arrived, including my room-mate, Bhanu, a beautiful Indian doctor from Los Angeles. As luck would have it, Bhanu and I ended up being compatible. We were close in age and both loved hiking. Having common interests and working in the medical profession made it easy to converse and get to know each other. I was blessed to have been paired up with Bhanu. I couldn't have chosen a better roommate myself.

Twenty-five American trekkers had come to Nepal to participate in the once-in-a-lifetime adventure. Four of us had signed up for the Camp 2 experience, 3350 feet higher than Base Camp, which sits at 17,650ft or 5380m in elevation. If the extra elevation wasn't enough to stress me out, climbing up through the deadly Khumbu Icefall sure was. My nerves started causing my thoughts to repeatedly stray into the danger zone.

I was anxious to learn more about the other three people going up to Camp 2, trusting that they too might be feeling overwhelmed. However, after I started getting to know the members of our group, I discovered most everyone felt uncertain about their decision to be here. It was good to know I wasn't alone.

The insomnia that had started months ago was now eating up half of my sleep as D-day neared. I had read too many mountaineering tales, such as Lincoln Hall's story, *Dead Lucky*, where he was pronounced dead and left overnight near the summit of Everest, or Joe Simpson's terrifying account of climbing in the Andes. Besides, I had Googled way too many pictures of the unnerving Khumbu with its multiple ladder crossings. Of all the sections on Everest, the famous Khumbu Icefall receives its fair share of headlines for the danger lurking there.

During our introduction meeting, I realized I knew one person in the group, a physician I had met a few years earlier in Flagstaff, Arizona, during another wilderness medicine course. Otherwise, I knew no one in our small party, which was made up mostly of doctors. Average staff nurses can't usually afford to make such a costly trip.

There was one couple in their sixties that I started sitting with during breakfast: Carol, an ER doc, and her husband, Brad. Brad did not work in the medical field but loved hiking in the mountains. One afternoon while hanging out in the lounge, Brad said, "Jo, I'm so envious of you getting to go to advanced BC (the other name for Camp 2)."

I eagerly replied, "It's not too late. You could still come along," hoping he would say yes. Brad wanted to go to Camp 2 also, but he was apprehensive about his abilities and getting altitude sickness, so he didn't sign up.

Every day Brad would ask me if I was ready for Camp 2. "Are you scared? Are you nervous?"

"I am nervous. I have been losing sleep for weeks." Brad's comments were so getting to my head. He meant no harm, but his constant reminding me of how dangerous it was made me super edgy. Not only was I struggling to sleep, but my nerves were also affecting my appetite, causing me to be nauseated during meals. This was the last thing I needed. In reality, I should have been trying to increase my calorie intake. I started to wonder if I should even follow through or only go as far as BC and return with the others. What if I wasn't strong enough, developed altitude problems, or fell in a crevasse? The icefall was full of crevasses.

The WMS group spent two days in Kathmandu, getting to know each other and touring the city. My co-worker at Rumaila, Lee, had been to Kathmandu and described it as a magical place. I couldn't have said it better—so many interesting attractions.

Influenced by Hindus and Buddhists, the city offers multitudinous cultural sites, everything from palaces, temples, shrines, sculptures, pagodas, and stupas. Having the opportunity to see so many architectural treasures was fascinating. Although I had researched Nepal and its people before arriving, I had focused on the mountain. Getting immersed in the culture opened my mind and piqued my interest. I had never been that fond of history until I started traveling internationally.

Our group visited many highlights. Three, in particular, have been etched in my memory, which I will always cherish. The first of these is Boudhanath Stupa, a massive white spherical building that dominates the skyline; it is one of the largest stupas in the world and is one of the seven UNESCO

World Heritage Sites in Kathmandu. A stupa is a mound-like structure that holds relics and remains of Buddhist monks or nuns. It is recognized as a spiritual place of peace and meditation. From high up on the central tower of the Boudhanath Stupa are a set of colorful eyes said to be Lord Buddha's, watching over the world. As I walked in silence around the stupa, a sense of serenity could be detected in the atmosphere. As I inhaled the burning incense, I thought it must be laced with some magical substance, and I was graced with a feeling of calm and peace.

Swayambhunath Stupa is Nepal's oldest Buddhist Stupa. Our visit began by climbing the 365 steps from the road up to the main stupa. So much for being a fit bunch of trampers. The ninety-degree temperatures and the ninety percent humidity meant we all sweated our way to the top.

Making my way up the stairs, I passed several small Buddhist shrines decorated in white and gold flowers, lit candles, and burning incense. Strung above our heads were rows and rows of colorful prayer flags. Stopping half-way from the top, I wiped the sweat from my eyes and took out my camera to snap photos of the numerous fidgety monkeys frolicking in the shade of the giant evergreen trees, hence the reason Swayambhunath is nicknamed Monkey Temple. From the top, where the mystifying stupa sits, was a mag-nificent view of Kathmandu city. The ambiance was completed by the sound of drums, cymbals, and horns, along with chanting monks echoing in the background.

Encircling the white dome of the Swayambhunath stupa are 211 prayer wheels. A prayer wheel is a cylinder-shaped wheel placed on a spindle, made of wood, metal, stone, or sometimes leather. Each wheel is inscribed with a Buddhist prayer, the mantra "Om Mani Padme Hum," which I was told has an in-depth meaning, basically good karma.

Walking the circle, I set the wheels into motion as I traversed around the stupa, spinning the wheels in a clockwise direction so they would turn in the same direction as the written prayers and the same direction as the sun's movement through the skies. I spun a few hundred wheels during my time in Nepal, hoping for all the positive energy I could soak in. I had a big mountain waiting for me.

Pashupatinath Temple is one of the four most important religious sites in Asia for followers of Shiva. Shiva is the third god in the Hindu triumvirate. Pashupatinath Temple was built in the fifth century, and the site is reported to have existed since the beginning of the millennium, a period of a thousand years. As Nepal's most significant temple compound, it stretches on both sides of the Bagmati River, which is also considered holy by Hindus.

Pashupatinath Temple is the one I remember best of all the places we visited. It was an out-of-this-world kind of experience. Walking beside the dirty gray Bagmati River toward the largest temple complex in all of Nepal, we encountered an eye-catching figure. Doing a double-take, I looked at Bhanu and then back at the powdered-sugar-white man standing on the stone steps in the shade. However, it was not powdered sugar but ashes covering the man. The first thing that sparked my attention was his light-brown matted dreadlocks that were as long as he was tall. The shirtless man wore a white knee-length loin cloth and stood barefoot next to a small brick hut. He looked around sixty years old, just a guesstimate though.

The man we encountered was a holy man, a religious ascetic, who the Hindus call a *sadhu*. *Sadhus* forsake their earthly life and all of its worldly accessories, including home and family, to live a life of religion. They rely on the generosity of others and the monetary donations we tourists provide for the opportune photo.

More *sadhu* were seen sitting around the many temples along the river. Some wore saffron-colored clothing, and most had their faces painted white, orange, or red. None were shaven; a few had gray beards twisted into waist-long dreads. I found these devout homeless souls amusing. They reminded me of mimes or statues instead of human beings, for they just sat quietly as the crowd gawked and shot photographs.

We walked further up the river and arrived at the main temple's premises. Regrettably, only the two practicing Hindus from the group were allowed in; non-Hindus are strictly forbidden entry. So the rest of us remained on the east side of the river, observing the ongoings around us, while Bhanu and Kanak relished their once-in-a-lifetime opportunity.

As we sat waiting and chatting in the morning sun, someone pointed out that two cremations were about to take place across the river. The group leader had warned us that we might have the chance to witness a public funeral. I didn't know whether to be horrified or buoyant.

Where in the world can you publicly watch a body being burned? Kathmandu, that's where. It felt like I had been transformed into a medieval place in time; witnessing such a ghastly sight was spine-chilling.

In the Hindu religion, cremation is a part of their tradition. Cremating a body after death alongside the holy Bagmati is thought to remove all sins, allowing the person to be sent to Nirvana.

From our seats we watched intensely as two separate altars, forty feet apart, were prepared for the ritual. First, the funeral pyre, or a stack of wood, was arranged on an elevated platform, just a few feet from the river. The deceased body, wrapped in a white sheet, was then carried out and placed on the pyre as a handful of family members stood close. An older woman approached and kissed the dead man's uncovered head then filled his mouth with rice to provide nourishment for the departed. Next, the two sons circled the body, and then the oldest son lit the body on fire. The funeral was over in a matter of fifteen minutes. Once the body started burning, the family left, but the burning continued for more than an hour. The remaining ashes are then swept into the polluted Bagmati, where they will eventually merge with the Ganges River in India.

As an onlooker, I was both fascinated and embarrassed. It felt so wrong and disrespectful to sit glaring as though this was just a Sunday afternoon football game.

Unlike a sporting event, I felt intensely guilty. A few times, I looked away to prove to myself I wasn't staring. But my eyes kept tracking back to the mesmerizing affair. As a result, I had to tell myself that it was a daily occurrence, and those involved in the ceremony were not bothered by our presence.

Pashupatinath Temple was like being in a cultural classroom. My brain became filled with the local ethnological facts.

It was easy to understand why this sanctum was so influential to the Hindu people. Hindus believe that those who die here at Pashupatinath would be reborn as a human, regardless of their past misdeeds. Hundreds of elderly followers come to Pashupatinath Temple to meet death and stay here until they die, just to be cremated and have their ashes swept into the holy river.

Talk about culture shock. This event took the cake. To this day, I have not experienced anything more formidable.

What a thaumaturgic city Kathmandu was, history, legends, people, and culture. So much to see and experience. If I had only made it as far as Kathmandu, my trip would have been declared prizewinning and unforgettable, but this wasn't the real reason I was here.

Tuk-tuks on the street in Katmandu

Boudhanath Stupa in Katmandu

Buddhist monks

Cremation at Pashupatinath Temple

Public cremation along the Bagmati River

Sadhu-holy man

Everest, Here I Come

The moon rested right above the mountains, a place I call home.

~ Daniel Wallock

Flying from Kathmandu to the most dangerous airport on the planet was a nail-biting ordeal. However, I was happy to know we were flying in one of the most reliable aircrafts, a Twin Otter.

During the short thirty-minute flight, Dr. Ken, our group leader, motioned for us to look out the windows on the plane's left side. For the second time, I was able to catch a glimpse of the noble snow-capped Himalayan peaks poking through the clouds. It was breathtaking seeing the highest mountains in the world. "Hey, look there, that tall peak in the back is Everest," Ken shouted over the roar of the twin engines. A few people unbuckled and positioned themselves where they could click a photo or two of the impressive three-sided pyramid kissing the heavens. A tear slid down my cheek, and I gently brushed it away. My heart took up all the space in my chest. My pulse quickened as a surge of adrenaline filled my veins; I felt so alive. I was really doing this. I was going to walk the same trail, cross the same suspension bridges, and stay in the same tea houses as the world-class climbers I had read about.

As the plane approached Tenzing-Hillary Airport in the mountain village of Lukla, I dug my fingers into the armrest of my seat. I forced myself to break away from the beautiful scenery long enough to pinpoint how many rows I was from the emergency exit. "Three, OK," I said out loud. My eyes returned to the window as the pilot descended into the narrow canyon. It was an uneasy feeling to be flying below the rim of the gorge. I can't say that I was scared, but I was on alert. I held my breath as the pilot made a sharp dogleg right then quickly touched down on the short runway, braking immediately. I took a deep breath in and released my clutch as we came to a complete stop. Everyone clapped as a sign of relief.

Having the title of the most deadly airport in the world is not something anyone wants to brag about. Nevertheless, Lukla has hosted seven crashes since 2000, totaling fifty fatalities. As of the time of this writing, Lukla's deadliest crash happened in October of 2008, when eighteen passengers and crew died, and only one person survived.

Tenzing-Hillary Airport maintains an extremely short runway limiting a pilot's distance to land and get off the ground. At the end of the runway, there is a stone wall and a steep mountain. The runway literally sits on a cliff with a 2000-foot drop-off. In addition, the weather is highly unpredictable, often causing flights to be canceled or delayed.

A buzz was in the air as part two of our quest was about to kick off. Before leaving Lukla we met up with the Sherpas, who would serve as our guides and porters during our entire trip to BC and back. The Base Camp venture was organized by Peak Promotion, a local expedition company that furnished our Sherpa guides and provided logistics for our trekking adventure. A highly experienced and skilled agency would be the difference between a good trip and a great one. Besides, once I enter the Khumbu Icefall, my life will be in their hands. Wilderness Medicine had employed Peak Promotion to support their trips to Nepal for years.

Sherpas are one of the ethnic groups native to the mountainous regions of the Himalayas. These people are highly skilled and knowledgeable climbers and highly sought-after mentors. Since mountaineering has become popular, Sherpas have been able to find work leading climbers into the mountains safely. They must be half goat and half yak as they're naturals at climbing and are self-sacrificing, tenacious, and inhumanly strong. I soon learned that these people are everything they are reputed to be.

Once the Sherpas had loaded our duffle bags onto the sturdy yaks, we set off down the trail. Everyone, except for the Camp 2 climbers, was limited to a thirty-three-pound bag to be carried by the furry bovine. Climbing higher meant additional gear. The extensive list included some rather pricey equipment that I chose to rent in Nepal rather than buy, such as a pair of plastic climbing boots, an ice ax, and a climbing backpack, which is different from a regular multi-day backpack. Along with the expense of the travel, guides, evacuation insurance, and the medical course, the required paraphernalia inflated the cost. We were expected to have two pairs of a specific type of gloves and a pair of mittens, a jacket for minus-40°, base layer clothing, and a damn warm sleeping bag. Even after finding a bag on sale, I still spent $600. However, it ended up being my favorite piece of gear I took to Nepal.

It's not an easy feat to haul two large fifty-pound bags to the other side of the world and back by yourself. First, I had to drag all this crap to the Middle East before I even came to Nepal. Then, smartly, I worked it out so that I could leave everything at the JW Marriott in Kuwait City for the duration of a twenty-eight-day work rotation.

Hiking poles in hand at a leisurely pace, we left the mountain village of Lukla. Within a few meters, I was immediately aware of the 9300 ft. elevation. I was glad we only had a four-hour walk planned for our first day in the mountains. Although the thirty-three-mile journey to BC wasn't considered taxing in a technical sense, the elevation would make the trek tough. Given we had eight days to cover the distance, I hoped it would be adequate time for acclimatizing to the additional 8200 feet of elevation. No one can say how they will respond to altitude until they're in the situation.

I wasn't sure what to expect as far as the trail conditions or how the terrain would be. The trail began in a pristine alpine forest; it wandered alongside a roaring river and crossed over nine long, shaky suspension bridges, which we shared with donkeys and yaks. The awe-inspiring scenery helped soothe my Khumbu nerves as I walked the footpath. With each step I took up the trail, I had to pinch myself; it seemed unbelievable. My emotions were raw, in a good way.

Each morning we were awoken with the delivery of a pre-breakfast cup of tea, a sign it was time to get up and move. The routine was the same each morning: packed bags needed to be dropped with the Sherpas, daypack organized, fill your bladder with purified water and inspect your supply of snacks. Once breakfast was over, it was time to start walking toward the next destination.

Ascending higher and higher, we passed through iconic Sherpa villages stopping to rest, have an energy bar, and use one of the grungy pit toilets. The itinerary was designed to go slowly, enabling us to take plenty of pictures and acclimatize more adequately.

Half of us struggled to trek at the slow pace that our guides suggested. My long legs had a habit of moving with purpose; dillydallying was like nails against a chalkboard. I did my best to comply, but a few of us always arrived ahead of most of the group.

Hiking for only five or six hours each day allowed us to arrive at our accommodations by mid-afternoon. Time enough to enjoy a warm cup of tea while the daily CME lecture was given. Rustic teahouses provided us with basic lodging and hot meals. There is no such thing as a motel in this remote region. The multi-colored teahouses were a plain and simple setup. Some had private rooms with two or three single beds; others were dorm-style with five beds in one room. The further up we hiked, the more basic the accommodations became. As for showers, they were generally only available at the lower elevation teahouses. The rooms where we slept weren't heated. The higher we went, the colder it became.

Thankfully, every teahouse had one large communal dining area with a yak-dung stove burning, which kept this large room comfortable. However, I found the food to be dull. Every restaurant seemed to all have the same food. Dal bhat is Nepal's national dish. It's made with lentils and rice, and I found it dry, bland, and flavorless. Other choices included cheese and veggie pizzas, garlic soup, omelets, and chapati. The higher I climbed, the less I felt like eating.

The villages en route were so enchanting. I loved their poetic names: Tengboche, Dingboche, and Lobuche. Namche Bazaar was literally a full-sized town situated on the steep side of a mountain at an elevation of 11,200 ft. It hosts multiple restaurants, bars, and stores, and it even has an ATM and a Saturday street market.

The landscape changed from evergreen forest to alpine tundra to a barren, rocky, moonlike region. The last stretch was tough walking; it was uneven with fist-sized rocks making it hard to avoid tripping. The trail consisted of everything from stone steps to single-file dirt paths. The scenery was absolutely breathtaking, with endless blue skies surrounded by the most beautiful snow-capped mountains I have ever seen.

By the time we reached BC on day eight, we had lost four souls from our group.

One poor guy had gotten up in the middle of the night to go pee, became dizzy, and fell, fracturing several ribs. Luckily, we were in Namche Bazaar, where a helicopter could be summoned to evacuate him out to Kathmandu. Another gentleman thought he was getting HAPE (high altitude pulmonary edema), a condition that affects the lungs. Even though our lead physician examined him and found no evidence of this condition, the man mentally wigged himself out and requested to leave. We were only a day away from Base Camp when this occurred. Another couple decided to turn around when the wife started developing severe shortness of breath. The best treatment for any altitude-related illness is to descend.

I found BC to be much different than I expected. The landscape was rocky and rough. It took all my energy to walk a short distance. In some places, the terrain was slick with ice and snow. It felt like I was walking in a landmine zone as I cautiously placed my boot down with each step. It frustrated me that no one else seemed to be bothered as much as I was. Maybe it's my big feet, or perhaps I'm just clumsy, but I didn't enjoy having to navigate over this obnoxious turf.

When we arrived at BC, the Peak Promotion team already had a post set up. The WMS group was only one of many customers they oversaw each season. The company bears an outstanding track record and has worked with many famous mountaineers.

The triumph of reaching BC felt incredible. Though tired to the bone, the thrill of being so close to Mt. Everest filled me with happiness. Everest couldn't be seen from BC due to being surrounded by many statuesque peaks.

There were no warm and cozy teahouses to gather in at BC; instead, tents provided shelter for visitors and guides alike. Consequently, each expedition was grouped in a cluster. At the center of our plot stood an oversized communal tent where our gang gathered for meals or to hang out and share stories while sipping a hot mug of tea. It was the warmest place to be, yet the yak-dung stove was hardly adequate to take the chill off. The room never got warm enough to remove my goose down jacket, and the frozen glacier beneath the canvas floor caused my feet to throb. But this was still a big step up from our frigid dome tents where we slept.

The tent Bhanu and I shared was located several yards behind the shared hut on the other side of a small frozen pond. Walking back and forth across the slick, jagged rocks to our three-person tent annoyed the hell out of me; it was energy-consuming. Using the toilet tent was a whole other experience. You learn to be fast when your bathroom is smaller than a telephone booth, being just big enough to stand in and zip the door closed. With temperatures ranging from below zero at night to 45°F during the day, I dressed in layers to stay warm. So when it was time to head to the loo to "spend a penny," it was a challenge. First, it required removing your hundred-dollar pair of gloves and shoving them into a pocket to avoid dropping them in the shitter, followed by peeling through three layers, then being quick, boy was that seat a frosty one. I could imagine my bum freezing to the seat. Wouldn't that have been embarrassing? "Help! Help, I'm stuck!" I'm thinking about writing a book on the art of using toilets around the world.

After two nights at BC, the people not going on to Camp 2 had to head back down the mountain. It was a sad morning saying goodbye to the people I'd come to know, especially Bhanu. She had been a great tent mate, and we'd become good friends. We promised to keep in touch. Everyone shared a hug and wished me luck. They would be waiting to hear the news of our success or defeat with the Camp 2 climb. Brad gave me a peck on the cheek and then whispered in my ear, "I know you're going to make it. I'm sure of it." I watched them turn and head out. I know I lost a couple of tears as they disappeared.

Four of us were left behind to finish our expedition and hopefully achieve our quest. Kanak, Hulbert, Mathias, and I were instructed to rest as much as possible, hydrate, and consume calories while our bodies tried to adjust to 17,500 ft. of elevation.

Back in my tent, it was so quiet that I could hear my hair grow—too lonely. Snuggled in my cozy mummy-style sleeping bag, I closed my eyes and tried to slow my breathing enough to allow my body to let go of the tension it held. Between the high elevation and the anxiety, I hadn't gotten much sleep in the past few days. On top of this, I had now developed a continuous, throbbing altitude headache and fought my lack of appetite. Finally, I had to force myself to eat solid food.

Preceding our climb to Camp 2, the Sherpas felt it was imperative that we did a rehearsal run. This was for our safety and the safety of the entire team. The question was, could we physically and mentally handle the imposing icefall?

Fully geared up in the burdensome attire—heavy plastic boots with crampons, three layers of clothes, climbing harness, helmet, ice ax, and a day pack heavy with water, food, and extra gear—standing on two legs felt difficult. I started to doubt my strength, and the excess weight increased my work of breathing even before I took a single step. How was I ever going to climb? In addition, there is little oxygen available at 17,500 ft. In fact, the percent of O_2 at this height is only 11%, compared to 21% at sea level. All of this upped my anxiety about climbing through the icefall to Camp 2.

At four-thirty a.m., we started moving. The less time we were in the icefall after the sun rose, the better. Once the sun begins warming the ice, the risks increase. During the early morning, the ice is frozen, but with the sunrise the ice starts melting and can become unstable, slick, and likely to cause an avalanche. The time had come to see if all those sleepless nights had been justified. My teeth chattered as we headed off into the dark. I surmised it was the cold and not nerves. As we started across the glacier toward the seracs of the icefall, I breathed a quick prayer. "Please, may I be able to keep up, and let me return in one piece."

Essentially, I was the oldest and the only female in our team of eight. Luckily, we each were paired with a Sherpa for support. Brad's words echoed in my head, "Jo, you can do this."

We soon came to the first fixed line, where my Sherpa guide gave me a quick lesson on clipping in with my safety carabiner, a device that supposedly would prevent me from falling to my death. A few short and steep sections followed. At this point, the multitude of climbers ascending was forced to slow down, and a conga line was formed. There were few places where the faster climbers could pass; tempers flared as impatient mountaineers rudely demanded to pass. This behavior disappointed me and made me feel sad. This was a well-known problem higher up the mountain, but I hadn't anticipated being a part of it. I thought to myself, you should not make Sagarmatha, "Mother Goddess," angry since your life is under her power.

The sun had broken the horizon by the time we came to the first ladder. We stood to the side, watching wide-eyed as two adventurers crossed with ease. Now it was our turn. Matthias and his Sherpa went first single file. Only one person at a time is allowed on the ladders. Moving into position, I could feel my knees trembling. Standing on the edge of the crevasse in front of the aluminum ladder that bridged the gap, I first had to bend over, grab the fixed rope, and snap my safety clip on. I hesitated for a few seconds as I focused on the rungs where I needed to place my feet. Another impatient line had started gathering behind me. Finally, I couldn't stall any longer. With my eyes focused, I took a deep breath, lifting my left foot outward over the second crosspiece and cautiously securing the toe of my crampon before setting my heel down on the rung back of my toes. With only a flimsy little rope to hang onto, I focused on balancing as I slowly moved my right foot forward with my left foot following suit. Toe then heel, toe then heel, suddenly finding myself suspended over a deep dark void. Mirroring these tactics, I managed to traverse several death-defying ladders crossing that day. This was the most difficult thing, physically and mentally, I had ever done.

A one-third of the way through the Khumbu, we stopped for a break, drinking and eating before heading back to camp. Seeing BC from high above was heavenly. No matter how precarious the situation seemed, I still was not lost in the grandeur of the encompassing landscape.

In addition to the rehearsal trek in the icefall, three hours were spent teaching us the art of climbing on a wall of ice. Learning how to walk up a hundred-foot ice curtain while simultaneously hanging onto a rope was compelling. The technique involved using two ice axes to claw yourself onto the icy surface while kicking the teeth of your crampons into the rock-hard glacier. Then, without losing your grip, you move upward one step up at a time. Next, we practiced using an ascender and Prusiks to pull ourselves up the fixed rope. Although physically arduous, it was such a fun afternoon.

Our playtime had a purpose, of course. We were learning lifesaving skills. If the unforeseen should happen, and God forbid we fall into one of the many crevasses, being able to rescue ourselves by using the technique we had just been taught might be the difference between making it home or not. Another disturbing fact that wasn't helping my insomnolence.

As we were gripping a wall on the glacier, a white-haired man appeared and asked to join us. Mathias turned toward us and remarked, "Hey guys, that's David." We had already been introduced to Mr. Breashears, as he shared our meal tent. David Breashears is an American mountaineer, filmmaker, author, and speaker. If you know the story *Into Thin Air*, David has a part in the tale. David is credited with filming the Everest Imax documentary. He was also the director of the 2015 movie *Everest*. David was currently at Base Camp to work on a new documentary on how climate change is destroying our glaciers and mountains. It's not every day you get to hang out with such a cool guy, let alone share the same wall of ice.

Breashears wasn't the only other well-known climber hanging out in BC. Another famous American, Conrad Anker was there guiding a summit climb. Understandably, these names won't have much meaning to you if you're not into mountaineering, but try to think of a famed celebrity or athlete you admire. How cool would it be to hang out with them in their natural environment?

Our training helped to prepare us both bodily and cognitively for what lay ahead. It was a silent warning to take the climb seriously and stay focused.

As I mentioned earlier, the Khumbu Icefall is a death-defying place. This renowned landmark is part of the Khumbu Glacier. The glacier starts high up the mountain on the Lhotse Face. It is a 10 mile/17 km river of melting ice. The icefall is at the lower end of the Khumbu glacier; the 2.5-mile section sits just above BC and ends just below Camp 1.

So why is the Khumbu Icefall so scary? The melting glacier can move as much as 3 ft./1 m per day. The icefall comprises crevasses up to 150 ft./45 m deep and includes towering seracs, or ice towers. The moving glacier pushes on these ice towers, which will eventually break and fall into one of the crevasses.

Dozens of aluminum ladders are used to cross over the crevasses. Sometimes up to three ladders roped together are used as a bridge crossing over the deep, black holes. The hazards within the icefall include falling into a crevasse, a section of the icefall collapsing, and avalanches. From 1953 to 2016, forty-four deaths occurred in the icefall. Everyone is expected to be clipped into a fixed rope at all times while climbing through this hazardous zone.

A week before we arrived in BC, there had been a fatal accident in the icefall below Camp 1. A Sherpa didn't bother to clip into the safety rope and fell off one of the ladders into a crevasse. We were warned that the wall was still painted red with the poor man's blood and not to wig out when we got to that spot.

D-Day had finally arrived. It was time to start our climb toward Camp 2. Proceeding with the same routine as the training day, we would head out in the dark a few hours before sunrise. Optimally, this would put us at Camp 1 by early afternoon, where we would camp for the night. The following morning, we would trek through the Western Cwm to Camp 2, reaching our goal of 21,000 ft. Then we would return to Camp 1, overnighting before returning down the icefall to BC. "Easy as mate."

At the last minute, one of the guys in our foursome changed his mind and decided to abort this challenge. However, the three remaining believed we had what it took both mentally and physically to succeed. The practice run had not only given us a taste of what was to come but also improved my confidence. I was ready.

At 0300, I heard the Sherpas approaching to deliver my wake-up tea along with my unneeded wake-up call. I had not slept well between excited anxiety, altitude sleep deprivation, and the intermittent crashing avalanches in the distance. Nevertheless, I was glad the day had come and was feeling pumped about my decision to be facing the biggest and most deadly showdown of my life.

Unlike test day, today we would be towing more weight. Spending two nights out on the mountain required additional equipment. A thorough gear check was done by our Sherpas, making sure we had not forgotten any essential items. Thankfully, these kind souls volunteered to carry part of our belongings, reducing our loads. With headlights in place, off we went again toward the treacherous Khumbu Icefall. Our small party was one of the dozens heading up the mountain that morning, as well as teams seeking to stand on top of mountain numero uno.

The icefall consists of a maze of cumbersome obstacles. There were walls of snow and ice that required using a fixed rope to pull oneself upward while kicking your crampon-fitted boots into the slippery surface. These features sucked my energy to near depletion, but the true demands were crossing those darn ladders over the crevasses. The simple task of bending over to clip into the safety line tuckered me out. My waistline seemed to have doubled in size with the addition of the six layers of overlapping clothing, three on the bottom half and three on the top half of my body. It was like leaning over a barrel, lessening my already-low oxygen level. Before I could continue with the tightrope act, I was forced to pause in an attempt to catch my breath.

I had decided early on that it was best to avoid letting my eyes drift any deeper than the actual ladder, so I refrained from looking into the black abyss. To illustrate the scene, the edges where the ladders rest on the banks of these crevasses were not perfectly flat, nor were they straight across to the other side. In most cases, the ladder was angled either uphill or downhill and tended to wobble side to side a few inches.

In some places, finding a good position to step off the slick sloping ledge was nearly impossible. Thus the same went for stepping off at the other side. The whole ladder thing was insanely intense. I felt so vulnerable with nothing solid to hold onto or grab if I lost my balance or slipped, which I did. I fell three different times in the icefall. During our return trip, Mathias and I fell at the same spot. We were coming off a ladder and had to climb an icy embankment chest high. I think we both thought we were going to tumble off into eternity.

Eventually, I became too fatigued to stoop and pick up the anchored rope, so my escort had to do it for me. One minute I was sweating, and the next I was cold depending on whether I was climbing up a wall or stalled in line waiting to cross a ladder. Finally, the terrain started to level out, a sign we were getting near Camp 1. My weary body couldn't wait to drop the hefty pack and stretch out. Only two more crevasses to conquer.

Seeing the blood-soaked wall of the latest victim made me think about how real the dangers were here. I felt lucky to have made it up the icefall in one piece, but our journey was far from over. We still had to get to Camp 2 and then back down to BC, walk back to Lukla, and fly to Kathmandu.

Camp 1 had already been set up with three tents. The two guys got to share one of the tents, two Sherpas took the second tent, and I was asked if the third Sherpa could share mine. "Of course." There was no toilet tent here. You were to just wander out a little way and use the small shovel provided. No trees or shrubs to hide behind, just open ice. It was a bit weird being the only female, but I have never let this stop me from going or doing whatever I wanted to do.

As I lay in my tent resting from the exhausting morning hike, I thought about my dad back in Indiana fighting his battle with cancer. I knew he would be proud of me, and he, too, would be thinking about me. This is the kind of adventure he would have loved a few years ago. I prayed my family wasn't worrying too much. I had only been able to send a few messages since leaving Kathmandu more than a week earlier. My family was aware that I should reach my goal on May 8, which would actually be the seventh in America.

That night in Camp 1 was dreadfully cold. I could feel the freezing ice beneath my sleeping bag. I took all my extra clothing and anything I could find suitable and placed it underneath my sleeping bag. It was a sin to even think I was cold with my -40 bag as the Sherpa sharing my tent didn't even have a sleeping bag since he had carried half of my shit. He edged his shivering body toward mine, and we snuggled together. I had brought an extra jacket that I gave to my tent mate, which he greatly appreciated. It was another restless night.

The sun was just starting to warm up the tent when my morning cuppa was delivered. The few hours of rest did little to restore my energy. I could have been content lying there all day. Opening the tent door, I was greeted with a beautiful morning, cold and crisp, but the vibrant sun promised to warm the day. Gazing at the vast panorama, I could hardly believe my eyes. Flanked on all sides by 8000 m jagged peaks was a spectacular sight. The previous afternoon, the mountains had been hidden by cloud cover.

Camp 1 sits at the mouth of the Western Cwm, a broad, flat-ish glacial valley stretching 2.5 miles to the bottom of the famous Lhotse Face, the fourth highest mountain. Halfway through the Western Cwm is Camp 2, our ultimate goal. Standing egotistically above Camp 2 was Everest looking down on her children. It was a "wow" moment. I remember calling out, "Hey guys, you need to see this!" as the other two men hadn't crawled out of the sleeping bags yet.

My soul was happy. This was the most astonishing place I had ever been. Standing below the Mother of the World was such an emotional experience.

Following our breakfast of soup, a protein bar, and more tea, we geared up for the walk to Camp 2. I was hoping our cooks had found some clean snow to use for our water and tea, as the area around our tents had evidence that visitors had not walked very far to relieve themselves.

Being able to see Camp 2 across the valley was encouraging. But this confused me. I thought we had to climb up to Camp 2. If so, why did it look like the camp was downhill? Besides, it was less than two miles away. Yeah, this was going to be a fun, easy day. How long could it possibly take to walk just over there? I don't even see any hills to climb. So why do we need all of our climbing gear?

Twenty minutes into our easy stroll, we approached a large canyon. My thoughts quickly changed. Ok, maybe this was going to be difficult. We had to climb down to the bottom, cross the floor of this ice canyon, and climb up several ladders roped together to reach the top of the glacier. Oh my God, there was no oxygen here. Each step I took on the ladder, I had to stop and breathe. It was like I had a plastic bag on my head. No matter how hard I tried to draw in air, I couldn't get enough to make my lungs happy. At this point, my guide started prodding. I had to keep going slowly, slowly. When I got to the top, my Sherpa asked, "You OK?"

Bent over, hands on my knees, breathing eighty times a minute, I mumbled a "Yeah."

"Ok, let's keep moving then."

My brain continued questioning the information my eyes saw based on what my body was experiencing. The ground looked to be flat, and it seemed we were heading downhill. This can't be Camp 2; it's supposed to be 2600 ft. or nearly 800 m higher than Camp 1. Continuing became a struggle. I started counting twenty steps before I allowed myself to stop and breathe. I could have understood feeling short of breath if I had been climbing up a big hill, but this was a mild incline not even noticeable to the naked eye. After a bit, I could only walk ten to twelve steps before stopping to catch my breath. With the sun shining down and all the glare of the snow, it was like being in an oven. I started sweating and stopped to remove a few layers. I felt like my blood was thick as syrup. Crap, I thought I was in really good shape. And what's up with the Sherpas? They act like, well, like they've done this a hundred times.

Then at long last, I was there, four hours later, 21,200 ft.—Camp 2, my highest yet. I had no power left inside to do the happy dance, yet I was crazed with joy. I dreamed it, I wished it, I did it, but not without suffering.

Our little group hung out for an hour and a half, resting and rehydrating while lying on the floor of a large tent. Tired and dizzy, I forced myself to drink as I knew dehydration at this elevation happens quickly. Our threesome was filled with happiness, victorious after months of training, planning, and stressing. We would celebrate when we got back off the mountain. For now, we had to focus on safely getting back down.

Prior to heading back to Camp 1, I needed to use the loo. I had refilled the tank and needed to unload. The guys had already found the toilet tent and pointed me in the right direction. "Don't bother to close the door and be very careful. It's pretty slick over there." They weren't kidding. The loo tent was at the top of a small hill that was ice covered. I opened the door to the toilet and found a shallow crevasse that was being used as a makeshift porta john. It was a terribly, icy-slick, uneven surface about ten inches wide.

A tricky process, trying to squat and pee while teetering over a poop-filled pit. I definitely got what they meant about not closing the door. I left it open, undid my pants, waddled backward a few inches, and hung on to both sides of the door to keep from sliding into the trench behind me.

After a couple of pictures, off we went back in the direction of Camp 1. I had screwed up and didn't capture a picture of Mount Everest when I first arrived at Camp 2. At the time, I was too exhausted and figured I'd get one when we got ready to leave. Unfortunately, it had clouded over and was snowing. Our Sherpas wanted us to get going as they were concerned about the snow covering the small crevasses we had to leap over on our way to Camp 2. In fact, on the return trip, I was tired and not focusing well while following my Sherpa. I nearly stepped into a narrow crevasse, maybe eighteen inches wide. I don't even want to think how this might have ended.

Reaching camp safely, a wave of gratification flowed through my veins. I couldn't wait to share my victory with the world. Conquering the 21,000-foot climb surpassed anything I had recreationally executed. This was for sure the gold medal of all previous winnings in my stockpile.

I slept well that night and didn't even notice the cold. In the midst of relief and exhaustion, I relaxed and fell into a tranquil coma. The next morning we packed up and set off for BC. We were about halfway down the Khumbu, and I heard it before I saw it. First, it was a muffled rumble and then the sounds of rocks and ice crashing and tumbling. I didn't take the time to stop and watch, although I was able to observe out of the corner of my eye, to my right, part of the wall framing the icefall was avalanching. My heart hurt with fear as we rushed to keep moving as fast as we could downward. As quickly as it started, the rumble stopped. Thankfully, it wasn't any closer and hadn't disrupted our path to BC. This was the same noise I had heard a few times while lying in my tent at BC. I wasn't scared there, as I knew my tent was in a safe location.

"Only those who will risk going too far can possibly find out how far they can go."

— *T.S. Eliot*

"You can never conquer the mountain. You can only conquer yourself."

— *Jim Whittaker*

"Somewhere between the bottom of the climb and the summit is the answer to the mystery why we climb."
— Greg Child

May 9 was spent relaxing at BC. For the first time in several days, I was given the opportunity to take an almost-warm shower and wash my hair. I felt refreshed and in high spirits, like a new person.

It was a perfect day for a party, but not just any party. It was, in fact, Buddha's birthday. Vesak or Buddha Day is one of Nepal's most celebrated holidays. Everywhere I traveled in this country, it was apparent how important Buddhism was to the local people.

The story of Buddha is fascinating. He was born in Nepal, something I never knew until this trip. Legend said he was born 2600 years ago, but research shows it was probably sometime during the sixth century. He was born into a royal family as Prince Siddhartha. The prince grew up in great luxury and was sheltered from the cruel world. At age twenty-nine, he started venturing off the palace grounds in his chariot. During one of these trips, the prince saw an old man, a sick man, and a corpse. Since he had been protected from the miseries of aging, sickness, and death, he questioned his charioteer, who explained what they were. Siddhartha came across a monk, and the prince was impressed with the man's peaceful demeanor. So he decided to go into the world to discover how the man could be so serene amid such suffering. Siddhartha secretly left the palace. After a long spiritual search, Siddhartha reached enlightenment, becoming a Buddha at age thirty-five. He formulated the Four Noble Truths and hence became the founder of Buddhism. Buddha is not a name but is a title meaning one who is awakened or enlightened.

Buddha's birthday is celebrated on the full moon, generally in May. So how do you celebrate Buddha's birthday at Everest Base Camp? To start with, we gathered under a large open tent that became flooded with people. Luckily, our group got there in time to get a seat under the canopy.

At the front of the tent, an elegant shrine set the stage. A golden statue of Buddha sat among burning incense, orange and white marigolds, and plates of candy bars. The earthy aroma of sandalwood lurked in the thin air. The gala started with a low humming chant and was then followed by a prayer spoken in Pali. Plates of candy bars, cut into pieces, were passed around to the guests. I presumed it represented a birthday cake. We were shown to cup our hands as a small puddle of beer was poured into each person's hand. Mimicking our leader, we slurped up the beer and then wiped our hands off in our hair. I doubt this is how Buddha's birthday was honored in Kathmandu, but it was the most unusual birthday party I've ever encountered.

Although it had been by coincidence that we had been a part of the special celebration, it felt like the perfect way to seal the milestone. During our trek to BC, we had stopped at many different monasteries where we received blessings for a safe journey from the Buddhist monks. Today we honored their founding father and a culture of gentle, selfless, and simple people.

Freed from my icefall anxiety, I expected the rest of my trip to be relaxing and pleasant, with time to embrace my greatest physical accomplishment and soak in all the glory. But regrettably, this was not the case. An atrocious GI monster instead attacked me. So the first night back in BC, I was awakened with my guts rockin' and rolling. Having to make my way over the rocky terrain to the toilet half a dozen times was not cool.

I hoped this would be short-lived, as the following day we would be trekking all the way back to the village of Pheriche, 23 km/14 mi. away. Plus, it wasn't like there was a bathroom every mile. As if this wasn't a problem enough, I had developed two walnut-sized blisters underneath the nail of each of my big toes. My beautiful purple plastic climbing boots were too loose, and climbing down from 21,000 ft. gave me large blisters. At least they weren't terribly painful, and thankfully I was back to wearing my regular hiking boots for the rest of the trek.

Nearly everyone in our original group had traveler's diarrhea at some point. Most dealt with their symptoms for only forty-eight hours. I crossed my fingers. I did well on the hike down to Pheriche. I only had to squat along the trail twice. I didn't feel bad, just a few stomach cramps here and there. I figured in a day or two I would be better.

Trekking to BC, we had spent eight days getting there and returning to Lukla took only four days. We reached Lukla at dusk on May 13. After checking into our accommodations, we headed back out to take advantage of a special invitation we had received. Our threesome had been invited to go to the home of one of our Sherpas and try some home-brewed Sherpa beer. I was excited to check out a Sherpa house, and the guys couldn't wait to try the secret brew.

The house was made of stone, simple as can be. In one corner of the main room were a fireplace and cooking area. Near the fireplace was a small wooden table, a wooden bench a foot wide followed the walls around the entire room. There wasn't anything else in the middle of the room except a wooden support beam. The floor was stone, and the house was frigid. The Sherpa's wife welcomed us and invited us to sit at the table. The couple had one young child aged fifteen months. He was so cute, running around smiling with his plump red cheeks. All Nepalese children had these characteristics: black eyes, rosy-red chubby cheeks, and always happy.

Sherpa beer or Tongba is a brew made from millet. The millet is left to ferment in a jug for several weeks. The art of enjoying this yeasty beer is to pour the ripe millet seeds into a mug and add hot water, allowing the alcohol-rich grain to leach into the liquid. A reusable metal straw is then used to slurp the potent drink. It wasn't the best beer I've ever had, as it was pretty intense. I avoided indulging too much as I wasn't feeling too well. My GI symptoms had gotten worse, and I was dealing with off-and-on nausea. I had never heard of anyone except the well-known climbers and maybe some of the American doctors ever being invited into the private home of their Sherpa guides. Our threesome had bonded quite well with our special friends, and their hospitality showed it.

Our flight back to Kathmandu was uneventful, and it was wonderful to be back at the Yak and Yeti, sleeping on a comfortable bed and having a hot shower. However, before the three of us headed off in different directions and returned to the real world, we were honored at a celebration dinner. The owner and founder of Peak Promotions, the late Wongchu Sherpa, took us to the well-known Rum Doodle restaurant. This is where most mountaineers come to commemorate their Everest experience. This restaurant pays tribute to the spirit of mountaineering. In fact, Edmund Hillary, along with every other world-class climber, has more than likely shown up here. Walking through the doors of the bustling Rum Doodle made me awestruck. The place was beautifully decorated with framed signatures of the greatest Everest summiteers adorning the walls. It is virtually Kathmandu's hall of fame for climbers.

Our farewell celebration dinner with Wongchu was the icing on the cake. Mathias, Hulbert, and Chhoti Sherpa—one of Peak Promotions assistants and two of our Sherpa guides, and I raised our glasses to a blessed adventure.

Although I didn't summit the mighty mountain, I did summit my goal. Sitting in the Rum Doodle, I sincerely felt like I belonged to the climbing community. I could relate to the mental and physical hurdles of high-altitude climbing. I still wasn't feeling physically great, but I wasn't going to let this destroy my fabulous evening. Wongchu thanked us for being Peak Promotions clients and told us we did a fantastic job. Wongchu gave me a big hug as he boasted, "Jonea, I knew you could do it. I was betting on you." He reminded me I was the only female on his tours this year to make it to Camp 2.

Before our evening adjourned, the three of us clients were asked to write some memoirs of our adventure. Traditionally, at the Rum Doodle, climbers are given a paper cutout of a Yeti's foot to write down something from their time on the mountain. Our paper foot included the date we reached Camp 2, our names, and our Sherpas' names. In addition, the following words were printed on each toe: Lukla Landing, Base Camp, Khumbu Icefall, Western Cwm, and ass-over-crevasse, with ladders drawn connecting the space to each toe. We agreed these were our highlights to remember.

Safe on the ground at the world's most dangerous airport

Our group on the trek to Everest Base Camp

Sherpa carrying lumber up the trail

Mt. Everest in the background. Bhandu second person
from the left and Brad is on the far right

Nepalese children at Namche Bazar

Sherpa stopping to rest while carrying load twice his size

One of the many prayer wheels along the trail to Base Camp

Everest Base Camp

Looking up at the Khumbu icefall from Base Camp

Camp 2- 21,000 ft. Sherpa, Mathias, Herbert, me and the other two sherpa's

Climbers in the Western Cwm headed toward Camp 2

Mathias in the Khumbu icefall

Camp 2 on Everest

On the ladder crossing another hair-raising crevasse

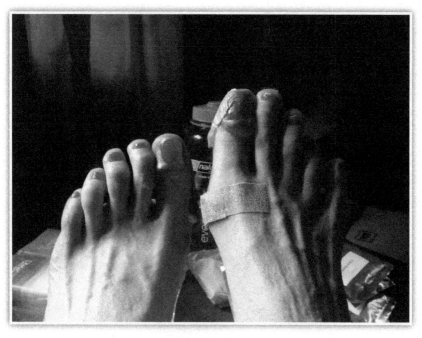

My feet took a beating

Touched with Inner Peace

One night the moon said to me,
if loves makes you cry why
don't you leave your lover?
I looked back at the moon and said,
Would you ever leave your sky?

Т he following day Mathias left, and a day after that Hubert flew out. Now alone, my quieted soul reflected, both heavy-hearted that this long-sought-after quest had ended yet gratified to have conquered a lifelong dream. Growing up a common rural American farm kid, who would have ever thought I would have achieved so much? I knew that I would have never made it this far if I had not rolled up my sleeves and challenged my fears along the way.

With a week left before I needed to be back at work, I decided I should see more of the world, but where? Instantly the Taj Mahal popped into my head. I was already scheduled to travel through India on my way back to the Middle East, so changing my flight would be no problem. However, with my decision to stop in India, I first had to obtain an Indian visa, a three-day process. Peak Promotions assistant, Chhoti Sherpa, was so helpful in shuffling me back and forth to the visa office and walking me through the paperwork.

While waiting on my visa, I planned my three-day jaunt to New Delhi. I was somewhat nervous about heading to India solo. My good friend Jacob, a native Indian, had once told me how hard India is to travel through. Being a veteran traveler, I knew I could figure it out, so I said goodbye to Nepal and left for New Delhi.

Since returning off the mountain from Base Camp, I had contracted some nasty GI organism. I pondered if I might have gotten this awful bug from the dirty snow at Camp 1. No, it was too soon for it to have come from that source. More likely it was food or water at BC or one of the teahouses. I had been pretty careful when I chose my meals, and our water was supposedly boiled before refilling our bottles. I will never know for sure. One day I would be OK with no symptoms, and the next I would have bouts of cramps and diarrhea; it would strike most inappropriately after going to bed. Every other night I spent in the john. How it was cycling in my body didn't make any sense to me. My appetite would come and go. Sometimes I could eat, and sometimes I was just plain nauseated. I was thankful for the hours when I did feel fine. I was starting to realize I would need some antibiotics to kick this thing. In the meantime, I started taking my anti-nausea medication, which did give me some relief.

When I arrived at Indira Gandhi International Airport in New Delhi, I was lucky enough to find a pharmacy in the airport that had a pharmacist on duty. I was relieved that she was able to sell me a bottle of antibiotics based on my symptoms. With my luggage in hand, I caught a taxi to my hotel. It was May, and the weather was steamy and hot. After checking into the hotel and throwing my bags in my room, I headed out to explore. I had a list of things I was interested in seeing. However, the front desk encouraged me to hire a cab and not try walking alone. So, taking their advice, I caught a taxi to the India Gate, originally named the All-India War Memorial. This local icon is a monumental sandstone arch dedicated to the troops of British India who died in wars fought between 1914 and 1919.

Before arriving in New Delhi, I had booked a single-day private tour to see the Taj Mahal. Early the next morning, I was picked up in front of my hotel by a well-dressed Indian gentleman driving a spiffy black sedan. He opened the door to the back seat, allowing me to get in, securing the door once I was seated. The driver took his seat behind the steering wheel, and we headed north. He introduced himself and explained our long days' itinerary, clueing me in that we had a lengthy, five-hour drive each way to get to the city of Agra. The scheduled stops included Agra Fort, followed by the Taj Mahal, along with both a lunch and dinner break, plus stopping at some souvenir shops along the way.

Thirty minutes after leaving the hotel, we met up with the impossible jammed traffic. Before long, we were crawling, and the two-lane byway had become a five-lane nightmare. Cars honked their horns constantly as if that would help speed things up. People were insanely impatient, and everyone was trying to squeeze into the packed expressway. There were a few times I had to look at the floor as I thought we were going to be rammed. I wasn't even driving, but my knuckles were white from gripping the seat. I could feel the driver's frustration. He was doing an excellent job and had common sense. However, this culture's drivers were unreal. Besides all the crazy vehicles, water buffalo would be standing on the road, adding to the insanity. I saw buses overflowing with people, and there were even people riding on the roof. Then there were the sizable open-topped livestock trucks transporting humans. I could imagine one of these transport vehicles crashing and rolling over, dumping dozens of people onto the road.

My driver was friendly and spoke English well. I must have asked five hundred questions, which he tirelessly answered.

After pausing for a quick lunch, we finally arrived in one piece. Our first stop in Agra was the historical fort, also known as the walled city. It was constructed in the sixteenth century and stood near the gardens of the Taj Mahal. This beautiful red sandstone fortress was built by Akbar, one of the greatest Mughal emperors of India.

Exploring the great citadel with my knowledgeable chaperone, I was impressed with not only how huge the ninety-four-acre complex was but also with the historical events that had taken place within the walls of the mighty fortress. I tried to imagine how difficult it would have been to hand chisel huge boulders into perfectly-sized blocks, then stack them like Legos to build such a massive stronghold. My arms ached just thinking about it. It was an eight-year process for the 4000 laborers.

Agra Fort and the Taj Mahal are some of India's many UNESCO World Heritage Sites. I pondered how many I had been blessed to visit so far. My list was definitely growing. However, a better question is, how many will I be able to tell great-grandchildren about when I'm ninety?

I got my first glimpse of the majestic Taj while touring Agra Fort. My guide led me to a room within the fortress and pointed to the palace perfectly framed by the window. Looking at the Taj in the distance reminded me of Cinderella's Castle at Disney World. I was a child in awe.

I'm not exactly sure what ignited my spur-of-the-moment decision to come to India and explore the Taj Mahal. Before my visit, I had no concept of the deep history of this region or who had even built this spectacular ivory landmark. For several years I had hoped to get a chance to travel to India, possibly after watching one of the Indiana Jones films, or because India's jungles are populated with man-eating tigers. Agra was nowhere near the tiger-filled jungles nor the location where Indiana Jones was filmed. But here I was checking out another country.

A fifteen-minute ride and we were at the gate of the distinguished mausoleum. I had chosen well by selecting a private tour with a well-versed, English-speaking guide. If I had opted out of having a tour guide, I would have probably never discovered what I think is the most touching love story on earth.

The Taj Mahal is an ivory-white marble Islamic mausoleum. It has been proclaimed as one of the most significant monuments of all-time. The Taj symbolizes love from a great emperor to his beloved wife. The setting couldn't be more perfect. The mausoleum is situated amidst beautiful gardens on the banks of the River Yamuna.

This place surprised the bejesus out of me. How was it possible to construct such a magnificent establishment without modern tools? With great effort and dedication, 20,000 workers completed the complex in twenty years with the help of a thousand elephants. Thousands of precious stones and gems, along with copious amounts of gold and a boatload of Mughal wealth, were needed to bring this one-of-a-kind structure to life.

Emperor Shah Jahan chose the name, Taj Mahal, meaning the Crown of Palaces. The original name was Roza-e-Munawara, which translated to Unique Building. I'm happy he decided to rename it. Plus, the Taj Mahal sounds more elaborate and fitting. Besides, as one of the Seven Man-Made Wonders of the World, it should be supported with a striking title.

Although impressive on the outside, the story behind this magnificent shrine is that of immense love that ends tragically. Personally, I know of no greater tale of devotion.

When Jahan was fourteen, before becoming an emperor, he met Arjumand. She was fifteen at the time. They soon fell in love. Five years later, they were married (1612). Arjumand's name was changed to Mumtaz Mahal after Jahan became the Emperor of India in 1628. The couple had fourteen children, seven of whom died in infancy. Unfortunately, Mumtaz died shortly after giving birth to her fourteenth baby.

Jahan cried for eight days without stopping. When he emerged, it was said his hair had turned gray. On Mumtaz's death bed, Jahan promised he would not remarry and would build a monument to honor her. Jahan and Mumtaz's story stirred my heart.

Viewing the Taj is something I'll never forget. When I left the charismatic cultural site, I felt different inside. My soul had been touched with inner peace.

When the driver dropped me off at my New Delhi hotel, it was late. It had been a sweaty hot day touring around Agra in the bright sun. I showered and retired to the comfort of my bed. The following day I packed my belongings for my journey back to Iraq.

I was traveling with more luggage than when I left. Peak Promotion had given us an additional ex-large duffle bag with its logo printed on the side. I managed to fill it with fifty pounds of souvenirs. Wong-Chu had encouraged me to purchase an additional warm jacket and some other gear as he was concerned with the quality of the jacket I had brought from the US. I never used the $40.00 jacket as my Mountain Hardware coat was just fine. I did leave my favorite hiking boots in Nepal as they had many hundred miles on them, and I was hoping that some large-footed Sherpa could use them.

My other purchases included three Tibetan rugs. These beautiful hand-woven carpets are an ancient, traditional craft. Tibetan rugs are traditionally made from Tibetan highland sheep's wool, called *changpel*. They took up most of the space in the extra duffel and weighed as much as a small boulder. I thought a Tibetan rug would make a unique wedding present for my son and daughter-in-law. The second one would be a fabulous Christmas gift for my daughter. The third I planned to keep for myself.

I was apprehensive about how much the bags weighed when heading to the airport. I knew I would be paying extra as I was now traveling with more than allowed. Sure enough, when I got to the check-in counter, "Ma'am, you are only allowed two bags on this flight. Are you sure you want to check the third bag?"

"Yes, sir."

"That will be $100.00." I reached into my wallet and handed over my bank card. I wondered what he thought I would do with my bag if I decided not to take it? But at least they allowed me to have an additional bag. Money talks, as the saying goes.

From New Delhi, I connected through Dubai and then to Kuwait City, where I overnighted at the luxurious JW Marriott. BP had prepaid my room and arranged my transportation to and from the airport. On my last night of freedom before returning to ROO, I have to say I was ready to settle back into a work routine and reconnect with my buddies. Maybe I would even devise a creative plan to get Tane's attention. He was never far from my thoughts.

The India Gate, war memorial in New Delhi

Agra Fort

View of the Taj Mahal from the Agra Fort

My guide and me at the Taj Mahal

Handcrafted gemstones decorate the Taj Mahal

The Taj Mahall

Water buffalo crossing the street in Prahesh, India

Para-Abnormal Parasite

If a star fell each time I thought about you, then the moon would truly realize what loneliness is really like

A cheerful reception awaited me when I walked into ROO's clinic; everyone stopped what they were doing and approached me to share a kind embrace.

"Well, how was it?"

"You survived!"

So many questions. It was good to be back home, my Iraqi home, that is.

I was disappointed when I realized Tane was out on leave. But on the other hand, I didn't have the energy to flirt as I was soon feeling ill again.

I had only been back to ROO for three days when the gremlin living in my guts returned. Disappointed, as I thought I had finally gotten on top of it, I didn't hesitate to visit Dr. Leon to share my symptoms. He put me on three strong antibiotics and sent me to my room to rest and recuperate. Lee took my place in the ambulance for the day. I didn't want to be in my room and felt guilty about not pulling my load. I have always been this way. My philosophy: if you become injured or ill while out playing, then suck it up. I have repeatedly reported to work with broken bones and painful injuries that occurred while I was off enjoying some thrilling activity.

Once I fractured my foot before the start of an adventure race in Arizona. Yep, it was painful when it happened, but we had a race to run. Eight hours later, my team finished FIRST. In adventure racing, you only quit if you think there might be permanent damage or you're truly dying. So I limped along, ignoring my sore foot. I knew I would be paying for my decision to keep racing.

When I awoke the following day, my foot was purple, and my leg was swollen up to my knee. My nurse friend Shelley took one look at it and said, "Yep, you probably broke something."

A day later, I had it X-rayed, and sure enough there was a crack in one of the bones in my foot. I was given a nice walking boot to wear for a few weeks. This happened during the time I was working as a flight nurse on a helicopter. I never missed a day of work, nor did we miss a transport because of my injury.

Being sent to my room to miss work was frustrating. I only hoped that the medication would take over soon. I had already lost 15 lb./7 kg during my Everest trip, and I didn't need to lose more. The middle of the Iraqi desert was not a good place to be while dealing with this ongoing GI illness.

Ten days later, I was still sick. Whatever was plaguing me was a nasty critter. Just like when it started, I would feel fine, and at night there would be a full attack on the GI tract. I didn't sleep at night because I spent half of it in the can. Thankfully, I had a shortened work schedule for this particular rotation. I was returning to America a few days earlier than usual because Nicky and I had adjusted our schedules. Vic, our Ops lead, had considered evacuating me out as I looked terrible and wasn't getting better. Instead, I said I would be fine and would soon be going to the States to get some proper testing done.

Three months later, after self-diagnosing myself and finally getting on the proper medications, I was able to slay the monster. Giardia fit the picture, per the signs and symptoms I was experiencing. Giardia is an intestinal infection caused by a parasite. So how did I get this? Giardiasis can be spread through contaminated food, water, or person-to-person contact. It's common in areas with poor sanitation and unsafe water. It can also be transmitted by touching surfaces, doorknobs, or sharing blankets. I'm not exactly sure where I picked it up, but I know if I ever get it again, I will get the correct treatment sooner rather than later.

My short two-and-a-half-week vacation to the US was over in a heartbeat. A few days were spent in Arizona, including a quick trip down to Tucson's government travel center so I could get an expedited new passport. My current travel book was running out of unmarked pages, and I didn't want to be denied access while roving the world.

Giving up possession of my passport in order to have a new one left me feeling weak in the knees. This was the way a parent might feel handing off their newborn to a mentally deranged babysitter for the day. It kind of made me want to spew. "Ma'am, you should receive your new document in seven to ten days."

"Thanks, sir. I hope so. I have to fly back to work in eleven days."

When your income is directly related to being able to travel to the other side of the world, being separated from the fundamental resource that makes this possible is disquieting.

As promised, my new navy-blue passport and my well-used old one arrived on time. Flipping through the embossed pages of the tattered book brought a smile to my face and spun my memory into reverse. Canada, Mexico, Tanzania, South Africa, Costa Rica, Namibia, England, Kuwait, Iraq, India, and Nepal all had a notch in my worn ledger and a spot in my heart.

I split my leave time between Arizona and Indiana. Since my dad had become increasingly more ill in his fight with cancer, I tried to visit my Hoosier family as often as I feasibly could. Besides, I was excited to share my tales of Nepal, knowing my dad would be eagerly waiting to hear of my venture.

I stayed in Indiana long enough to enjoy my tribe's Fourth of July BBQ. It had been a couple of decades since I had experienced such a gleeful Independence Day. My parents, two of my siblings and their kids, three of my four offspring, and my six-month-old grandson were in attendance. We indulged in the typical American Independence Day provisions—grilled hamburgers, hot dogs, potato salad, mac and cheese, watermelon, iced tea, and lemonade. Funny how food is always ten times better when consumed with family.

I hated eating and running but had to catch my flight from the local regional airport, so the family would have to partake in the evening fireworks display without me. Attempting to be strong, I hugged everyone goodbye. Saying goodbye to Dad was incredibly hard. His health had taken a nosedive. He held me in a tight embrace and whispered, "Be safe, kiddo. I love you."

I kissed him on the cheek and whispered back, "I will." I knew we both were hoping that there was still time left on his clock.

Deported

For the moon never beams without
bringing me dreams.

~ *Edgar Allen Poe*

July 2012 was the start of my second year in Iraq. I had re-signed my contract and currently had no plans other than to continue working for Frontier along with picking up a few casual shifts back in Phoenix during my leaves.

On Friday, the sixth of July, I found myself sitting in the visa queue at Basra's International Airport. I was feeling pleased to be starting another year at Rumaila. Even though the job had its frustrations, I loved my adventurous career and couldn't imagine doing anything else.

Like the first time I came to Iraq, I needed the same crucial documents to be granted a new visa. Frontier's responsibility was to prepare the forms and email them to us before leaving our home base. Before clearing customs, the Iraqis would collect all the passports and LOIs (letters of invitation) of those needing a new visa. Then, they would call your name one by one, and you were to step to the desk and pay the $202.00 in crisp, new bills.

Sitting there on the uncomfortable plastic seat, I wondered why this took so long. My bum ached from all my sitting over the past thirty-six hours. I was growing restless and found myself checking my watch every few minutes. How come I ended up at the bottom of the list when I had been one of the first to hand in my passport? It had now been forty-five minutes, and nearly everyone else had been given their passports and sent to the customs window. Didn't they know my security team would be getting antsy since I hadn't made it through customs yet? My delay would hold up the entire transport back to camp.

Then, at last, one of the agents attempted calling my name, Janeea Mouzsey, finally. I stepped to the window with the cash in hand. "Do you have a copy of your LOI?"

"Yes, I do." I pulled out the two-page list I had recently received from Frontier's office. Because it was my one-year anniversary, and having a new passport required a new visa, I needed a new LOI from the Iraqi government saying I had been approved to travel into the country to work.

Two uniformed Iraqis scanned the paper, and I pointed out my name. The list was written in Arabic and listed everyone receiving a new visa. The only English on the paper was each person's name beside their Arabic registered name. All the other information was in a language I couldn't read. So when the men told me this form was outdated (July 2011), I was none the wiser. Not good. They then brought over a ledger with a handwritten list and asked me to see if I could find my name in their records. I held the book, believing I would no doubt find Jonea Mounsey USA, amidst the other characters. My eyes slowly scanned each line. My heart was racing when I checked the list for the third time. "Nope, it's not here." My biggest fear wasn't my safety but how to get in touch with someone who could actually email my correct LOI. Frontier had mistakenly sent me the outdated one.

Getting my hands on the correct LOI wasn't going to happen quickly. I was able to contact ROO's document officer, Mac, who in turn tried to get a hold of Frontier's office in England. Finally, he reached the on-call duty manager, who was at home taking emergency calls. The document I needed was in Frontier's office, which was shut.

When I gave the news to the Iraqi customs agent, he smiled at me and stated, "Now you go to jail."

My response, "Is there TV and good food?" He laughed out loud. No, I wasn't taken to jail but was deported back to Kuwait with the charter jet. Mac had informed me to get a room at the transient hotel at Kuwait's airport, reassuring me it would only be for a night or two. I never imagined being deported from a country. Doesn't this only happen to criminals? Circumstantial grounds for deportation, include being found with drugs, firearms, smuggling other illegal substances, human trafficking, and not having a valid visa.

At first, I thought, cool, I will just chill and enjoy a few days relaxing. Hey, I'm on the clock, so no problem. But, on the other hand, I couldn't help feeling guilty that someone at ROO would have to cover my position, whether Nicky would have to hold over or one of the other medics would need to fill in. At least it wasn't my fault.

When I arrived back in Kuwait, I was taken to the Safir airport hotel and checked in. My room included meals, so at least I wouldn't starve. I found my room. It was about the size of a shoe box, with a tiny window so high on the wall that you couldn't see anything from it, and my TV didn't even work. The room creeped me out. The shower was disgusting with excess hair from a previous guest. The sheets looked OK, but I felt the room had not been thoroughly cleaned between customers. I was confined to the hotel and unable even to go outside as it was set up for travelers transient to another airport. Unfortunately, neither the pool nor the exercise room was available. Both were closed. Now I understood why the window in my room was so small. It was to keep deranged people like me from jumping.

I was exhausted from three days of travel and the excitement of my first deportation, but the sandman was too freaked to come to visit me. All I knew was that I wasn't planning to spend more than one night at this cesspit.

The next morning I emailed Mac, asking what was happening and if he had any updates. I was informed I would have to wait until Monday. Without hesitating, I booked myself into the Marriott Courtyard, hired a taxi, and relocated into the city.

Kuwait is a small country nestled between Iraq and Saudi Arabia and is situated in one of the driest, least-hospitable deserts on earth. It lies next to the Persian Gulf, also known as the Arabian Gulf. In the eighteenth century, Bedouin tribes from the interior founded a trading post, now Kuwait City.

This small nation was a British territory from 1899 until 1961. Then in 1990, Kuwait drew the world's attention when Iraqi forces stormed over the border and attempted a takeover. The United Nations coalition led by the US drove Iraq's army out of Kuwait and, within a few days, launched a counterattack in February 1991—the Persian Gulf War. Before retreating, Iraq looted the country and set most of its oil wells on fire. Today Kuwait has recovered and is a bustling modern city.

Over the past year, while passing through Kuwait City, I have taken the opportunity to investigate the local streets, malls, and sights. As part of our travel stipend, BP put their expats up in the plush JW Marriott, near the Soup Sharq Pier and Shuwaikh Beach Park, only a short walk from the hotel.

I remember the first time I walked to the beach park. It was a Friday, which is the first day of the weekend in the Middle East. Muslim families were out enjoying the day. Men dressed in their long white robes and women in abayas by the dozens sat on the grass having picnics and were cooking on mini charcoal BBQ grills. Children ran wildly around the park kicking balls and riding tricycles like any Western country. I chuckled when I saw one group grilling hotdogs on a hibachi grill. I was impressed by how friendly everyone was toward me. I was notably the outsider here. I'm sure it wasn't a regular sight to see a lone Western woman walking in their park. The locals would look at me and wave or give a cheerful nod. Their gestures made me feel most welcome in this distinctly foreign land, and they seemed pleased that I had taken an interest in interacting with their community.

During one of my visits, I stumbled onto the Kuwait fish market. The crowded warehouse positioned next to the port was noisy with chatty customers. The doors opened each afternoon at 4:00 p.m., allowing the public to buy the freshly caught seafood. Even before walking inside the market, I was overpowered by the pungent odor of seafood. Inside the massive building were row after row of stalls overflowing with fish, prawns, crabs, and squid. Wandering through the aisles, I was fascinated by the myriad of seafood, some species I had never seen before. As I continued along, one vendor abruptly shouted. "Lady, lady, you want to buy a fish?"

"No, no, I have nowhere to cook a fish, sir." Looking directly at the peddler, I shrugged my shoulders with hands in front of me, palms up, implying I had no good solution. I smiled and walked off.

The Kuwait Towers are one the most famous landmarks in the city after the Grand Mosque. These three blue spheres first caught my attention from the airplane's window. With my curiosity spiked, I longed for a closer view. It was a hot 100° day when I walked along the seafront to the towers. The closer I got, the taller the towers became, with one standing above the others. The ocean-colored spheres looked like giant Christmas ornaments twinkling in the sun. They were situated on a peninsula that juts out into the Gulf, making them especially easy to see from miles away.

After paying 3 dinar/9.50 USD, I was escorted to the top by an informative local Kuwaiti. Built in the 1970s, one of the orbs is part of a water storage system. The largest and tallest, 187 m, and the one I visited has an observation deck and a restaurant. The view of the sea and the city was splendid from the top, even though it was a hazy, humid day.

Three days after being deported, Frontier emailed me the correct paperwork. With my correct LOI in hand, they bestowed a new visa and granted me entry into Iraq. Being an international contractor could be trying at times, as I was finding out. There was always some new drama, be it canceled flights, a paperwork tragedy, or work site exigency. Sometimes I found all of this exciting, other times emotionally taxing. If I thought things were compelling at this point, I only needed to wait for a few months for the true eruptions to unfold.

Fruit market in Kuwait

Kuwait City fish market, "lady you want to buy a fish?"

Kuwait towers

Kuwait City from the harbor

Opened a Can of Worms

Don't worry if you're making waves just by being yourself. The moon does it all the time.

Although happy to be safe and sound back in the sandbox, I returned to find the world at Rumaila was quickly evolving. First, construction had begun at the Qarmat Ali (QA) water plant, meaning a medic was needed to be positioned at the site. With this in mind, Lilith decided her best option was to relocate the medical trainers, Galvin and Cain, the newest hires, to QA until something else could be arranged.

When Doug, our Ops lead, unexpectedly turned in his resignation, roles quickly changed again. Once more, Cain was shuffled and given the position of clinic manager, replacing Doug.

The days were filled with chaos and divulging information. I was lucky to be spending my days at Lion and away from the main camp during this hectic time. I hoped being out of sight would also mean being out of mind as Lilith looked at who else she could place at the QA.

The next move involved Nicky. She had drawn the short straw and chosen to go to Qarmat Ali, where she would now function as a trainer and medic. This left me without a back-to-back or a reliever. Suddenly our team was understaffed. So Frontier frantically started the search to find someone to fill this spot

I had escaped being removed from my job and continued to operate the ambulance, providing medical coverage as usual. I was relieved that Lilith had chosen Nicky, and I was allowed to stay where I was. But there was talk that I, too, would be moved to a different camp in the future. I held my breath and hoped it would only be a short-lived notion. Besides, I was a woman on a mission and had Tane in my sights. Yet I had not thought up how I would pounce.

Another expansion had also commenced. Just a few miles north of ROO HQ, the construction of a supersized supply warehouse and pipe yard had broken ground. The new Rumaila Supply Base (RSB) would include a small housing block and a new clinic. Lilith had mentioned that she wanted the north field medics to relocate to the new post.

Progress on the new build was advancing at full speed. Every other day, I was told RSB would be ready to be occupied within a few weeks. So naturally, I was perturbed at the thought of possibly having to shuffle to another place. But, for now, I enjoyed my daily routine and crossed my fingers that the new camp would get delayed or Lilith would devise a different plan. Things were going gangbusters on Rumaila.

Fortunately, Frontier found and hired a new medic to fill the trainer position. For his first rotation, Lilith planned for the new guy to stand in as the north medic taking my place while I went on leave. Frontier aimed to have the new hire processed and on board by the time of my scheduled departure.

Regrettably, the news came that he wouldn't be arriving until August 22. I was scheduled to go on leave on the ninth. Frontier's office contacted me and asked if I could hold over until the new medic arrived. Knowing I needed to keep Lilith happy, I agreed.

I had only had a two-and-a-half-week break on my last leave due to scheduling issues. I remained optimistic that my relief would show up on time. I couldn't wait to return to Arizona and spend time with my loved ones. My only grandkid, CJ, was now eight months old. I looked forward to giving him a big squeeze. My oldest son, Drew, was getting married in October, and there was planning and preparation to do. My daughter Angela and I had registered to run the Disneyland half marathon in California in September. It would be her first long-distance race. *Inshallah*, it would all work out.

In addition to the trainer, there was still a vacancy for a permanent medic to take Nicky's place as my reliever. Frontier put their nose to the grind and soon scored. An American paramedic, Larry, signed the one-year contract and started compiling his paperwork.

Besides the two medics, we were also getting a new physician from Germany. As usual, I was the last to hear that a female provider had signed on as an occupational health doctor. I didn't even know what exactly her role would entail.

It was getting hard to keep track of who was coming and going. My head was swimming, and ROO's medical staff was quickly expanding.

My initial plan for this rotation had been to avoid the limelight at all costs. With all the disarray and tension, I wanted to stay in the background and out of the way. However, it was August. Temperatures were soaring, and so were tempers. Sadly, Mark and I found out the hard way. Unintentionally I got sucked into an unpleasant situation. The following is the letter I wrote in my defense.

I need to report an incident that took place this morning. My driver Mark and I were given a departure time of 0700. We always receive our time the evening before. Mark is given the time by the Team Leader of the QRF, which is our escort for the morning. Mark then calls me and gives me the time.

When I arrived at the clinic today at 0647, Mark was readying the ambulance. Mark said we would meet our QRF, TL-Isaac, at the loading bay at 0700. I packed the ambulance with my gear, taking 5 minutes or so. When I got into the ambulance to leave at 0656, Mark told me Isaac had now called him 2 x asking where we were. Mark said he radioed at 0650 the first time. It's a 1-minute drive to the loading bay. As we are pulling up to the bay, Isaac is on the radio asking where we are; I answer him we are here. I look at my watch, and it's 0658.

When we reached Lion, Mark and I came into my office, and Isaac was there. He tells Mark that we caused the team to depart late, which meant the clients had to wait. Mark asked why we were told 0700 if the time was really earlier. Isaac then stated we should have been there at 0655 because that's how it's done in the military. Mark reminded Isaac that we aren't working for the military here. Isaac then lost his temper and said to Mark, *"You f----n idiot, you need to be there 5 minutes earlier." I then told Isaac that we aren't going to be talked to like this and asked him to cool it. I explained, "We don't have a problem being flexible. We just need more notice if we need to leave sooner." Isaac still raised his voice to me when we were trying to settle this issue.*

This is the first issue of this nature I have encountered. If anything, we often have to wait for the QRF team and leave 5-15 minutes later than told. I will not allow my coworkers or myself to be disrespected in this matter.

Sincerely
Jonea Mounsey
Northfield Medic

I can tell you I opened a can of worms. Isaac probably felt the heat from someone higher up and decided to hand the blame over to us. As the letter states, we were the ones waiting most of the time. On this particular day, when Isaac reported we needed to get going, it was only ten minutes at the most the client would have had to wait. No one should have gotten into trouble over ten minutes unless someone was dying.

I will tell you that I'm generally not a shit-stirrer, but when Isaac started in on Mark, I jumped in without even thinking. It was reflexive self-defense, I reckon. I was shocked at myself and couldn't believe this was even happening.

Of course, there was an extensive investigation that went up the ladder to top management. In the end, Isaac kept his job, but he was pissed with me for several days. Mark's boss felt that I was too "chummy" with Mark. I justify my actions with the fact that we were a unified crew. I routinely spent seventy-five percent of my time with the drivers, and I would say I was friendly with all of them.

Nevertheless, I was getting tired of listening to everyone harass Mark. Somehow the guys started calling him *bawbag*. I'd never heard this vulgar word before. As I discovered, the term *bawbag* is Scottish slang for scrotum or a worthless person. Mark never acted as if it bothered him. Obviously, he was used to being teased yet never attempted to stand up for himself. I have a feeling Mark had been picked on most of his life. Being of small stature, Mark would never throw a punch and expect to come out ahead.

Welcome, Dr. Angela

Be the moon and inspire people even when you're far from full.

~ K Tolnoe

When Frontier had asked if I would hold over, I felt I could not refuse them. I had literally only spent eighteen days at home since the middle of March. I needed a break from the ongoing tension on the oil field. Sharing a home-cooked meal, having a glass of wine, and going out hiking were definitely on my to-do list. I was counting down the days until my leave.

Guess I had too many things in my head when I figured out I had made a big boo-boo. One week before my leave, I realized I had forgotten that I needed to get an exit visa in my new passport before I could leave Iraq. To obtain this specific travel document required that I hand my passport over to Mac, who would in turn prepare the paperwork and then forward the passport over to the Iraqi officials. This typically took about a week. The problem was the day I remember was the first day of Eid al-Fitr. As a result, the government offices would be closed for three days before my passport could even be handed over.

So now, instead of leaving on the twenty-second of August, I was pushed back until the twenty-seventh. It was my own fault this time. Despairingly, I wouldn't be allowed extra time at home, and I would get two weeks of leave, not the regular four. I was just thankful it happened in August and not in October. It would have been harrowing to miss Drew and Jocelyn's wedding.

Dr. Angela and Sam arrived as scheduled. With Sam in country and available to cover Lion, I was allowed to spend my extended time hanging out in HQ. Having five days in camp was a nice change, something that had never happened in the year since I started working there. Along with more gym time, I spent most of my days helping out in the clinic and chatting with my coworkers. But the highlight of my week was getting to know Angela. Yay, another woman.

Until now, Nicky and I were the only females working on the healthcare team. But, because we replaced each other, we only crossed paths for a few minutes coming and going and sometimes not even then.

Dr. Angela had an impressive professional background, including having a long list of credentials. The woman had clearly worked endlessly at advancing her medical career. She reminded me of myself. We both strived to boost our vocational experiences, and having only one job never cut it, not because of finances necessarily but because it was always good to have a backup. Angela's second job was one I also longed to do, repatriate patients to their homes. In other words, if someone was on holiday and became sick or injured and needed to be medically escorted home, a medical representative, such as Angela, was flown to the patient's location and ushered them home. Since she was a single parent of young adult twin boys, we had a lot in common.

Angela was grateful I was there when she arrived. We had first connected via email prior to her coming to Iraq, so it worked well that I could show her around and provide information about the current happenings.

Like myself, Angela arrived in the dead of summer, and she thought it was bloody hot at 50°C (122°F). However, I reassured her that by her next rotation it would start cooling off and by November she would need a jacket in the evening.

At the end of Angela's first day, she asked if I would walk with her. She was unsure if she could find her room in the dark. As we strolled down the sidewalk chatting, I spotted a creepy camel spider. I was excited to finally see one. It was relatively small, about the size of my palm. The hairy-faced spider with oversized jaws almost got stepped on as its light-brown coloring was perfect camouflage. Unlike me, Angela was less than happy to have come across the arachnid. The little guy just sat on the narrow path, refusing to move. Hoping to encourage him to run off, I picked up a few small rocks and dropped the first stone near the spider. Nothing, it did not budge. I held the next rock above the critter, but my aim was off, and I crushed the poor creature, "Oops, sorry."

Camel spiders had gotten a bad rap from when the US military was in Iraq. There were all kinds of stories about how camel spiders would chase the guys around the desert. The fact is these creatures are arachnids but not true spiders. Camel spiders are sometimes called wind scorpions. Despite their fierce reputation and gnarly looks, they aren't harmful to humans and are not poisonous. However, they run very fast, up to ten miles per hour.

One good thing about being stuck at ROO, I got to know Angela and spent time with her. I didn't realize how much I needed a female cohort until I had one. Angela and I became good friends from day one.

During the day, there was very little to do as I patiently waited on my visa. The clinic had plenty of staff, and the camp was tranquil with the Iraqis on holiday. Thank goodness there was a fantastic gym to occupy my time. I went every morning and often again in the evening.

Surprisingly, I was still getting full pay. I felt lucky because I had been in the wrong. I ended up working fifty-seven days on this particular rotation, the same as working two cycles in a row. It felt like I was never going to get home. I wondered how the security guys dealt with their long rotations of eight weeks and often as much as twelve weeks without a break.

Before going out on leave, I was told to have all my items packed up so they could be taken up to RSB. The camp was to be finished during my break and would be ready for the north field medic to move in upon my return. This didn't really make me too happy, but it was what Lilith thought should happen.

Pump It Up, Girls

Tell me the story
About how the sun loved the moon so much
That she died every night
Just to let him breathe . . .

~ Hanako Ishii

E venings in the Iraqi desert could be most enjoyable. When the sun fell from the sky and the
moon replaced her, a calmness claimed the land.
Summer's heat decreased to a tolerable ambiance, and in
winter the darkness sucked the warmth from the milieu,
necessitating a jacket.

Following our evening meal, I would try and convince
my teammates to come out and join me for some recreational
activity. Sometimes I won their attention, but most of the time
they had an excuse and would reject my offer. Angela occasionally joined
me if she had her work caught up; otherwise she spent her evenings working
in the clinic. Unfortunately, Dr. Ang was not a big gym fan. So instead, we
walked laps around the complex, chatting and sharing gossip.

One of the evening pastimes we all loved was playing tennis. ROO was
blessed to have three superior courts to play on. The problem was lots of people
liked playing, so the courts needed to be reserved in advance. Nevertheless,
it was great fun when our gang got together to play. We would take turns
playing doubles, rotating in and out. Lee, Vic, Angela, Galvin, Leon, Mark,
Seth, and I joined in on the sport. Just like with everything else, Vic was an

amazingly talented player. He cracked me up as he was a play-by-the-rules guy. The rest of us would get silly and laugh so hard that we could hardly breathe. Poor Vic.

ROO had employed a very cool and talented engineer, Gina. The first few times I saw Gina were during prayers, shortly after arriving in Iraq. I'm ashamed to say, the small group I sat with during the security briefs started discussing whether Gina was male or female. We knew nothing of who this person was, only that we were confused about Gina's identity. A mesomorph body, muscular arms and legs, no body fat, and broad shoulders. It was simple to tell that much gym time had been the factor in carving this admirably structured physique. The person in question had a masculine appearance, and her hair was in a short butch cut.

Gina could be found every evening either in the weight gym or in the circuit gym boxing. As time went on, I was lucky enough to get to know Gina and the super awesome person that she was. We shared the same birthday, both Saint Paddy's Day babies. Gina had competed on the USA Powerlifting team and at one time was ranked seventh in the world overall and was second in the world in the bench press, impressive. Gina also has made a name for herself in the competitive boxing arena.

Gina asked Angela and me if we were interested in doing some training in the weight gym. Absolutely. Gina was already lifting with several of the security guys. She shared her knowledge of correct technique, incorporating an attitude to drive us to train hard, all while enforcing a positive spirit into our brains. I learned a great deal from this devoted expert. To this day, I use those methods taught during my training sessions at ROO.

Although Gina had muscles that any bodybuilding freak would die for, she was the kindest, most considerate person you could ever meet. Few people respected the Iraqis and loved their culture more than Gina did. I've always felt fortunate that our paths had crossed.

Rocky, Balloonie, Meanie, and Theresa

I am the Lone Wolf and the Moon is mine.
~ Avijeet Das

I'm not sure how it all started or why we were first given Balloonie, Rocky, Meanie, and Theresa, but one of our Iraqi coworkers brought them to us from a pet store in Basra. Balloonie and Meanie were orange-colored goldfish, and Rocky was a black goldfish. Our fish started out sharing a small fish tank, but as their popularity grew they were given a deluxe tank with lights, bubbler, plants, and decorations. The colorful tank was set up on the physician's desk in the clinic at HQ.

At the end of my day, I would return from Lion to find Lilith kneeling on the desk, butt in the air, playing with the fish. If fish could be spoiled, these were.

The solution became clear when the fish started fighting, hence the name Rocky, as in Rocky Balboa. Dr. Angela thought it would be a great idea to send Rocky to live on my desk at Lion. Poor Rocky was moved into a small fishbowl without all the bells and whistles. Rocky did receive some plants to hide in and was well cared for by Nicky and me. Every few weeks, his fishbowl required cleaning. He would be removed and placed in a Styrofoam cup until his bowl was fresh again. I always worried this procedure would stress him and that I would return the next day to find him belly up. But, he did fine and was still there when I moved on. I guess he was a fighter, ha-ha.

Once Rocky left, the other two fish then started fighting. Finally, Meanie was removed to the transport building next to the clinic. These fish were so territorial.

Balloonie became Miss Personality. If you told me that a fish could learn tricks, I would have bet against it. The clinic staff and Lilith spent so much time playing with her that she learned to beg for food. She would swim into your hand and devour the fish food. She soon fit her name perfectly. Have you ever seen a really overfed cat? Well, Balloonie was a very overfed fish. I'm surprised she could keep afloat.

Theresa was a red-eared slider turtle. This species is from North America, but somehow Theresa ended up moving to Iraq, or maybe her grandparents were originally American. When Theresa first came to ROO, her name was Terry. It was later discovered that Terry was not a boy, so the name Theresa was given to her.

Theresa didn't have a proper terrarium to live in, so Lisa hid her in her room. I didn't see much of Theresa, but Lisa and Angela became very fond of her.

Pet passports are a real thing. Just like people, a pet passport allows pets to be able to fly between countries with their owners. This document includes official information, such as the owners' details, specifics about the animal, and a vet-signed paper showing their health record.

I mention this because Dr. Angela decided that Theresa should be taken back to Germany to live. Dr. Angela went to the effort to try and get Theresa a passport. I'm telling you, these critters were loved. Theresa ended up having a fake passport of her own. Angela was never allowed to take Theresa back to Germany as immigration wouldn't allow a turtle to pass through.

It was delightful to have our little pets around. We even befriended one of the stray dogs in our camp. The gang started feeding him, even though it was against the camp rules. Sadly enough, there was a mass slaying of all the stray animals in the camp. This was for the safety of the staff and the guard dogs. Wild strays could easily have rabies and become aggressive if cornered.

Rabies was a genuine concern in Iraq, and we all had to be immunized for it before our first deployment.

Autumn

I'm such a "look at the moon" person.

D
eparting Arizona for Iraq after my fourteen-day
visit was tough. For the first time, I wasn't ready
to go back to work. I had received word that the
north field medics had not been relocated to RSB yet but
to expect it to happen within the first week of arriving
back to work. I decided I would try and stay optimistic
about the whole situation. Dr. Angela, my new comrade,
encouraged me to remain positive.

The routes to and from Iraq always varied. It seemed
weird to fly so far north, transiting through Seattle to get
to Dubai, several hundred miles north of Phoenix, where I
started my journey.

Once en route, I relaxed in my comfy business class seat, leg
stretched out in front of me, sipping on my glass of Chateau Montrose. I ma-
nipulated my private TV screen to the flight tracking page. I was bewildered
why our jet was flying north over Canada. Dubai is in the other direction, so
this seemed odd. I was fatigued but was not even close to being inebriated.
The route finder showed our aircraft would be flying over the North Pole!
Wow, this was so cool. Too bad it was dark outside, or I'd probably had a
chance to look out at the icy landscape.

In reality, it's much shorter to fly over the North Pole from the west coast
of the United States to get to Dubai than to fly straight east. These routes are
called polar routes, and Emirates is one of the few airlines that use this route.

It was nearly midnight as I stood at the visa counter in the Kuwait International Airport. I needed to have a visitor's visa stamped on my passport before I could clear customs, find my driver, and be taken to the JW Marriot for a few hours of sleep before my morning charter flight to Basra.

I waited my turn among the loud, impatient crowd, which was made up mostly of Middle Eastern males. Eventually, I reached the counter and waited for one of the Kuwaitis to take my details and stamp my passport. Next to me stood a short Asian woman who glanced over and saw my navy-blue American passport.

"Hey, are you American?" the female voice called.

"Yeah."

"Me too."

Both of us were shocked to bump into another American, let alone a woman. We introduced ourselves and asked what the other one was doing in Kuwait.

Autumn lived part-time in Kuwait City with her husband, who worked for Kuwait Oil. The couple had homes in both Alaska and California. Autumn asked me if I had a place to stay, and she tried to talk me into coming and staying at her place that same night. I told her I couldn't really, as my company had prepaid for a driver and my room at the Marriott. I told Autumn that I traveled through Kuwait regularly and would love to meet up next time. We exchanged contact information and promised to connect.

My September 2012 rotation was better than expected. Due to communication issues at RSB, I didn't end up moving. However, my new back-to-back, Larry, had been cleared and was ready to get his boots in the sand. Sixteen days after I arrived on ROO, I was again traveling west, homeward bound. Since I had spent extra time at work in August, I ended up with a shortened trip. This was a kind reward that Frontier did for me after my previous elongated rotations.

I had gotten in touch with Autumn, and we made plans to hang out in Kuwait on my way back through. I had a twelve-hour layover before my midnight departure, so I had time to waste. Autumn picked me up at the airport, and we drove to Kuwait City for lunch. I didn't envy her driving in the city as the traffic was insane. She took me to the Souk Al-Mubarakiya market. What a fascinating place! There were rows of shops selling spices, fruits, vegetables, fish, jewelry, nuts, garments, and electronics. Oh, the smells.

Autumn had a favorite open-air restaurant she wanted me to try—lamb and chicken kebabs fresh off the grill along with Iranian flatbread, known as *taftoon*. Delicious! The bakers invited us to come and watch how they made the flat dough. Once it is rolled out, they throw it onto the sides of the domed oven. Then they insisted we practice throwing the raw dough into the oven. Everyone laughed and joked at our skills. The proud bakers grinned ear to ear as they posed for photos.

Autumn's husband, Thai, came to the market and met up with us. They both were born in Vietnam but met after each had moved to the United States. Thai was familiar with the Rumaila project and had recently been asked if he would consider coming to work in Iraq. However, the couple reported they were concerned Iraq was still too dangerous, so Thai had decided against taking the offer.

My new friends escorted me to their flat, located in a beautiful high-rise overlooking the Arabian Gulf. "Jo, would you like a glass of wine?"

I was shocked when Autumn inquired. "Sure, that would be great," I said.

The country of Kuwait is supposed to be a dry country. Alcohol is illegal in Kuwait, but as I learned, it is still snuck in and often cultivated in people's private homes. Punishment for trafficking or consuming alcohol can be harsh, including hundreds of lashes, imprisonment, or deportation. When they returned from visiting France, my friends had gotten the wine through customs. They had a friend who worked at the local Kuwait embassy.

At first, I hesitated to indulge, but Autumn reassured me it was fine as long as we drank in the privacy of their home. That was all I needed, to get into trouble and be held in Kuwait. I'd already been deported from one country.

It's funny how we humans enjoy doing things we know we shouldn't. Even the most conscientious people probably have bent the rules at one time or another. Maybe it was as simple as using a fake name, drinking underage, or eating something at the store before paying for it. Don't tell me you've never made an illegal U-turn.

It felt good to be sitting in my friend's apartment, consuming a couple of glasses of illegal drinks. "Why is alcohol illegal in Kuwait?" I questioned.

"Because Kuwait's majority is Muslim," Thai explained. The Muslim religion teaches against the use of alcohol for spiritual reasons. Drinking is considered an iniquitous act. I presume partaking in alcoholic beverages could lead many good men and women to commit ungodly deeds.

Later the same evening, Thai drove us around the city. Previously I had avoided being out on the streets after dark, as it is frowned upon for a single woman to do so. The city had come to life, skyscrapers brightly illuminated; it was like looking at a giant Christmas tree, not quite the Las Vegas strip, but still impressive. I was asked what I wanted to see. "A grocery store." I always like to check out the food markets when I travel. I find them fascinating. Thai took us to the expansive Lulu's Hypermarket. The store was super clean and had everything—so many yummy choices. I purchased a small package of Barazik, a Middle Eastern pastry with honey and pistachios. I planned to enjoy it somewhere between Kuwait and America.

A hypermarket, also known as a big-box store, is a retail store that includes groceries, general merchandise, and even clothing. In the US, it would compare to Super-Walmart or a Costco but with much more interesting food items; this was the Middle East after all. Besides, I've never seen camel meat for sale at either of these places in the US.

I had a great day hanging out with my new friends and felt privileged to have randomly bumped into Autumn. As I traveled the world, I was blessed with a conglomerate of new acquaintances. Having the chance to meet people from all over was awesome and such an honor. Autumn and Thai had been great hosts, and I looked forward to meeting them again.

Rim to Rim to Rim

*Love is like the moon. When it does
not increase, it decreases.*

I was much relieved when the wheels of the Boeing A320
braked on the runway at Phoenix Sky Harbor Airport.
It felt odd to be arriving in Phoenix later than some
of the wedding guests. It was only four days until Drew
and Jocelyn's wedding. My dear friend Shelley and her
mother, Mary-Jeane, had arrived from Canada a day before
me. Life was full-on, prepping for a wedding, entertaining
family and friends, all while trying to get into the groove of
being back home and trying not to be overcome with jet lag.

The wedding went off without a hitch, other than being
disappointed that Brock, my middle son, was unable to attend
due to the Navy denying him leave for the event.

Drew had been introduced to Jocelyn through his brother-in-law Bill.
Jocelyn and Bill were both math teachers at the same high school. Drew and
my daughter Angie were also teachers who have degrees in history. Drew and
Jocelyn had dated for three years before they decided to get married.

Their wedding was perfect. It was held at an outside venue in Phoenix.
Smartly they chose to have it on a Monday evening instead of on the weekend,
saving themselves some money by doing it this way. The wedding occurred
on Columbus Day, a national holiday in the States. Columbus Day celebrates
the anniversary of Christopher Columbus discovering the Americas. The cool
thing was most of their friends already had the holiday off from work. Perfect

weather, great food and drink, music, dancing, and making merry with many special people. It was indeed a momentous occasion.

I couldn't have been happier for my son and his beautiful bride. I felt he had wisely chosen the perfect mate. I tried not to cry during the mother-son dance as I reflected on how my oldest son had grown into the man I hoped he would be. He had practically become the man of the house when I became a single parent. I relied on his judgments, good sense, and financial wisdom. He had been a rock when I floundered with difficult life decisions.

I was undeniably going to maximize my time, and I had much catching up to do. So I planned to squeeze the most out of every minute of every day.

For starters, I volunteered to be medical support for a large group hiking through the Grand Canyon. Two days after the wedding, I drove 230 miles to northern Arizona, where I met with the trekkers. The band of hikers had gathered as a part of the Project Athena Foundation. The Athenas had been founded a few years earlier by four of my world-class racing friends. These four women had a vision of empowering other women who had encountered medical setbacks. Thus the Project Athena campaign was born. In reality, it is an adult make-a-wish crusade for women.

The idea is to help women who have suffered a life-debilitating illness achieve an athletic dream. For instance, a woman might have survived cancer and had always hoped to run a marathon. The Athenas take the hopelessness out of these women's lost aspirations. Project Athena would choose a candidate and provide sponsorship, providing everything from a training strategy, shoes, and race entry fees, to see her finish her goal.

As a fundraiser, the foundation organized the Grand Canyon hike twice a year. This involved a paying bunch of eager people signing up to cross the canyon and back over two days. The epic tramp includes walking down the South Kaibab Trail to the Colorado River at a distance of 6.3 mi./10km, descending 4860 ft., and then continuing across the floor of the canyon and up the North Kaibab Trail to the top of the North Rim for an additional 14.3 mi./23 km and a climb of over 6000 ft. The exhausted hikers would then overnight in rustic cabins at the North Rim lodge only to get up in the dark hours of the early morning on day two and backtrack to the other side.

Excited to be doing my fifth rim-to-rim-to-rim crossing, or r-r-r as it is known, I was enthralled to be a part of this physically grueling challenge. This test of endurance was right up my alley. That said, I was distinctly aware that I would be on the trail for no less than sixteen hours on the first day and probably fourteen more on day two.

Melissa, the woman I befriended during my Kilimanjaro trip, was one of the four founders and had introduced me to the other co-founders. I joined the Athenas during the inaugural hike and participated in many of their other events. Meeting these women has been a life-changing experience, as they encouraged me to push myself beyond what I thought was possible.

I had been asked to come along as an Athena support person. My duties were to bring up the rear, making sure no one was left behind. I carried medical supplies to treat anything from blisters, sunburn, abrasion, sprains, and sore muscles to heat stroke. The participants were warned well in advance that they needed to get in shape and be prepared for a long, grueling workout.

The hike is super tough, even for seasoned athletes. It's a long and trying day. Never mind being exposed to the hot sun during the day and the freezing cold pre-dawn and post-sunset. The last few miles up the steep Kaibab in the dark have been nearly impossible for some. I've held women's hands while carrying both my pack and theirs, telling them with every five steps, "Come on, you can do this." When finally reaching the top, tears of success, joy, and pride run down their faces. I'm known as a trail angel for my patience and encouragement that I have shared freely. Being the trail sweep, I have always arrived at the top hours after the leaders. My reward is a slice of cold pizza and a beer, which energizes me long enough to start two or three IVs, infusing a liter of NS into those who are badly dehydrated.

The Grand Canyon is my favorite landscape in America, and I never get tired of visiting or exploring it. However, every trip and crossing are different. Each time I've made this trip, a handful of hikers have difficulty reaching the North Rim on day one. Luckily, there was a support vehicle to escort anyone who changed their minds about hiking the twenty-plus arduous miles back.

On the morning of day two, we retraced the same trail down to the Colorado River but ascended the Bright Angel, which is 9.6 mi. and 4500 ft. of stepping up. Eventually, we reached the top of the south rim. Ta-da! A total of 44.5 miles/ 72 km and 21,400 ft. of elevation change which is even greater than Alaska's Mt. Denali, the tallest peak in the United States.

Back in Phoenix, I attended the Arizona Cardinals vs. Buffalo Bills football game, American football. My European coworkers would talk about football, but they were referring to soccer. I had held season tickets to the

Cardinal's NFL team for several years. But since working abroad, I could only get to half the games. I first purchased season tickets in 1998, which was fourteen years ago. Pitifully, the poor Cardinals never really had been a top team in the league; even so, I loved going to the games and cheering them on. On this particular day, the Cardinals lost to the Bills in overtime, 19–16. It made for an exciting game. In football, there is a saying, "It ain't over till the fat lady sings."

This expression means to hold on. Anything can happen right up to the exact second the whistle blows, ending the event. I have seen American football games won with two seconds on the clock. I was curious about where this saying originated, and it seems it first was associated with the opera. Then in the 1970s, sports commentator Dan Cook used the phrase when reporting an NBA playoff game. It took off from there and has become a popular phrase in sporting events.

I had always been determined that one day I would run the Bisbee 1000, The Great Stair Climb race. So deciding that I wouldn't put it off any longer, I signed up. For years I had hoped that one of my running mates would join me for this challenging event. Or that I would find someone who might be interested in traveling down to this small historical settlement in southern Arizona. Neither ever transpired, so off I went to the colorful and entertaining old mining town nestled in the Mule Mountains. Bisbee was founded in 1880, becoming a booming copper mine in its heyday. Now, it was a tourist haven with art galleries, shops, and good dining options, hosting ghost and mine tours.

The settlement survived nearly a century of mining. Eight million pounds of copper, 102 million ounces of silver, 2.8 million ounces of gold, and tons of zinc, lead, and manganese were extracted. Later the open-pit mining operation was closed down. As a result, Bisbee is an authentic Old West town, just like in the cowboy movies. Bisbee is only twenty-three miles from the famous town of Tombstone.

Bisbee sits on the side of a mountain. Nothing in the town is flat; when the settlement grew, it grew upward. To access all the various levels of the town, stairs were built throughout the city. There are ten staircases comprising over a thousand steps. Every October since 1990, Bisbee holds a unique fitness challenge where participants race or walk the 4.5-mile course, which features 1000 steps.

To help fill my camping fix, I arrived a day early and set up my tent in a campground just outside of town. That evening before calling it a day, I wasn't thrilled to find a large bark scorpion crawling around the bathroom. I'm not afraid of these creatures but am aware they would often find their way into campers' sleeping bags and shoes. Though poisonous, they rarely cause any fatalities. I have heard their sting is quite painful, and I had no intention of finding out. When I packed up my gear a day later, I was cautious, checking that no venomous animals had found shelter under my tent, whether a scorpion or a snake.

Although it had started drizzling rain, the cooler weather made for a comfortable temperature to run. It was a beautiful autumn day in southern Arizona. The trees had changed their attire from green and yellow to orange and brown, the perfect outfit for the season.

Standing at the starting line, I bumped into a friend from Phoenix. The crazy thing was that his half-sister was one of the Project Athena founders, the group I'd hiked across the GC with a week earlier. We chatted about the canyon crossing until interrupted by the starting pistol cracking off a round. We gave a quick handshake, and wished each other good luck, then down the street we went.

With the roadway and the steep, narrow steps now wet, I focused on my footing as I chased dozens of runners up and down the stairs and twisting alleys. I had come to complete the run and just to have fun. But it never fails. I think I don't care about my time, then something kicks in and the word "race" gets a foothold in my subconscious. Suddenly I became competitive and felt the need to pass as many competitors as possible. This has happened countless times. I can't deny my love of competing.

The 1000-step race was a blast. Being in the presence of like-minded strangers, minus one, is so heartwarming. You know in reality that they are not aliens but nameless friends. Finishing in less than an hour, I ticked another box off my bucket list.

It seems I have this problem where when I complete a box on my list it sometimes goes right back on the list again. Bisbee's 1000-step race is one of them, but next time I would love to share this event with another person.

Drew and me at his wedding October, 8, 2012

Drew and Jocelyn with wedding party

Grand Canyon view from the top

There are nearly 100 switch backs on the Bright Angel trail

At the Bisbee 1000

I Saw Her, Yet
I Saw Her

Drink in the moon as though
you might die of thirst.

~ *Sanober Khan*

O n my arrival back to Iraq on the last day of
October 2012, I was pleased to find out the move
to RSB had been further delayed. There were ongoing issues with the supply camp's communication system, which was to be figured out before I relocated.

I stepped back into the ongoing drama regarding staff
and their roles. Lilith was again revisiting the idea of sending
me off as the medic at the QA water plant. The latest plans
were that the north medic would again start teaching the Iraqi
clinical staff, and Lilith seemed to want Nicky to carry out this task.

Nicky and Lilith got on like a house on fire. Both were from the UK,
which made them more connected. It wasn't hard to see that Lilith favored
my back-to-back over me. By now, Lilith couldn't fool me. I saw her, yet I
saw her. What I'm getting at is she couldn't hide her intentions from me. She
wasn't the first boss I knew to be ruthless. I can't say that I didn't get along
with this catty woman, but I had lost respect for her over the past few months.
Her insolent behavior was starting to sicken me.

Lilith talked so revoltingly of the Iraqi people. I often wondered why in
the hell she took on this contract. I guess earning big money spoke loudly. My

buddy Mac had told me he knew her when she was still married to her first husband. He said she was a "manipulative bitch." The story has it that she was working offshore on a drill rig when she met her now-husband. The current spouse was reportedly a kahuna in the British Petroleum Corporation. I was told Lilith left the first guy and ran off with the current husband. Maybe this is hearsay, or maybe it's not.

It was good to know a few people who did not worship the ground she walked on. Half of my coworkers also felt she was contemptible. We witnessed her unprofessional actions so many times. One of her favorite things to do was to come into the clinic at the end of the business day. In front of all of us, she would sit on Dr. Johannes's lap with her arms around his neck. His face would redden, and he never once put a hand on her. His arms remained at his side. She did all the touching. I felt bad for him, and it was an awkward situation. I think it would have shown if the man was enjoying Lilith's playful behavior. He would not have had the look of discomfiture. Lilith seemed always to get her way. She was an insensitive soul. I wondered if she had ever loved anyone other than herself.

I knew I would have to get assertive if I was to have any chance of remaining as the north medic. I lay awake at night, trying to decide on an attack to rescue myself. I communicated back and forth with Dr. Angela seeking her ideas and support. Angela had only spent two rotations on ROO, so she was still green to the drama.

My coworkers, including Angela, kept telling me maybe it wouldn't be so bad being relocated. However, my classified secret crush remained airtight. I knew if I got moved to the water plant, I would rarely get back to ROO HQ to see ANY of my friends.

The Ops leads were untrustworthy when it came to standing against the demon. They needed to protect themselves if they wanted to continue receiving attractive paychecks and avoid the dreaded phone call from Frontier's office.

After a long debate with my conscience, I decided to contact my employer and convince them that I could do the same job Lilith wanted Nicky to do. So I wrote them the following letter. I knew I was well-liked by our project managers and hoped they would stick up for me.

Dear Jen,

Before you decide on moving me to QA, I have some questions and a few things to share with you.

When I was in the Frontier office during my project briefing, I was told I would be expected to do teaching and that this was a part of my role. On my second day at work here on the ROO, I taught First Aid to a group of non-English-speaking Iraqis. I wasn't given any material to instruct with; Joc just told me a few things I needed to cover. Since that first day, I have taught several different classes here. I have not been notified of any negative feedback. I currently hold instructor certifications in ACLS, BLS, and ITLS. However, I haven't done much instructing in the last couple of years due to working over here.

Jen, I asked if you could send me the details of the education plans. I'm still waiting to receive this. Nicky did tell me she thought it was an EMT-B course. I believe the students will be the North Clinic staff, PAs, and nurses. Are the students coming to Lion, or will the instructor go to the clinic? In the past, I've been told it's not secure enough for us to spend much time there. When are the classes to begin? Will the material be in UK or US format?

When I first came to Iraq, I was afraid to tell the locals that I was American. I believed this might put me at a greater security risk. This has not been the case at all. Within a couple of weeks, I was told, "You are different, and you are a warm person, not cold like everyone else from the West has been." I have built a trust and a bond with the local nationals. The Iraqis, including our doctors, EMDs, security teams, and people of Lion, all get so excited every time I return from my rotation. There is, in fact, one person who actually sheds tears when I leave; my kids don't even cry when I leave. These people have shared their culture, history, language, and personal lives with me. I understand and respect these people. I believe in the LNs and care about them and their future.

Teaching and working with the LNs takes a great deal of patience and understanding. I watch daily at everyone's frustration working here. I hear the negatives and see how impatient many expats are. It's like moving one grain of sand at a time, and there's a whole desert to be moved.

Jen, there are so many inconsistencies that have been communicated:

For example, when I talked to Nicky last Friday, she told me she likes being at QA. Not sure why she would consider taking a pay cut to move.

On Friday, you told me you wanted experienced instructors. Dr. Angela said she hadn't taught before!

I was told over a year ago that the client didn't want anyone with a military background doing the teaching.

I was told over a year ago by Lilith I would be having my own clinic in the north (RSB).

I thought Nicky and Larry were hired as medics the same as I.

Jen, I feel like I'm looked at as the weakest one out here. This doesn't do anything for one's self-esteem. I think there are a few reasons for this. First, I haven't got to know the folks in the UK; I have only been into the office once since being hired over a year and a half ago. Second, no one knows how I will perform because I haven't had any real in-the-field trauma emergencies. Third, I don't get to spend much time in the clinic to build my skills here. Finally, I'm usually the quiet one around the clinic and don't come across as very confident; I'm hardly ever aggressive unless I need to be.

Jen, if I didn't think I could do this, I wouldn't be asking. However, I feel I deserve a chance to give it a try. I understand I'm not as experienced as the others, and I will have to work hard to deliver what is expected. Can you believe anyone would turn down a raise but choose to do more work and have more stress in their life instead?

I understand you have hard decisions to make, and this is a challenging project. However, I want you to know that I appreciate the Frontiermedex staff's hard work. Jen, if you still believe you need to relocate me after reading this, I will go. Maybe you could consider allowing Nicky and I to be the north medics (btbs). Just a thought.

Sincerely

Jonea

A few days later, Frontier contacted me and said that it had been decided that I would remain as the north ROO medic. I was so relieved, but I also knew I would need to prove I could perform the tasks asked of me. I knew Angela would be supportive and help where she could.

Remaining the north field medic also meant I would transfer camps. Lilith decided to move forward with her plans, communication dilemmas or not. I was officially removed from ROO's main headquarters. Luckily, it was only as far as the RSB compound, a twenty-minute drive from HQ. Maybe I would like it there. For starters, I would be out of the direct fire of all the drama at the main camp. Life at ROO had gone from being uninvolved to being a convoluted atmosphere.

Deep down, I was sad and felt lonely even before packing my belongings. Whenever Vic, Lee, or another cohort questioned if I was excited about my move, I smiled and lied, "Sure, besides, I get to be in charge of the new clinic."

With that said, I moved to RSB before the communication issues were fixed. I found this concerning. My cell phone didn't work, I had no landline, and my radio had lousy reception. If I needed to talk to the clinic or anyone at the main camp, I had to go to the security office at the front gate. On the other hand, if I were needed for whatever reason, the security personnel would have to come find me.

I still crewed the ambulance and traveled each day to Lion, but now my accommodations were at Camp Solitary. All the structures at RSB were new, which I will admit was nice, including the clinic. For whatever reason, Lilith thought I would be elated to have an infirmary to manage. "Jo, you'll have your own clinic to organize as you wish."

I wanted to say, "Lilith, I don't give a damn. Why do I need a clinic?"

The whole clinic thing didn't make sense to me. I wouldn't even be around during the most likely time of an accident. I would be up north at the same time the construction crew would actively be working on the warehouse. By the time I returned in the evening, their day would also be finished. How busy would the clinic be with only twenty-five people residing there?

I had only spent six short nights at RSB prior to going out for leave. Just enough time to get my feet wet and start arranging the clinic. With multiple boxes of medications and equipment to unpack, I thoughtfully organized each item, placing it in a designated spot, inventorying every single object as I went—needles, aspirin, scissors, and boxes of gauze. I wondered if Larry and Lilith would approve of my layout. I had my doubts. Lilith had embarked on a micromanaging warpath; nothing or no one was out of reach.

Now or Never

If I were the moon, I would like you to be my sky.
~ Alexandra Vasiliu

I stepped out of the camp hospital and into the Iraqi moonlight. The crispness of the evening compelled me to draw up my jacket's zipper. As I headed toward my room, I pulled the phone from my jacket pocket. Taking a deep breath, I crossed my fingers as I hit the speed dial setting on the company phone labeled AB south. I was nervous and unsure of my decision, but what the hell? It was now or never. It took me over a year to get the courage to make this call. I stopped breathing as the phone started to ring.

"Hello, Tane speaking," he said, answering as if he had no clue who was calling or hadn't looked at the phone's caller ID before answering.

"Hi, it's Jo," I paused, holding my breath, and without thinking, I blurted, "Hey, you want to meet up for a coffee?" I drew a big gulp of air into my lungs and again held my breath, anticipating the answer.

"I'm already back in my room for the evening," Tane replied.

"Okayee, just wondering. See ya later. Have a good night." Embarrassed, I quickly hung up the phone and continued down the path to my room. My stomach tightened, feeling disappointed, stupid, and second-guessing myself all at the same moment. He was probably wondering what that was all about. Now he would never realize that I had a secret crush on him. What a foolish move! Guess this didn't work out as I had hoped for. I figured if I at least attempted to get his attention, he might notice me.

Tane's vocation was working in the protection sector. His duties varied from gate control, fire duty, camera surveillance, writing daily reports, and occasionally filling in as the ambulance driver. He had spent many years working in the Middle East and was well-versed.

I had been surveying Tane since first meeting him more than a year ago. Our paths crossed during my second hitch on the oil field. It was by coincidence that we even met.

It was the highlight of my week when Tane showed up at random times to drive the ambulance. Interestingly, he was often reserved, a man of few words who seemed always to be pondering some profound notion. Yet, at other times, his verbiage charmed my soul and amused my brain.

Every so often, he would catch me off guard, asking or saying something that would either puzzle my mind or make me laugh. I remember one such day when we were returning to camp. As the ambulance had a good number of flies buzzing inside, he asked, "If we are driving sixty mph, are the flies flying at sixty mph also?"

"Humm, I have to think about this one."

Unfortunately, the evening of my courageous phone call was my last night at Rumaila's main camp. The following day I would be heading home for my twenty-eight days off. Not only that, but I now had also been permanently relocated to the new RSB camp. I was only allowed to stay at HQ on the nights before going on leave.

I settled into my cozy room in the hotel (sometimes it was referred to as the high-rise) and switched on the TV. This wasn't exactly a hotel but a housing facility for visitors and expats transiting in and out of Rumaila. The standard procedure was for the person heading on leave to spend their last night in the two-story hotel. This allowed your reliever to take over the quarters you shared when it was their turn in country.

The incoming person was to arrive a day before the outgoing rotator so that there could be a face-to-face handover of assignments, preventing any gap in work coverage.

Lying in bed, I tried to ignore my pangs of disappointment. I wondered how I should have played out this plot so that it might have ended better. Then unexpectedly I hear my phone ring that all familiar sound, dududu

dududu dududu du. I expected it to be my good friend and colleague, Dr. Angela, calling to invite me to meet up for breakfast before I was to head out the following day. I answered to hear a familiar male voice. "Do you really want to meet for coffee?"

Hell yeah. "Umm, sure." I could feel my heart speeding up.

Tane asked, "Where do you want to meet?"

"How about the main coffee shop?"

"OK, see ya in ten."

Wow, he changed his mind. I jumped up and straightened myself out, my heart beating hard in my chest. OK, stop it, calm down. He'd probably show up for fifteen minutes, and we won't have anything to talk about and decide to leave.

I stepped outside and noticed it was drizzling. *Damn, he's probably not even going to show up.* As I approached the coffee shop, I observed it was closed. In the same instant, I looked up to see Tane walking up. I spoke first, "Hey, guess the place is closed. Now what?"

Tane's comeback, "How's the hotel? What floor are you on? I've never been over there before."

I said the only thing I could think of. "Do you want to see the place?" Whoa, where is this going?

Together we quietly sauntered through the guesthouse, not wanting to expose ourselves to any possible visitors. Stopping on the outside landing of the second floor, we took advantage of a minuscule overhang. Facing the countryside, we paused to chat. Standing higher than the concrete barrier T-wall, we freely viewed the barren landscape of the expansive oil field. In the distance, the streetlights dimly lit the new construction underway on the outer wall. The orange glow from the giant stacks burning afar interrupted the night sky.

The mizzling rain had become a steady shower. There was a chill in the wet November night. The slight awning barely protected us from the weather. I was still feeling anxious, my chest tight. My train of thought led me to wonder how this would conclude. Why had he agreed to come out? I was afraid he was going to query my intentions.

In previous encounters, Tane had been quieter than not. He was a man of few words. But tonight was different, and I was awestruck by how talkative he was and super thankful. I yearned to decode this mysterious man with the onyx eyes. We stood in the storm for a long time. He told me comical stories that had happened during his childhood. It was fun listening to him and the way he used his dry sense of humor. We talked about work and all the daily drama that happens on Rumaila, how the oil field was expanding and all the crazy things that had happened. It was interesting to hear something from the security side and what goes on, which almost everyone is unaware of.

Our chit-chat was going smoothly. I sensed there might be a bit of mutual fascination developing as the evening progressed. As the minutes passed, the night became colder. Standing with our backs pressed on the metal building, we gradually inched closer and closer to each other. Soon our arms were touching. Was it a collaborative effort, or was I blamable?

I was ecstatic our little rendezvous had panned out and hated for it to end. Tane started complaining about his soaking wet shoes and said it was time to get going. I turned, facing him, to bid farewell, and our eyes met. I couldn't control myself from gazing into those dark orbs. Trying to read what he might be thinking, at the same time, I was doing my best to coax them closer. Tane led off with, "Hey, have a great leave and be safe."

I responded, "OK, I will. Don't work too hard. Bye."

"Bye."

I ended with, "Thanks for coming out and getting your feet wet."

I returned downstairs to my comfortable, warm room and made my way into bed, turning on the TV. I needed to sleep as it would be a long journey home. A broad smile covered my face. I was overwhelmed with satisfaction. The evening played out better than I expected. My heart was overflowing. It was late, close to midnight, but my mind was racing with thoughts. I questioned myself as to why I liked this guy so much. Part of me knew the answer, and the other half would just have to wait.

Yes, he was handsome, witty, and a wisecracker. But he wasn't like any of the other men I've been attracted to. Hmm. This was not a good idea; being interested in someone at work can be dangerous. Besides, I was now living at RSB. How would it ever work? Dang, why did I wait until now! Why wasn't I more aggressive? I should have flirted sooner.

Lights out now. trying to sleep. My thoughts were soon interrupted. Beep, beep, beep, came the familiar sound alerting me that I had a new text message on my phone. "Hey, what are you doing?"

"Nothing! What are you doing?"

"Trying to get my feet warm, thanks to you for making me stand out in the rain all night."

"I didn't make you, and you wanted to. Remember?" Wow, fish on.

Tane flirted, "You should come over and watch TV with me."

I answered, "Why?"

"I don't know. I guess I enjoyed talking."

I so wanted to go but decided against it. It was late, cold, and rainy. Plus, I thought he was just teasing me. Besides, there was the fear of being seen wandering around in the middle of the night that could look suspicious. So our coltish messaging continued until it was nearly time for the sun to start her day.

Indiana Wants Me. Lord, I Can't Go Back There

The sun sees your body.
The moon sees your soul.

I remember well my November 2012 trip home. After being up all night messaging Tane, I was drained and animated by the thrill of the late-night correspondences. I wondered what I could expect on my next rotation back in Iraq. I slept very little during my flight west to my home country. Tired as I was, there was too much excitement within me to relax or sleep.

It lined up perfectly for me to fly into Chicago, pick up my son Brock from the Lake Station Military Academy, and head south to Indiana for Thanksgiving. It had been months since I had seen Brock as he was in the Navy's Pre-BUD/S training.

I landed at Chicago O'Hare International Airport and disembarked. I waited in line for nearly two hours to clear customs. I passed the time by conversing with those around me. Everyone was gleeful, openly sharing their holiday plans. It was the day before (America's) Thanksgiving holiday, also known as the busiest day to travel in the US. On average more than three million people take to the sky to visit family and friends for the four-day break.

I picked up the rental car and drove to Lake Station. Brock met me at the front gate of the naval base, where he greeted me with a tight hug and a big smile. "Hi Mom, how are you?" My heart was happy.

The five-hour drive to the family homestead gave us one-on-one time to catch up. We both had plenty of tales to share. Lake Station is located on the north side of Chicago, the third largest city in the US. I swear half of Chicago's 2.7 million people were on the road this particular day. Traffic was horrific and crawled as the sun set, and the temperature dropped. I was so glad I wasn't making the drive on my own. Jet lag was starting to set in. It was very much a cultural shock returning to America after spending time in the Iraqi desert, where I hadn't driven in a month.

I was eager to return to my parents' farm in northeast Indiana, where I had spent my childhood. Being raised as a farm kid taught me everything I needed to prevail. It didn't matter that I was a girl. I was expected to work hard, get my hands dirty, and respect family values. My rural experiences helped to develop common sense and self-pride. Growing produce, raising livestock, milking cows, changing the oil in the truck, and driving a tractor were only a few of the skills I acquired.

Thanksgiving was my dad's favorite holiday, and he loved having his family come together. To my father, not only was Thanksgiving a family celebration, but also a time to rejoice at the end of the harvest season. I treasured my father's gladness each November once the crops were successfully gleaned.

It was a memorable holiday with time spent with my relatives. Besides, my parents, two siblings, three of my four offspring, and nieces and nephews had gathered for the occasion. With such a large family and people spread out across the US, it was a special time and didn't happen very often.

I tried to visit Indiana as much as possible following my dad's cancer diagnosis a few years earlier. Family time with my precious kin was a treasured occasion. This Thanksgiving was no different. We enjoyed traditions, shared memories of times past, and created new ones.

My time in Indiana was short-lived, just four days and then it was time to head to Phoenix to catch up on life there. I always tried to work a few hospital shifts during leave. I liked keeping my foot in the door. Anything can happen when working as a contractor. Your job can vanish in two shakes of a lamb's tail. Plus, I also was concerned about keeping up my nursing skills, and this was a perfect way to do it.

While at home, I was overjoyed when Tane started emailing me. With his assistance, I set up a Skype account, allowing us to talk in real-time. His willingness to converse shocked me but also caused me to be aggravated at myself. Why didn't I make a move sooner?

It did not take long to see that this person was much different from other men I had encountered. Since he was not American, I enjoyed listening to his accent, and his word choices cracked me up. He wasn't afraid to say whatever crossed his mind. I'm pretty sure many Americans might find his sense of humor a bit offensive. I did not know how to take his silly racialism, mainly against myself as a white American. Soon I realized he was only playing with me to see if he could get me to react. It crossed my mind dozens of times that he might just be playing along. ROO can be a lonely place.

There was never a shortage of things to do in the great state of Arizona. I engaged my active spirit by running two races, the Runners Den half marathon and the Cave Creek Luminaria run, where I placed first in my age group. I hiked, biked, and spent time catching up with friends. In a flash, I was boarding a plane back to the Middle East.

Angie, Christopher, Jan, Dad and Mom in Indiana

Dad and Mom in the combine, harvesting corn

Mom at the family home in Indiana

Shelling corn on the farm

Me, Jan, Brock, Renaye, and Dad, target shooting.
Dad was always an excellent marksman

Yo Ho! Yo Ho! It's a Rotator's Life for Me

Go slowly, my lovely moon, go slowly.
~ Khaled Hosseini, The Kite Runner

Dozens of people have told me that I have the ideal job. Traveling to the other side of the globe, working for a month, then having a month off to do whatever I choose. Yes and no. This type of work is not for everyone. I must have been asked how I'd gotten this job a hundred times. Is your company hiring? Can you get me a job? No, but you can find your own. There are more out there.

There are plenty of benefits to this type of work. Every other month off, minus travel days, exceptional pay (including hazard pay), and having the ability to travel to fascinating places. But honestly, my favorite part was getting to meet and work with different people from around the world. On this contract, I worked with only a few Americans but several Europeans, Australians, Chinese, and a large number of Iraqis.

On the other hand, it was a long way from family and friends. You could not just decide you needed to get home for an ill family member or a death per se. On more than one occasion, my dad was hospitalized with complications related to his cancer, and I was 6,500 miles away. I often felt guilty and wondered if I was being selfish. My family wanted me to be happy, but I knew they wished I was closer to home. Weekly phone conversations were not the same as talking face-to-face.

While working in Iraq, I missed many special occasions and events—six or seven of Brock's military graduations, my grandson's first birthday, a nephew's wedding, and my favorite aunt's funeral.

The world on the outside goes on. You miss birthdays, weddings, births, and holidays. Christmas away from family just is not the same. While your family is together making new memories, you are in a far-off place feeling lonely.

This wasn't even the hard part. The hardest thing was when you returned to work; it was like closing the door behind you. You literally walked away from your life as you have always known it. You soon discover that your family and friends just keep on keeping on without you. Of course, you knew they wouldn't be sitting around waiting for you to return. But all of a sudden, you have missed six months. For half of a year, you have missed the happenings back home. No, I wasn't gone for six months, only a month at a time. I am trying to explain that what sounds like the ideal job has a dark side. One must fully understand this is what you have to be ready to leave behind. It truly is living two lives.

The folks at home cannot come close to perceiving what the opposite side of the world consists of. I'm sure most have drawn a picture in their head with the help of the media and tales from other influential sources. I discovered just how much media propaganda had swayed the thinking of civilians worldwide. Every time I returned home, I was asked if it was safe, was I afraid, did I have to cover my hair, etc. The answer was no.

I soon started to notice I was feeling culture shock every time I returned to planet America. I remembered thinking how green the grass was and how blue the sky was. After not driving a car for thirty days, being able to wear whatever you chose, going to a restaurant, having a beer, listening to music, petting your dog, or hugging your kids were simple pleasures. It was like the treadmill had been moving without you, and now you have to jump on and act like you were never away. It's not so easy. Your acquaintances talk about things you have no clue about. Often you feel out of touch and like an outsider. This can affect your psyche. As your best friend sits across the table from you, she hasn't an inkling. She can't come close to comprehending how lost you feel.

Then there's the jet lag. It was always harder to return to the US than going in the other direction. The first week back in the States is always messed up. Not much to do at 0200 when everyone else is sleeping. Then the unbearable ghost of absolute tiredness haunts you at 1600 in the afternoon, and keeping your eyes open is hopeless.

Hey, I have come to love this lifestyle of being a rotator. It works for me, until something or someone leads me to a better adventure! Yo ho! Yo ho! It's a rotator's life for me.

Banished to
Camp Isolation

Keep calm and look at the moon.

When I returned to work in mid-December of 2012, I was downhearted, for I could only spend a few hours at HQ. The time had come to be banished to my new accommodation at the supply base. As soon as I arrived at ROO, I headed straight to the clinic, where I received the usual warm welcome from the medical team. Everyone was eager to share a hug and ask the typical questions—how was your break, how are your kids, what did you do, etc. I was sure going to miss their smiling faces, even though I would only be twenty klicks (kilometers) away. Pretending to be blissful, I interacted with my colleagues, sharing the particulars of my time off.

I only had four hours to hang out on ROO before my transportation would be there to take me to the new quarters, my home for the next four weeks. Nicky, my reliever, would be brought to ROO HQ, and I would immediately move into the role of north medic.

During my brief visit, I had a chance to hear about all the latest news that had happened while I was away. ROO was a growing operation, and something exciting happened nearly every day. This project was massive, complicated, and full of challenges, including cultural issues, a harsh working environment, safety concerns, language barriers, knowledge deficits, logistical matters, untrusting players, and corrupted government agencies. The list went on and on.

I had been told that I would be able to come back to visit occasionally and get to spend a day or two at Rumaila's main camp. I said goodbye to my dear friends with a heavy heart. I knew that my chance of getting to visit would be extremely limited. The chance of seeing Tane could be nil, but I would not give up hope.

RSB was a new tiny camp developed as a facility for the construction engineers to live in while working on the new warehouse project. A new ginormous warehouse complex was being constructed near the RSB accommodation block. In addition, two supersized storage sheds were under construction. One was to be used as the pipe yard, and the second would house various other supplies used around the oil field.

RSB had the same portable-type modules for accommodations as the main camp. Although the rooms were small, they had everything you really needed. The units where the local nationals (LNs) were housed looked like all the other modules but had four people in a room and furnished two bunk beds.

My new camp was so confined that I literally felt as if I could stand in the center and touch the surrounding barrier with my arms stretched outward. It was as if the twelve-foot T-walls were squeezing inward on us.

Of the twenty-five of us living there, I was the only female, unlike at HQ. Besides the two Turkish construction managers, the security men, and the catering crew, there were several young Iraqi fellas, all of whom worked and lived at RSB.

The camp included a small dining facility with low-quality food options, including rice and chicken daily, unlike the main camp's lavish buffet dining. However, to my disappointment, our gym was a rusty old container trailer with second-hand equipment. The cramped recreation tin can was stuffy and hot as the air con struggled to cool the metal quarters.

The only good thing I could see about being here was that I did have a brand-new clinic supplied with all new equipment. But on the other hand, I was here as the only medical provider, meaning I would be on call every night. I would also be expected to respond to accidents on the north half of the oil field day and night. Supposedly, this was one of the reasons for sending me to RSB. Being told the clinic was my own to manage was a bribe—much the same as promising me visits to HQ. Lilith knew I was not happy about the move.

As time passed, I began to understand what Joc meant about Lilith. She became a pro at using her beguiling craft, easily putting a spell on many unsuspecting souls. She was super funny, a jokester. We guffawed uncontrollably at her choice of words and attempted pronunciations. But, sadly, another side was pitiless, sly, and manipulative—beautiful on the outside, dangerous within. Yet, in the beginning, all seemed well. Lilith spent a good bit of time hanging out in the clinic. We were her stepchildren, and she was there to keep us performing as she directed.

After shifting to RSB, I still traveled to Lion every day the way I always had. But now, the QRF had to leave ROO fifteen minutes earlier and come to Rumaila Supply Base to pick me up. At the end of our day, they would have to return me to my new location. RSB was situated four km off the main road. The road leading to the camp was a rough pothole-filled dirt road. The ambulance shook violently as we made our way to the main road. Everything in the back found its way to the floor. The vehicles kicked up so much dust you could not see ten feet in front of you. The security detail was not happy at all with this new procedure.

Honestly, this relocation scheme didn't make sense to anyone other than Lilith, who always got her way. Lilith decided that by putting the north ambulance medic at RSB at night, someone would be available during the evening to cover the camp and any emergencies. This wasn't reasonable. If there was an incident at night, the QRF still had to come from the main center and get me, which was a twenty-minute delay. But whatever Lilith wanted, she made it happen.

It was understandable why Lilith could so easily manipulate everyone, at least the men. As an attractive, petite, and charismatic gal, Lilith could easily charm anyone with her thick-tongued dialect, which we liked to taunt her about. We would have her say things and then crack up when she butchered the pronunciation. The f-word was absolutely her favorite word, interestingly enough. She loved to be the center of attention, and you could tell she was used to having it. Some of the guys saw through her controlling methods, but many got caught in her trap. She would bat her beautiful eyes and use her intelligence to dominate her way around the entire oil field. She stood out like a fly on a wedding cake. She, of course, had a perfect curvy body to keep the distraction going. It was hard not to notice the overly perfect silicone boobs. Her lips were hyperinflated with artificial material, and every time she returned from her leave, they seemed to have grown to the point it was the talk of the camp.

Lilith carried a large rusty knife that she used to stab people in the back. Eleven medical staff were hired and fired while I worked at ROO. These employees would be fired if she simply did not like how they talked or if she happened to get a wild hair. Wickedly, if she didn't care for you in some way or other . . . GONE. I saw people that only lasted one or two rotations, which was not long enough to give a person a fair chance. Not sure how I managed to last this long, but I tried my best to stay under the radar and not question her way. However, she put fear into every one of us, so to survive you needed to bow down.

0-Dark-Thirty

And if you're ever feeling lonely just look at the
moon, someone somewhere is looking at it too
                              ~ Night Vale

Tane's job was on the security side of things. The security guys worked a different schedule than the other expats. They worked eight weeks on and four weeks off. However, it wasn't uncommon for them to work longer than the scheduled eight weeks. I never thought this was healthy or safe. These people were responsible for our security; they worked much longer days than anyone else did. These men were ex-military and had experience living, working, and being on long, dangerous deployments. Still, I felt they were not given the respect they deserved. Many were married and had young families at home.

Tane had been on leave and returned a few days after I did. We started communicating via text message during the day and through Skype at night. We flirted back and forth and talked about the next time we would meet. Chatting with Tane helped to keep me from feeling so isolated.

Before long, Tane started asking when I would return to the main camp. "I wish I could, but not for a while." We were slowly building our friendship, only getting to know each other by telecommunications. I had no clue what this guy's honest thoughts were. This was a bit scary in many ways. Knowing what you can and cannot trust is hard without spending real time together.

However, we kept each other entertained.

"Babe, why didn't you pursue me when you were still living at HQ?"

My response, "I had no clue you would even be interested. Besides, I was scared and didn't know how to tell you I liked you."

Having a workplace fling could be a dangerous thing. Too-friendly relationships had gotten a few people on ROO sent packing, never to return. Knowing this, we would have had to be extremely cautious, as we were playing with fire. Also, because we used our company phones to message each other, we had to remember to erase the text before handing them off to our btb's.

An average day would start at 0-dark-thirty (0430) or earlier if I decided to go to the gym before work. Sometimes I'd go both before and after, as I was training for the upcoming Rome marathon in March. So each morning, I was expected to be ready with all my gear when the QRF arrived to pick me up.

Unfortunately, the canteen didn't open for breakfast until 0630, so I would pack my breakfast and lunch from the previous night's dinner and store it in the fridge in my room. It sucked on the days I forgot it on my way out the door. The food at RSB was terrible, plus we had the same-same, nearly every day. If you loved rice, then you were OK. But I got really tired of eating white rice after twenty-eight days.

The time we left varied daily depending on the QRF's daily assignment. The time could be anywhere from 0515 to 0615. Routinely, I would get a phone call from security the evening before informing me of the departure time. The QRF was directly responsible for the safety of the oil field. Although there were a few different private security companies around the oil field, the QRF team I was paired with was the lead team. Our team was first out and last in every day. I loved this part. It was fun to be involved in the drama. Plus if anything exciting was going on, I knew about it.

Early morning, the roads were quiet and empty. Most days, the sun would just be rising over the horizon. Generally, we drove north of the Lion up to the canal that bordered the edge of Rumaila. On other days we scouted around and went down dirt roads that made their way to various drill sites. I loved exploring Rumaila, except that it beat the hell out of the ambo due to its stiff suspension and the weight of the F350 Ford chassis. The QRF's Land Rover could cruise easily over the rough and bumpy terrain, but the ambo would have to putz along. The TLs were never happy to have to slow down and wait for us to catch up. I think this was why we didn't explore more often. However, depending on the team lead for the day, I sometimes convinced them to go for a drive.

We usually arrived at Lion around 0700 and stayed until late afternoon, 1700-1800. But, of course, times depended on how long the expats needed to be in the field. These guys and gals represented various departments within Rumaila's operation. All of the expats lived at HQ and had an office there. But many spent much of their time either at one of the degassing stations, drill sites, or visiting Lion to attend meetings.

During the time I was based at HQ, there were some occasions when we left camp at four a.m. This was due to the security level in our area being elevated. So going at this time of day meant I got up in the middle of the night.

The QRF would go out for an hour, do the sweep, then return to HQ. Because we got back before the DFAC opened at six a.m., we sat in our trucks and waited. After breakfast, we proceeded with our routine, heading back to Lion for the day. This made for a long day, especially if I had been on night call and had a callout. Sometimes I got no sleep.

Infrequently we were summoned to an emergency during the night. I only remember it happening twice while working on the oil field. One of these times, we went to a drill site managed by Shell Oil. The camp's medic, not a Frontier employee, had fallen off the step to the camp's clinic and broken his leg. Poor guy, how embarrassing. He had to be taken to the hospital at ROO to receive treatment and be medevaced. It's not good when you're the only medic and get evacuated.

There were two identical armored ambulances, 1aa and 2aa. If one needed repair, there was a backup, and also, if I was in the north during the day and there happened to be an emergency in the south, another Frontier employee could respond using the second ambulance.

It seemed one or the other ambulance was always in the garage, pronounced *garriage* if you're from the UK. Half the time, the air con wouldn't work, or there was an ongoing carburetor issue. The extreme heat and blowing sand took a toll on vehicles in this part of the world.

Another enthralling job I occasionally did was escorting ill expats to the airport when they needed to be medevaced. The security escort would be identical—two security vehicles as our protection. We would deliver the patient to the airport in the armored ambulance. Then, I would rendezvous with a medical flight team at Basra's airport and hand over the patient to them. These patients would be flown to either Dubai or Istanbul to receive medical care that we couldn't provide.

Atrocious black smoke from the ground flares

Camels are a common site on Rumaila

DFAC at RSB

Flare stacks silhouetting the sunrise

I Choose the Moon

The moon is a friend for the lonesome to talk to.
~ Carl Sandburg

I wish I could say that I had learned to be content in my new location. Nevertheless, that was not the case. The only good thing was I didn't have to be on night call for the largely populated main camp. Yes, I was the only medical provider in the camp, but with the few residents, I was never called out during the night to treat any patients, unlike when I lived at HQ, where I had to be on call three nights a week, and sometimes you would be called out twice in the same evening.

I started to feel extremely isolated at RSB. Unlike HQ, there was no socialization, no real friends. I would go to the gym every evening to avoid my estranged situation. It took several weeks to get a satellite installed, so there was no TV.

Eventually, I got approval to run in the field where the new warehouse was being constructed. T-walls secured the vast lot, and two Iraqi guards were staged along the perimeter. It was a perfect track, and one loop equaled three km. After work, if we got back before dark, I would go there to run.

This helped lessen my sense of confinement. Being outside the wall felt awesome. But it wasn't long before management at ROO found out and stopped our running. They thought we would hurt ourselves because some of the ground was being dug up. So I was forced to go back inside and run on the treadmill.

The gym was set up in a metal shipping container. It contained two stationary bikes, a treadmill, an elliptical machine, various weights, and workout benches. The equipment was old and worn but, for the most part, worked. However, the place was small, and I preferred to be alone, which rarely happened.

The gym was a popular place, visited by the expat security guys along with a handful of young Iraqis. These young males smelled of body odor and uncleanliness, but even more annoying was that they seemed infatuated with me. They stared while I tried to focus on my workout. I felt uncomfortable knowing I was the only female living in the same complex with these young horny dudes.

Each evening upon returning to camp, the Iraqi lads would be sitting in their boxers on the steps of their CHU (Containerized Housing Unit). It was baffling that Iraqi women weren't supposed to show any skin, and then these guys were close to naked. Some of the locals did seem shy, but others weren't at all. I read that Arab men often viewed contemporary Western women as being highly sexual. Western women were thought to be promiscuous and easy. The uneducated youth's eyes and actions said it all. I was sure they were intrigued by my gym wear, short running shorts and a short-sleeved t-shirt.

When my dear friend and colleague, Dr. Angela, was in country, I would talk to her a few nights a week. I felt I had to be cautious and not say too much about how uncomfortable I felt at RSB. Lilith didn't need much of a reason to send me home on a one-way ticket. She seemed to be keeping a scorecard of the numbers she had unemployed, as they were adding up. I did my best to try and be content. I still enjoyed my job, or at least while away from RSB. Communicating with Tane helped but was also a large part of my unhappiness. I was sad that I could not see him and started stressing that I would not get any chances either. I unknowingly was developing limerence for this man. The more we talked, the more he charmed and amused me, and the more interesting he became.

I lay in bed at night, thinking of ways I could go back to HQ for a visit without creating waves. But I needed to be patient. I had only just returned, and it was way too soon to ask for a visit.

Looking back, I envision how bleak my soul perceived the situation. My spirit felt I had been shunned and relocated to a godforsaken abode. It was a weird feeling to have no control over my circumstances. My hands were tied.

This was my first foreign contract and my first experience with social isolation to this depth. I was struggling to find my peace. I desperately needed to find an antidote.

I envisioned my situation by drawing a metaphor. Think of HQ as the mothership, a sizable, beautiful vessel able to ride the waves with little difficulty. And it featured many pleasant amenities and freedoms. The crew can enjoy fine dining, modern recreational facilities, and access to socialization. Now think of the small remote camp of RSB as a small yellow raft, getting pitched around in a stormy sea surrounded by scary sharks looking to feed. How long would it be before I got saved? This was the point where I needed a superhero to rescue me. I gazed upward and spied one—the moon!

Honestly, I had always been influenced by the moon for as long as I can remember. A selenophile, I am—having a fondness for the moon. For this reason, I have chosen the moon to be my comrade.

I Wish Me a
Merry Christmas

The moon made me do it.

2 5.12.12 Even though it was Christmas Day, we still had to work. Nevertheless, there was a cheerfulness in the air. Being in a Muslim country, Christmas is not highly recognized. The expats at ROO HQ had planned a huge holiday celebration. But, of course, I wouldn't be able to participate now that I lived elsewhere. I tried not to dwell on the fact too much, but it was hard not to. Besides knowing my family was home enjoying their holiday, I knew they would be missing me and I them.

Dr. Adel was the Iraqi physician working with me at Lion on this particular Christmas Day. He had purchased some goodies and sweets for me and the other guys working. Dr. Adel was such a kind, big-hearted person. It made me sad to think that the Western world had been brainwashed by our media into believing Iraqis and Middle Easterners were dangerous and not to be trusted.

I had grown very fond of Iraqi culture and its people. Yep, there were many dangerous, hateful, and mean people over there. This was not restricted to just one place in the world though; they are everywhere on the planet. However, I found the Iraqis to be some of the kindest, most caring humans I have ever known.

It was a weird day, as it was pouring down rain like I'd never seen in this country before. It had started raining early in the morning and was not letting up. We were like a bunch of kids when it snowed. Lion was very quiet like it was on the weekends. There were no office workers around, just Dr. Adel, Mark (my driver), the QRF team, and me.

Rain is the miracle in the desert, as I always said when I witnessed it raining back home in Phoenix. I think about this special Christmas Day frequently. When I replay the twenty-fifth of December 2012 over in my heart, I smile and envision the day's events. It remains one of my all-time favorite memories.

I sat in my office at Lion, watching the beautiful, precious rain from the window. Mark and I discussed our Christmas traditions, and Dr. Adel listened and asked questions. Mark, being from Scotland, and I, an American, were comparing and contrasting the ways we held our Christmas holiday.

Mark and Chase, the TL, would at least be treated to HQ's extraordinary feast when they return to camp. Dr. Adel worked a twenty-four-hour shift and would be stuck at Lion alone all night. As for myself, I would be back at RSB, where no special celebration was planned. There was no reason I should not have been allowed to go to HQ for at least Christmas dinner. However, Lilith said no, which made me feel like an unwanted black sheep and not valued as much as the other medical staff. I didn't need any more reasons to feel woeful. Such is life.

Tane had been texting me all morning. "Merry Christmas."

"Thanks, you too."

"How's the weather?"

"Pouring down here."

"Same here."

We messaged back and forth throughout the day. "Are you going to the Christmas party tonight?" I questioned.

"Naa, I don't like crowds. What are they having at RSB?"

"Leftovers, I think. No turkey for us, just cold rice as always."

It was early afternoon, and the rain had only slightly eased up. However, the excitement in the air was about to get even better. Mark said, "I'm starting to think the dirt road into RSB is going to flood, and you'll have to walk," addressing me. "The ambo will probably get stuck." Wow, could we be so lucky as to have the road washout? I jumped up and went into the room next door to where Chase was sitting.

Before I could even say it, Chase remarked, "The road to RSB will probably be washed out by now."

I replied, "That's what Mark and I think too."

My mind was racing, and my heart was exploding with excitement. Could this really happen? I might have to go to the main camp for the night. Chase asked me to call RSB security and ask them about the weather and road conditions. I finally was able to contact Clarkson, the on-duty security manager. He informed me that it had been raining heavily all day and that the dirt road was in rough shape. I also asked what he thought if I could not get back to camp for the night. He said he didn't see a problem with it, but it should be officially cleared by ROO security. I then contacted Vic, the Ops lead in the clinic, updating him on the situation. I told him I would let him know the final decision. He said he would wait to hear from me but planned to get me a room in the high-rise.

Chase voiced, "Ok, I'm going to call ROO security to let them know the road conditions and see if you can just stay at HQ tonight. Bet you're disappointed, huh?" Security thought it was a good idea, and I got the thumbs-up. After doing the happy dance, I updated everyone on what had been decided. I called Dr. Angela, who was excited that I was coming back for the Christmas party. This was one time Lilith couldn't have her way.

In all of my adult life, this was undoubtedly one of the most "over the moon" times I can remember. I did not tell Tane what was happening until we pulled into the gate. Then, texting him, "Guess where I'm at?"

"Where?"

"HQ!"

"REALLY?"

"Yep, the road to RSB is flooded, sad huh?"

"COOL— Where will you be staying?"

"In the high-rise, as far as I know."

I walked into the clinic. Everyone was excited that I was back for the evening, especially Angela. Rushing over, she gave me a hug and a big smile. Secretly she understood my delight. "It's terrific that you can have Christmas dinner with us." Angela reported she had asked Lilith again yesterday and was told no. "I think they should have allowed you to come anyhow."

A few minutes later, Lilith walked in to see me standing there. I could tell she didn't share the same joy. She had been overruled. She wasn't asked for approval this time. Mother Nature had chosen to be on my side!

Vic handed me a key to my room, lucky # 5, the same room I was assigned in November before going on leave. I smartly always kept a change of clothes and a toothbrush in the ambulance. At least I had clean duds for the night. I cleaned up before dinner, then updated Tane on where I was staying. No one knew about us, and it would stay that way. Even my best friend Angela had no clue. First, I knew she probably wouldn't have approved as this was forbidden in our work environment, or at least if you get caught. But, being the adventure-seeker I am, I loved the challenge. As long as we did not spend much time being seen together, I knew no one would even be suspicious. Cool right? Besides, I was no longer around enough to create suspicion.

Tane messaged me, "Do you want to see me?"

"Of course."

"OK, let me know when you get back to your room after dinner."

I questioned Tane, "When are you going to dinner?"

He replied, "I don't know, later."

I was so nervous and distracted and was sure Ang (short for Angela) would wonder what was wrong. Angela and I walked to the DFAC together. It was amazing. They had gone all out. The large hall was decked out in white and purple lights and gold tinsel. The tables were beautifully trimmed, and the lights were turned low to set the festive mood. Candles lit the tables. I had never seen such a spread of food, lamb, turkey, roast beef, everything you could think of, and more. There was even an ice sculpture. Wow, and to think I was not even supposed to be here.

I wanted to cry when I saw the decorated room and the fantastic food—how cruel to leave me out. Knowing I wasn't invited and that it was only by chance made me feel I was being punished and cheated.

I was happy Angela was there to share the celebration with. The room was crowded with people. Where did they all come from? In attendance were several Iraqi oil ministry people and other government representatives. I kept trying to scan the room, waiting for Tane to show up, but he never did, or I didn't see him anyway. I felt guilty because all I could focus on was getting out of there and getting to see my secret friend. I could not even really enjoy the feast of outstanding cuisine. I tried to relax and appreciate the company of my ROO friends I had missed since moving.

Finally, I wiggled away from Angela and the crowded scene after bidding a Merry Christmas and a good night to those sitting next to me. Part of me wished to stay longer and suck up every last drop of gala and companionship I could draw upon. How would this phenomenal day close? I was out the door to find the answer.

The butterflies in my stomach carried me to Room #5. I was keen on the rooms in the high-rise. They were new, quiet, and comfortable, but best of all the building was tucked away from the main complex. I'm not sure where the term high-rise started, but the oil field was full of unexplained names for things, i.e., Lion.

"Hey, I'm back in my room. What's the plan?"

Tane's response came a few minutes later. "How was dinner?"

"Great! How was yours?"

"I ate at the Iraq café."

"Why?"

"I don't like crowds. Can I come to see you later?"

"Yes."

"Are there many people staying over there?"

"No."

"I don't get off work until 10 p.m. I will let you know when I'm on my way."

Shoot, it was only 8:40 p.m. I should have stayed with Angela for another hour, but how was I to know?

I started thinking that this might not be a good idea to let Tane come to my room. What happens if someone does see him? Maybe we should meet somewhere else, but there was nowhere else. We had spent more than six weeks waiting to see each other, and who knows when or if another chance would come.

Ten p.m. came and went. *Crap, is he coming or not? Maybe he changed his mind, fell asleep, or had a security issue.* Finally, at 10:30 p.m., the familiar tone announced the incoming message. Tane teasingly asked, "You still want to see me?"

"Yesss."

"I just finished. I'll get a shower and be on my way." At 10:45, the message arrived. "On my way."

I watched out my window and saw a figure approaching in the shadows of the light. Then I could hear the front entrance door squeak open. I felt lightheaded and short of breath as I waited for the soft tap on my door. I was excited, like a teenager sneaking out after curfew.

I had no expectations for the evening other than getting to see each other again face-to-face. In a teasing gesture, I slowly cracked the door. Tane pushed the door open and rushed in, closing it quietly behind him. "I worried someone might see me."

Tane turned toward me with his big guilty grin, which reminded me of a kid who just got away with something and was proud of it. Without a word, he stepped toward me, encircled me with his arms, and drew me into his warm hug. He held me there for a few seconds and then pushed me a step back, leaned toward my face, and in a quick motion, kissed me on my cheek. He stood back and gazed around the room as if he needed to inspect every corner. "I have never been in here before," Tane exclaimed. "The first I was ever over here was when you tricked me into coming out in the rain."

I already started dreading him leaving in the first few minutes he was there. I wanted our time to go slowly and last but knew it would end way too soon. I was already trying to plan how I could see him again, and he had only been here eight minutes.

"Hi, how are you?" he said, as if he just walked in and the last two minutes never happened.

"Good, how are you?"

"Tired. You are making me stay up past my bedtime."

"I'm not making you. You wanted to, remember?"

Tane was on fire duty that night and reminded me he could be summoned anytime. I crossed my fingers that he wouldn't have to race away. He had his radio just in case.

We spent the next short few hours sitting on the bed side by side laughing and joking around. Tane told me stories about his childhood. Some were funny and some were sad. As he talked, I painted a scene in my mind and used the details he spoke of along with those I had researched about his native home. Tane was from a place near the bottom of our planet, a beautiful mountainous environment surrounded by the gift of an endless blue ocean.

As we talked, Tane sat holding my hand. I still could not believe this was not just something I dreamed up. It seemed everything I fantasized about in

my mind was coming to life. Obviously, some magical fairy dust was sprin-
kled on me before I arose from my sleep today. If I could think about it, I could
bring it to be. Or maybe there was a Santa, and I had been a very good girl.

"Hey, babe." (Tane always called me this.) Here it comes. "I have to go."

"No, you can stay."

"I wish, but I can't. I have to make rounds before 0200."

"OK."

Tane moved off the bed and started to gather his belongings. I stood up,
feeling lonely even before he walked out the door. I put my arms around him
to give him a big hug and told him thanks for stopping by. I looked into his
deep dark eyes and kissed him. His reply, "Anytime. Have fun at RSB's gaol."

OK, I'll try."

One last kiss. "Merry Christmas."

I softly responded, "Merry Christmas, baby." The door closed. He was
gone, and so was my fairy dust.

The next evening, I hoped the road to RSB would still be impassable, but
no such luck. It was in terrible shape, and we came close to being stuck. There
were enormous mud puddles with two feet of standing water. Mark looked
at me to affirm my wide eyes and grinning expression as his foot stepped
down on the gas. The awkward heavy ambo slipped and slid like a scene
from a cartoon. The muddy brown water sprayed with immense force from
the wheel wells, making it impossible to see out the windshield. Mark and I
laughed hysterically at the top of our lungs.

Ali, Noor, and Nael

If you are to love, love like the moon
loves. It doesn't steal the night—it only
unveils the beauty of the darkness.
~ Jasleen Kalra

One of the long-term goals of the SOC and BP was that someday SOC would have the resources to take over the management of the Rumaila field. At least, this was what had been conveyed to us employees. This was a mind-blowing concept and seemed a far from reachable goal. No one believed that BP would ever consider leaving the fifth largest oil field on the globe, leaving all the profit of the black gold to Iraq. Especially since they had both hands in the pot—they held the reins on this project. Would Jack the Ripper ever turn himself in?

Every department was to develop schemes to deliver this challenge to Rumaila and her native people. In addition, BP's Health and Safety team came up with some ideas of their own. These projects focused on improving the well-being of the oil field and the LN's lifestyle.

The medical team and clinic fell in direct line under the HS management, and we were a huge piece of the puzzle. Our team was the worker bees who were to do the task that queenie asked.

One of the principal projects was to hire and train local nationals to be ambulance drivers. This was twofold. First, three Iraqi men were hired to drive the armored ambo, replacing my Western expat drivers. The other half of this project included hiring and training another fifteen Iraqis to staff the newly purchased soft-skinned ambulances. The latter group's role was to be drivers and primary first responders. The idea was that the soft-skinned drivers would learn basic medical care and stage at all the different degassing and pumping stations on the ROO. Each site would then have twenty-four-hour medical coverage for the Iraqi employees working at these sites. Nine soft-skin (non-armored) ambulances had been purchased for this reason. Expats would not be allowed to travel or be cared for by Iraqi first-aiders as their skills would not be up to the standards of Western care. In essence, the Iraqis would care for their own.

My drivers were referred to as the north ambulance drivers. They worked a six-day-on, twelve-days-off schedule, rotating through all three men and then starting all over. They, too, would live at RSB during their scheduled time on. We could then park the armored ambulance at RSB, which was a huge convenience. The QRF would no longer have to wait for me to load my gear prior to heading up the road.

Each evening after I returned to camp, my crash bag, drug bag, and heart monitor needed to be stored securely in the clinic, and the drugs locked in the safe, firstly, to keep anyone from possibly borrowing the gear, and secondly, to hold the expensive equipment in the air-conditioned clinic. We did this practice no matter what camp we were staying at. At Lion, the ambulance was left running to keep things cool, or the gear was taken inside. The drugs were always kept in my possession when not safely locked up.

Shortly after 2013 arrived, so did Ali, Noor, and Nael. I desired to keep a positive attitude, but my wounds from my recent torture still wept with pus. Of course, I'm referring to being sent to resettle. I knew that the replacement of Mark and Mick was not a crafted personal stab, but it did not matter; it still sucked.

The three new drivers deserved a chance. I needed to try and put my emotions aside and open my mind to the changes I had no say in.

Noor and Nael were single, in their early twenties, and enrolled at the University of Basrah. Noor was studying computer science, and Nael wanted to be an engineer. Both of these young men displayed positive attitudes and were very thankful to have been offered a job on the oil field. In addition, they each proved to be easygoing and friendly and showed me respect.

Ali, at thirty-two, was married and a father of two young children. He was definitely in a different place in his life than the two younger guys. The stress of his family responsibilities was a regular topic of conversation.

The driver program unfolded ten days before I was to go out on leave. I was the one to help start the process of turning these men into competent employees in their new roles. It wasn't that they didn't know how to drive; they did. They had already been through driver's training with Roger, ROO's professional driving instructor. During their training, they were instructed to drive the monster-sized ambo around. Being behind the wheel of a large armor-plated truck is not the same as driving a car around the streets of Basra.

Noor and Nael at first lacked competent driving skills to handle the cumbersome ambulance. Smooth operators, they were not. During the first few weeks, I had knotted shoulder and neck muscles, tense from the drive to and from Lion each day. However, with time they both developed their skills.

Ali was a very skilled driver, and later I found out he had previously been employed with ROO's security team. He was familiar with the ways of Rumaila and had himself been victimized by someone within his department and fired. He told me that he had been falsely accused of something. We both suffered feelings of being belittled. He also was walking on eggshells.

A few times, he and I butted heads. I was considered his boss, and he was to follow my directions. He saw things his way and had difficulty listening and trusting that I knew what I was talking about. I don't think he appreciated having a woman direct him around. This was not the norm in this part of the world. Management got involved, and we finally worked things out with some adjustments. I liked him and did not want him to be fired again. He swallowed his pride, and I succeeded in the power struggle that was at hand.

Once the Iraqi drivers were in place, our routine also changed. The ambo now stayed with us at RSB. Our goal was to be packed up and waiting outside the security gate before the QRF arrived. The new procedure shortened the QRF's trip by at least ten minutes, since now they didn't have to wait for the ambulance to arrive. When they turned off the main road, they radioed me the signal to start heading in their direction.

Refueling after we relocated to RSB hindered our normal daily flow. There was no fuel at RSB, so every other day on our way home we would have to take the ambo down to ROO HQ and refuel. Occasionally I got to pop into the hospital to pick up something and say a quick hello. Otherwise, the QRF was anxious to escort me back to Camp Isolation as swiftly as possible (like a horse to the barn).

By February 2013, our fueling procedure had changed. We started getting fuel at a pump station in North Rumaila. The fuel station was located on the edge of a small village close to Lion. This was not a public station, and I rarely saw anyone else fuel there. It was a fenced area. Occasionally, the gate was closed when we arrived for our routine refueling. It was ridiculous, since we arrived at virtually the same time every other day, just like Groundhog Day. Pull up, no one around, honk the horn, wait, honk the horn, wait, five minutes later, the attendant slowly walks out of the shack from the far side of the lot, rubbing the sleep from his eyes. The QRF got so frustrated having to wait.

If Ali was driving, he would get out and converse with the attendant while we were fueling. One of the rules was that the driver was never to get out of the truck, and the doors were to remain locked at all times, a safety thing. BP didn't want the medics to be kidnapped.

One of the fuel attendants creeped me out. He would start fueling, then come over to my side of the truck or stand where he could see me and just flippin' stare at me. I never thought of getting out and always ensured my door was locked. I realized I may have been the only white woman he had ever seen. Here I was, a white Western female uncovered, not wearing traditional clothing.

A couple of the other attendants would try to get me to roll down my window and talk to them. Most of the time, the vent window was cracked, and sometimes I would lower my window just enough. After that, I realized I had to be cautious, but I was almost as curious as they were. They always wanted to know where you are from, the most frequently asked question while I worked there. I think that was the only English they possibly knew—where you from?

A few weeks after we started getting fuel at this pump station, Ali began looking closer at the fuel receipts. The receipts didn't match the liter amount indicated on the meter of the actual pump. The driver was responsible for keeping a log of the miles and liters. We guessed the pump attendants were selling or taking home a bit of extra fuel. We handed this information over to management to deal with.

One fuel guy in particular always had a lit cigarette between his pursed lips as he stood inhaling smoke and diesel fumes, and his asinine logic was amusing. Common sense had undoubtedly been robbed from a few of these simple-minded people. We tried to explain that smoking while fuel was leaking onto the ground wasn't an acceptable practice. It would take someone with more influence than us to get them to understand this.

After fueling up the ambo, we headed to Lion to settle in for the day. Traveling the short distance from the fuel stop to Lion's car park was a stressful task. Although the drive was only 1.5 kilometers on the main east /west road to reach the Lion turnoff, traffic on this road was out of control. A zillion laborers were traveling to their jobs. Scores of commoners rode on motorcycles; there were always at least two and sometimes three on one cycle. Many others were walking or on bicycles. Add this to the endless bumper-to-bumper cars, buses, and trucks. Iraqi drivers inarguably never had acquired a knowledge of road etiquette. Having no concept of safety, fear of being injured, or dying in a road accident seemed to be an inevitable thought.

Merging onto the road as a three-vehicle caravan was virtually impossible. One of the security rulings was that the QRF was not to let any vehicles get between the ambulance and its protective trucks. The lead truck would pull out and then pull off to the side until we could merge onto the road. My driver would maneuver in behind the lead truck and wait for the sweep QRF vehicle to fall in line. At this point, the drivers had to become aggressive and force their way back onto the busy road. The truck behind the ambulance would pull out first, blocking traffic and allowing the lead vehicle to pull out with us riding their bumper. The local drivers would honk, yell, and shake their fists at us. Our trucks were bigger, heavier, and armored. We were never rammed, but there were many times when I closed my eyes and readied myself for impact.

I have always wondered what the road crash statistics are for this country. When I researched the topic, I discovered that over three years, 2010-2013, more than 7,900 Iraqis died in road traffic accidents. A large majority (78.2 %) of the fatalities were male, and 2,272 (28.5 %) were children under eighteen years of age. Forty-nine percent of these fatalities involved pedestrians. Iraq was reported to have the second-highest road crash fatality rate within the Eastern Mediterranean Region. In 2014, WHO reported Iraq as the second leading country in the world for traffic deaths—interesting, huh?

Reckless and aggressive driving is the norm, traffic signs are nonexistent as far as I can tell, and the ROO's speed limits were routinely ignored. It was a common tendency to beat the traffic by driving up the wrong side of the road. The government did little to enforce traffic laws. I had been informed there were no age limits, no required driving education, and locals probably didn't even need a license. No highway patrol officers would stop you unless you're an expat and you hit and kill a local. Somehow, we always managed to arrive in one piece.

Ali, Nael and Dr. Adel

Ali, soft-skinned ambulance on the left, armored ambulance on the right

Noor and I

Business Class,
I Don't Need
a Paycheck

*I like to think the moon is there
even if I am not looking at it.*
                    ~ Albert Einstein

My twenty-eight days in the country slid to an end. Having had its emotional dark side since being exported to Camp Iso (isolation), as I referred to it, I was glad that this had been a busy and challenging few weeks setting up the RSB clinic, getting everyone adjusted to the new routine, and adapting to my new colleagues. The biggest reward of all, the Christmas Day miracle, somehow, I believe my heart willed it into happening, *inshallah*.

Maybe you're asking why I didn't quit and return home to the safety and comforts of my native land. Why would I, instead, choose to endure the emotional hardship of RSB? First, I'm not a quitter, plus I expected I'd eventually find peace in my new habitat. Besides the constant changes that were always happening, I could always end up being moved back to ROO's main camp. Knowing that I had been promised to have visits to HQ kept me optimistic. I did love my job, just not my current living situation. I was cognizant that most of my mood had to do with being separated from my newest fascination.

Vacation time always flew by; twenty-three days was a short time to adjust to the time zone and re-orient to the homeland. Fortunately, BP paid their contractors' full wages for our travel days. We were flown business class, and when we ended up overnighting while traveling a five-star hotel room was provided, along with compensating any travel expenses we incurred.

While back in Phoenix, as I mentioned previously, I worked a few hospital shifts for Abrazo Healthcare. Not for the money but because I didn't want to lose my status as a casual nurse. I knew it was a bright idea to keep a foot in the door. I never really knew when my Iraqi job might end unexpectedly. My expat job could vanish without warning, as it had for many of my coworkers. Lilith had a pointed dagger and was an expert at cutting jugulars and letting her victims fall to the ground. Most of them were attacked on a moonless night, unaware of their fate.

I aspired to make the most of my time off. During this particular holiday, I drove to beautiful San Diego, where I attended my son Brock's naval award ceremony at the Coronado Naval Base.

There are always many fun things to do in San Diego, such as walking on the beach, hiking, enjoying some great food, sailing, or touring one of the many other local attractions. Along with hanging out with Brock, I also loved spending time with my adventurous girlfriends who resided in Southern California.

Another favorite activity while roving around the Golden State was to visit Temecula and do some wine tasting. I held a membership to two vine-yards, which allowed me to take a group of six people along to enjoy sampling various locally produced wines. The membership also gave me a nice discount on bottles of my favorite vino. Wine tasting is an excellent way to spend a sunny afternoon while experiencing a few different wineries.

Tane remained in the picture. Occasionally we found a mutual time to chat, but our conversations mostly turned to texting. Meanwhile, he was still in Iraq, working long hours. The time difference was ten hours, which did not make communicating so easy. Still, I found myself adjusting my schedule in hopes of getting a few minutes to chat. With every online visit, I found myself becoming more allured and rapt. Nevertheless, my intellect was trying to impede my enthusiasm. It was too soon and too unknown to be this jovial.

My time stateside vanished, and I was once again sitting in my lavish business class seat aboard a Boeing 777 heading east. Each time I flew in these quality seats, I started to wish my fifteen-and-a-half-hour flight would be even longer, depending on which airline. Some were more extravagant than others with Emirates being on top. They were amazingly posh and always had an outstanding crew.

Business class is distinguished from economy class by the quality of food, drinks, seats, service, and amenities. I clearly remember the first time I flew in business class. I did not want to look out of place or as if I did not belong among the elite travelers. Once my carry-on was stored, I parked myself in the oversized seat assigned to me. I poked around, orienting myself to the luxurious space I had been provided. There were drawers and cubbies to conceal personal items. Each seat had its own T.V. screen with a controller to choose from a trillion movies, shows, or music titles to keep you from caring that you had fifteen-plus hours until the next touchdown. The confusing part was the seat control with its umpteen buttons.

After takeoff, you can adjust your seat to flat or nearly flat, depending on the airline you're flying with. Some seats even had massagers built into them. In addition, each chair is designed to provide passengers with privacy from their neighbors, which is great when you sleep with your mouth open or the guy beside you snores. The cherry on top of this, you get to accumulate thousands of frequent flyer miles with each trip.

Once inside the cabin, a beautiful flight attendant appears and offers you a refreshing glass of orange juice, water, or bubbling champagne. "Ms. Mousay, would you care for something?" Impressive. The flight attendants were required to learn their customers' names. Occasionally, I was tempted to shout, "Can't you wait until I put my crap away?" but instead I smiled and reached for the bubbling alcohol, then stored my gear.

A hot lemon-scented towel is given out to freshen up with after you're seated. Shortly after getting airborne, meal service menus were passed out. For each meal, you had a variety of food and drink choices to pick from, including an extensive bar list. Next, a small cup of warm succulent nuts was provided, followed by the beverage trolley. "I'd like a glass of the shiraz, please." There were always two to three red and white wines to choose from. Not the typical house wine economy class was being served.

Another furnished amenity was a clever travel kit. Inside, you would have a toothbrush, toothpaste, socks, comb, and a sleep mask to cover your eyes. Emirates had the best packs, which were the size of a small clutch purse, pearl white for women and satin brown for men. Heck, if they only had a gym, I could nearly live here.

In business class, you had your meal in front of you within forty minutes of the seatbelt sign being turned off. The ladies and gentlemen attending to this privileged class of passengers busted their butts to gracefully and swiftly get their customers ready to stretch out and relax, be it to sleep, enjoy a movie, or do some additional work on their laptops. The Emirates crew even placed a quilted seat cover on your seat for extra comfort before you closed your eyes.

When you fly business or first class (even a higher rank), you can use the airport lounges. Lounges are like an oasis where qualified passengers can go for peace and quiet while sitting in comfortable chairs and enjoying the complimentary amenities, including premium food and alcoholic drinks. It's a perfect location for business people to open their computers and get some work done before continuing the next leg of their trip. Complimentary high-speed Wi-Fi is always available. Many quality lounges even have showers, and some have sleep rooms or chairs where you can stretch out and get a nap. The restroom is well taken care of, and you won't find any pee on the seats here. Flight monitors are conveniently located, so you can avoid getting too comfortable or drunk and miss your flight.

One of the lounges I had the pleasure to use was in Frankfurt, Germany. Smartly planned, the business class hall had direct access to the airplane from the lounge. The hostess would announce the flight was boarding, and you were able to simply step over to a check-in counter, have your ticket scanned, and walk onto the jet bridge to the business/first-class cabin—sweet.

I have experienced some marvelous airport lounges: Kuwait, Houston, Dallas, Frankfurt, London, Dubai, Hong Kong, and more. My favorite lounge is the Star Alliance lounge in Istanbul, Turkey. It's almost indescribable. First, it's enormous. It has a movie theater, a library, a pool table, sleeping rooms, and a large self-serve bar serving made-to-order food with a chef preparing it. There's a room with a baby grand piano, sometimes with a human playing it, and other times it plays by itself. You can always find a quiet corner to sit and relax in. It's a place you could forget your onward flight and not even care.

It was definitely a privilege to receive the benefits of first-rate travel. First, BP made all their employees and contractors fly business to prevent deep vein thrombosis (DVT), a dangerous blood clot. Secondly, they wanted everyone refreshed and ready to go to work when they hit the ground at ROO. Finally, traveling for multiple hours, including layovers, is very wearing. Thus, having workers to fly in comfort left little excuse for being tired on arrival (minus the jetlag).

I always said I didn't need a paycheck. I'll just work for free if I can fly business. So this was totally a sweet deal. However, boy, were these tickets pricey. The dollar amount was always visible at the bottom of the flight itinerary. The cheapest flight I remember was $6700 and ran upward to $13,000. That was just for little ole me, one person.

It seemed that some of my fellow premium class (male) travelers did not feel I looked the part of a business professional. While traveling, I dressed casually and not in business wear. Often, I wore jeans or yoga pants and my gym shoes. More times than I would like to report, I was treated rudely by men while trying to board as a business class passenger. I would be standing in line trying to work my way to the jet bridge, and some dickhead would try to get in front of me, either saying in an arrogant tone, "This is business class only," or asking, "Are you flying business class?"

"Yes, I am." It's interesting how judgmental the world is. I found this so offensive. You can't gauge an individual by their outward appearance. If you do, be prepared to get shamed.

This was one of the most interesting things I ever saw while journeying home. I had just boarded the plane and was getting my carry-on stowed. I was on an Emirates flight heading to the United States. I noticed this round Middle Eastern man take a short stack of clothing and disappear into the toilet. I didn't really think too much of it until I saw him again. He was now dressed in a pair of red silk pajamas with an Emirates logo. He handed the flight attendant his business suit to be hung in the closet with other travelers' suit jackets. This guy was serious about getting into some comfortable clothes. When we neared our destination, he reversed the process and returned to wearing his handsome tailored suit.

Emirates was and still is the best-quality airline I've flown with. Of course, there are many good airlines out there, but if you travel outside the US, it's worth choosing an international brand. There's no comparison, just saying.

A Stealth Visit

The sun watches what I do, but the
moon knows all my secrets

~ *J.M. Wonderland*

On February 13, 2013, I arrived back in the Iraqi desert. Although I had the feeling of familiarity as our caravan pulled through the security gate at ROO's entrance, returning brought emotions of uneasiness. Lilith's sporadic decisions kept every one of us in a state of apprehension. Stepping back on Rumaila, I breathed a silent supplication, "Please empower me to stay out of Lilith's path."

Working in security, Tane knew who was coming, going, and when. I knew he probably already was aware of my landing, but he had asked me to let him know when I got there. So I forwarded him the news of my arrival before I left the reception hall.

I grabbed my gear and walked toward the clinic, saying hello to the familiar faces along the way. It was the normal hugs and hellos in the clinic. Doug was the current Ops lead in country. He told me I would not be heading to RSB until late afternoon. He suggested I chill out for a couple of hours as he handed me the keys to Lee's room, as he was currently off-site covering at the water plant. Cool, I headed over to the room to relax for a while. I looked at my phone and saw the message from Tane. "Hey, when are you leaving for your concentration camp?"

I messaged him back, "At 16:00, why?"

"Cool, I'm in my room. Can you come over and say hi? But I don't have long. I have to get back to work in thirty minutes."

"OK, are you sure?"

"Yeah, it'll be OK. Just don't let anyone see you."

"Umm, OK, where's your room?"

As I'm walking, I think how fun this is, and it's such an adventure. I knew no one was in the least bit suspicious of the two of us. One, it was a new thing between us, two, we were both sly, stealthily, and closed-lipped. Tane's room was back in the corner of the camp, ideally isolated from everything and everybody. I wasn't nervous or worried. If anyone saw me, they would just think I was out on some work errand. It wasn't unusual for me to be roaming around the camp.

Tane had instructed me to walk in, not knock, so I did. "Hello." Well, a few minutes was better than no minutes, and at least I had the opportunity to see him in person. Damn, it's those black eyes, along with that guilty-looking grin. This is what had gotten my interest running several months ago. My mind flashes a warning, and my ears hear an imaginary siren in the distance, STOP, WARNING, DANGER AHEAD! It was extremely easy to close the door and elude the caution signs. My head reminded me that one day all of this would get me into trouble or crunch my heart.

The twenty-two-minute hookup was heartening. It was hardly enough time to say hi, how was your leave and goodbye, but I left beaming. I wondered how I had been so lucky.

The next morning, I opened my eyes and found myself alone in my cozy room back in the RSB complex. In my dreams, I was still with Tane. I sat up and smiled. Time to get around for work. Maybe this will be an awesome rotation. It was looking good so far. I told myself I could handle anything for twenty-eight days, good or whatever.

I returned to find that the Rumaila saga continued, with more changes, rumors, and drama. Heaps of ongoing politics, as always. Lilith and the medical team had decided that the north field medic could be put to good use as the trainer for the new soft-skinned ambulance drivers. The plan was that the drivers would come up to Lion for training. Larry and I would run the sessions while we were staging out. All in favor say "Aye." I loved this idea. It would make the days go faster, and instead of sitting around we would be doing something productive. Maybe, we would even earn synthetic (fake) bonus points from our queen. More than ever, it was important we were earning our keep.

The role was handed over to Larry and me after firing our newest staff member. Sam had been hired to train the LN ambulance guys yet had only been here for one rotation when Lilith decided she wasn't fond of him.

Her latest excuse was, "I don't like the way he talks. His southern drawl is annoying." She also felt he wasn't catching on fast enough. Sam had left an excellent job at home only to get ejected. Can we say unjust and prejudiced?

Hiring fifteen qualified Iraqis to fill the role of ambulance driver turned out to be tricky. There were dozens and dozens of applications; everyone wanted a piece of the pie that Rumaila would potentially be offering. Of these applications, few met any of the requirements. To be considered, the individual had to be able to read and write in Arabic. English was not a requirement. They also had to be able to pass a security screening, for starters.

The successful ones would attend several weeks of medical training courses. It was mine and Larry's job to teach these individuals six days a week while hanging out at Lion. I was excited about my new task even though I did not have much experience in lecturing.

Fourteen men passed the requirements to become our students. Half of the class could speak some English, but the majority could not. To remedy this problem, Lilith cleverly figured out that the armored ambulance drivers would be perfectly suited to stand in as our interpreters. It made sense as they were there anyway. Moreover, the drivers all could speak both Arabic and English. So, Nael, Noor, and Ali were tasked with being the course interpreters. They weren't asked; they were told.

The training took place at Lion from 0900-1145 in a room we had been given as our classroom and medical storage room. The scenario went like this: the course lecture took two hours, and we did practical hands-on skills during the last forty-five minutes of class. The program was equivalent to a primary EMT curriculum in the States. The drivers were instructed on dozens of topics such as approaching a scene safely, patient assessment, taking vital signs, stabilizing bleeding, and how to transport patients safely. They would not be expected to give any medications but to take the ill person to a local hospital or one of the local clinics.

Four or five of the guys were great. They showed a genuine interest in learning and were highly motivated, but the majority were not. I think they were looking for a quick and easy paycheck. This was not a job for lazy employees, and there was a lot of responsibility in this type of work. They loved to get off topic and discuss their unfair working conditions, such as staying on-site for twenty-four hours without proper sleeping conditions. They wanted uniforms and were not paid to come to training but felt they should be. The list went on. I couldn't blame them for being frustrated, and I don't know anyone in America who would tolerate the same work conditions, so I let them vent. I collected their complaints and reported the list to Lilith and the medical team. Little did Lilith know, but I was siding with the Iraqis. Some positive compromises did come out of it. Larry, too, had a kind heart for these guys, and between the two of us we did manage to improve their working situation.

As for Ali, Noor, and Nael, Ali's English was excellent, Nael's English was not so good, and neither one of these two liked having to interpret. They were only interested in being a driver. Then there was Noor, a well-educated, motivated, handsome young Iraqi who was a natural in the classroom, so much so that I tried to encourage him to study to be a teacher. Noor made my job easy. We got along well, and he became one of my best friends.

Via the Back Door

Live by the sun, love by the moon

Since relocating away from ROO Headquarters, I started having symptoms of anxiety. I felt out of control. This was an agonizing emotional affliction. My mind kept dragging me across a pile of hot coals. I feared losing Tane's interest and knowing Lilith was always looking for her next target. I did my best to conceal this issue, even from Angela. I thought if she became too worried about me, the information might get leaked, and I could be seen as a liability. Lilith needed little reason to cut the cord and send you home.

Nights were the worst. I tossed and turned instead of dozing. I spent volumes of time walking through my mind trying to answer my own whys and wherefores. I practiced trying to slow the thoughts by telling my mind to pretend it was in a black hole, concentrating on only the blackness, and slowing my breathing. My unique technique was in lieu of counting sheep. Unfortunately, I was not strong enough to mentally overcome my brain for more than a few minutes. The gym was a great counselor, but the best source of succor was my friend, the moon.

> Dear Moon, I choose you. You are my soulmate
> My best friend, my perfect companion
> You know my heart
> You know my darkest secrets

You follow me around the world and back
On the coldest and warmest nights, you are there
Of this life and in the next, I choose you.

—Jonea Mounsey

After moving to RSB, I picked up a pen and started putting words on paper. I had just finished reading *The Diary of Anne Frank*. So I decided to start my own Dear Kitty journal. Kitty was the name Anne gave her diary. She wrote as if Kitty was her friend. I credit the text I scripted with shaping this very book.

Life at RSB was status quo. Besides staying busy teaching during the day, I focused on getting ready to run the Rome marathon, which was scheduled during my upcoming leave. I hit the gym nearly every day, sometimes before going to work and again after work. I hoped I wouldn't disappoint myself on race day. I knew I could knock out the 42 km/26.2 miles, but would I be satisfied at the finish line? Just finishing wasn't necessarily enough. I needed to feel appeased.

Tane and I talked and messaged back and forth. He continuously asked when I would make a trip back to HQ. The only answer I had was, "I don't know." Tane's dry, comical humor would cause unconstrained giggling, producing tears as my cheeks constricted. Sometimes I'd still be laughing aloud hours later as I remembered certain hilarious tales. He enjoyed telling stories about his youth. I was so entertained; he was obviously a little hooligan. Tane and his siblings no doubt drove their parents crazy. He tells the story that for his tenth birthday he requested a chainsaw. His father gave him one, took him to the forest, and left him alone to enjoy the day cutting up the woods.

One afternoon while working at Lion, I got a surprise visitor. Dr. Angela showed up. She informed me that our Ops lead wanted her to take my place for the rest of the day and night. I then would be allowed to go to HQ and spend the night so that the IT department could do some work on my laptop. Angela would go to RSB and stay in my room, filling my place as the medic until the following day, when we would change back to our routine.

I had been requesting for a few days to have my laptop repaired. Vic promised that I could bring it down to the main camp one of these days. Today was the day. Speechless, I didn't hesitate to hand over my role, keys, and equipment. Angela had only had a couple of quick visits up to RSB. I had shared a few facts about my new living arrangements, and now she would get to experience it for herself.

I returned to ROO HQ with Angela's security team. Much like when I traveled in the ambo, all the expats around the oil field traveled in armored vehicles with an armed security detail. I arrived back at the clinic and received a pleasant welcome from Vic. After dropping off my computer, I returned and spent some time catching up with the medical team. Next, I went to dinner with Lisa, one of our ambulance supervisors. I loved this gal and was happy to have some time to chat.

Lisa had come to join our tribe two months earlier in December. Finally, another female to add to our team of twelve, eight men and four women. Lisa was a kind, big-hearted, fun-loving person. She got on well with the Iraqis and brought a positive influence to the sandbox. Lisa was born in the UK but lived with her partner in Tanzania, East Africa. Lisa, like myself, became passionate about the local Iraqi people. We often stood up for them when others did not. I enjoyed spending time chatting and confiding with her.

Vic had been so kind as to get me a room in the high-rise. I messaged Tane before going to dinner, "Guess where I'm at?"

"Where?" He was surprised to hear I would be staying the night in HQ. Tane's job required insanely long hours. He sometimes got up as early as 0400 and worked until 2200 or later. He asked if we could meet up when he finished.

"Yes, of course, I was hoping you would say that," I replied.

Using the back-door approach, Tane came to see me, as invisible as Harry Potter's magical cloak. Ta-da and we were chilling once again in person, eye to eye. It was marvelous to have a few hours to let me forget about the world on the other side of the door. The night was too quick. I savored the minutes of flirting, storytelling, and companionship. The long day stole my friend's eyes. I held on to all the minutes, and sleep did not take me. The early morning light meant our time had ceased. Tane thanked me with a big, tight embrace and vanished into the new day.

There Will Come a Time

My favorite thing on earth is the moon.

I stood outside underneath the dark sky, looking at my bright friend high above the earth, the same as I had done a dozen, or more like a hundred-dozen, nights before. I imagined that somewhere out there underneath this great dark sphere, someone else was looking upward, admiring the moonbeams and hopefully feeling less alone.

I had settled into my new routine and had accepted Camp Iso as best I could. I told myself I can do anything for twenty-eight days. It's really a short time in the big scheme of life. I knew one day I would look back and trea-sure this time. This life won't always be available. There will come a time when I will be sad not to be able to return to this ruthless land. Things were bound to change, and no matter how much wishful thinking we do, we have no power to lasso the sun.

Rome to Run

I've never seen a moon in the sky that,
if it didn't take my breath away, at
least misplaced it for a moment.

~ Colin Farrell

M arch had arrived, and my days continued to be filled with teaching the Iraqi men medical skills with the hope they would one day be able to manage health-related situations long enough to get their patients to a hospital. Some of the ambulance drivers were doing surprisingly well. In reality, most trainees were not focused on learning the required material. *Inshallah,* these guys never have to deal with a serious situation.

I was getting excited about my upcoming trip to Italy. I would be running my fifth marathon through the streets of Rome. The race would take place on St. Paddy's Day, which would also be my birthday. How cool. It was fantastic to have this pilgrimage to look forward to. I had not yet been to Italy, and the journey would surely be memorable.

Before I knew it, I found myself at the HQ, ready for another crew change. Only one more night in Iraq, and then I would be on a plane to Dubai, where I would start my holiday. It was so divine getting to have a superb dinner with cherished comrades. Tane was home on leave, so no secret squirrel meetup was happening tonight.

After our evening meal, a small group had arranged to meet at the newest coffee shop. Nicky and her back-to-back, Ignatius, were there. Nicky and

Ignatius were now working as medics at the water facility near Basra airport. Unfortunately, they were temporarily moved to HQ due to a security issue. Dr. Angela, Lee, my past driver Mark, and I made up our group. It was a blast hanging out together, chatting, and telling stories of our many ROO adventures. This gathering was a unique opportunity for all of us. Sitting together was a first and a last. I'm sure we were all aware of this as we laughed the evening away.

Ignasius arrived in December 2012. He was an excellent medic from South Africa and had worked with Frontier since 2003 doing various projects, mainly offshore on seismic assignments. He decided to leave his sea legs behind and came to join us in the sand. I wish I would have gotten to spend more time hanging out with him, but that wasn't the case.

The next day I headed out on leave. My first stop, Dubai, where I booked into the beautiful Habtoor Grand Resort. The deluxe accommodations were located on Jumeirah Beach, fronting the Persian Gulf. I had three days to kill before I needed to be in Rome, so I decided to spend it at the beach. The resort was pricey, but I splurged anyway. It was located near the Dubai Marina and a tram station. The hotel had multiple restaurants—Thai, Italian, Lebanese, a British pub, and an upscale steak place. There was no shortage of watering holes—a beach bar, a poolside bar, a Cuban bar, and the list goes on—three swimming pools, a private beach, a spa, and tennis courts.

I had had a few layovers in Dubai but had not seen many sights. This happened to be the perfect time to look around. I started my holiday by spending a few hours lying by the pool, enjoying cocktails purchased by a talkative British man. Next, I wandered down the beach only to be amused by a local Arabic man encouraging me to take a camel ride on the beach while sporting my bikini. I'm not thinking so. After sundown, I strolled along the gorgeous Dubai Marina, an artificial canal city that was built along a two-mile stretch of the shoreline of the Persian Gulf. Upscale bars, restaurants, and shops lined the waterfront canal, with skyscrapers in the background and million-dollar yachts docked in the marina.

I had two things on my list that I wanted to check off while in Dubai this time. One of which was Ski Dubai. I just had to do the touristy thing and check out downhill snow skiing indoors. It was ninety degrees outside at the beach, so what better way to spend the afternoon than skiing at the 22,500-square meter indoor resort in the Emirates Mall? I found the place to be fascinating. After purchasing a ticket for approximately $70, I got in line for the much-needed winter attire. I was deeply humored seeing Muslim women enter the changing room in their burkas and exiting with ski pants and jackets, a sight that brought me happiness.

The indoor resort has a nice-sized hill of snow to slide down. First, you had to get on a small chair lift and ride to the top. The snow was slippery and a bit icy, as it was artificial—no powder to ski here. The two runs were short but entertaining. I was astonished at how flippin' cold it was in the place. In fact, I stayed for less than an hour as my hands became painfully frigid.

While there, I noticed an older Muslim woman, maybe about sixty-five or seventy years old. I first saw her on the chair lift, sitting in the seat ahead of me. She did not have any skis. I thought she forgot to get them or maybe didn't know she needed them, but something seemed wrong. She didn't get off the lift at the top and kept circling. I was concerned for her until I realized she was there just to ride the chair lift around and around and around. I could see she loved the ambiance.

Visiting the famous Dubai Gold Souk was the second thing I planned to do. A souk is a traditional market. Dubai Gold Souk is known for its exquisite jewelry, not just gold but silver, diamonds, and other stones. More than three hundred markets are here, and even if you aren't shopping, it's reported as a must-see sight.

I had mapped its whereabouts out on my city map. It looked like all I needed to do was take the tram to a station near the Deira district and then walk a few blocks to its location. Riding the tram around Dubai is a breeze, but when I got off at the station, it seemed like there was nothing except apartments in the area. Oh well, I was determined to figure it out now on foot. I walked and walked then came to a wire fence that put me at a dead end. I so badly wanted to climb over it as I knew this would shorten my route, but I wasn't in America and didn't want to go to jail here. The laws in the Middle East are stringent, though UAE is more lenient than other countries, I didn't need to be the next *Locked Up Abroad*. I continued walking but wasn't getting any closer. It was starting to get dark. I was tired and starving by now, plus I needed to find my way back to the tram station. I realized the souk would have to wait for yet another trip.

I found myself back at the Habtoor. I was famished, so I decided to give the Lebanese place a try. It was a pleasant evening, so I requested a table outside. It's interesting as a solo woman traveling alone how you are treated in different places around the world. Sometimes you are pampered, and others you are not so much appreciated. But, of course, this highly depends on the cultural attitude toward women.

My waiter showed me to a table close to the pool and waterfall. At the table next to mine, I noticed two other English-speaking women dressed in Western-style clothing. I asked the waiter to help me decide on what to order. I told him I loved lamb, and he then pointed to a selection he thought I would enjoy. I wanted a glass of wine, but it only came by the bottle. "That's fine. I'll take a bottle of rosé." I soon found myself in conversation with the ladies sitting beside me. They were Europeans working and living in Dubai, which was no surprise. Dubai is not only the richest city in the world, but many expats call it their home. The waiter arrived at the women's table with an interesting-looking contraption. I knew what it was but didn't know exactly how it worked. Without staring, I gazed in their direction, observing. I asked them about the *shisha* pipe a few minutes into the smoking. They explained that the steamed flavored tobacco was delightful and that I should give it a go. Why not? I had wanted to check it out, so tonight seemed like a good time. I informed the waiter I'd like some *shisha*.

"What flavor?" He listed them off from memory

"Green apple, please."

A few minutes later, he returned with the three-foot-tall water pipe. He placed a couple of chunks of red glowing coal under the lid on the top. Soon I was drawing in my first ever hubbly bubbly, shisha, or narghile. I've never been a smoker, other than smoking dainty foo foo cigars with my female friends while sitting around a campfire or, on a rare occasion, taking a drag off someone's cigarette when nearly drunk. So I was quite surprised by how enjoyable the sweet, flavored mist was. Smoking *shisha* (tobacco) is a traditional social activity common throughout the Middle East. It often follows the evening meal. A pipe can last forty to fifty minutes and is generally shared by a group of friends. It also has become trendy in the States, except it's better known as hookah. Originating in India, hookah is the name for the large water pipe that uses indirect heat to produce the warm fruit-flavored mist.

This had been the first holiday where I had spent it all alone. I had traveled alone before, but after arriving at my destination I usually had someone to meet up with. It felt satisfying to have explored a foreign metropolis companionless. It would have been more enjoyable having someone to share dinner with. On the other hand, the male servers were very attentive to my needs once they realized I was all alone—drinks two-for-one, for example.

The Dubai holiday was lovely—such a captivating city. I could spend a month here and never see half the sights. Maybe next time I'll make it to the Gold Souk and the camel races, but for now I had a plane to catch, a friend to meet, and a race to run. So off to Rome I went.

I landed in Rome on Thursday, the fourteenth of March. As part of the trip package, a driver had been prearranged to meet me at the airport upon my arrival and delivered me to the boutique hotel, The Grand Hotel del Gianicolo Rome. Here I would join my fellow runners and nonrunner group. Best of all, Dr. Angela had decided to come along to cheer me on and be my roommate. I was stoked to have convinced her to join me. Sharing this magical experience with a good friend would complete the trip.

Run Italy was an annual event led by the famous Jeff Galloway. It combined the opportunity to run the Rome marathon with a week of touring Rome, the perfect runner's holiday.

Jeff Galloway, a 1972 American Olympian, is the nation's leading running coach. Jeff has written more than twenty books on running, having sold over a million copies. He is the founder of the method run-walk-run, proving that nonrunners can become successful at the sport.

Jeff being one of my heroes, I was super excited to have the chance to hang out with him and his wife, Barbara. It was a privilege and honor to be on holiday with Mr. Galloway. I had met Jeff a couple of times before. Once I attended a lecture he gave in Arizona. Jeff autographed a book I had that he had written. I also bumped into him at a couple of different running expos. He always remembered me and gave me a warm handshake.

I checked into my room. It was a quaint little hotel on a hill above St. Peter's Cathedral. Three hours later, Angela arrived. We were giddy as teenagers. Angela, like myself, had never been to Rome. She mentioned that it had been high on her bucket list. Doctor Ang was a seasoned traveler. She worked part-time for a German health insurance company doing medical escorts for German citizens. She got to travel to destinations around the globe, accompanying ill Germans back to Germany.

Following the introduction meeting, a small group of us explored the area outside our hotel with Jeff and Barb. After a short walk, almost everyone decided to head back to the hotel. Angela and I were the only ones who had not arrived from the States. So the two of us decided to venture off independently as the others were suffering from jet lag.

It was a historical time to be in Rome. Pope Benedict XVI had just stepped down, and a new pope was soon to be named. The world was impatiently waiting. Popes are chosen by being voted in by the College of Cardinals, which consists of more than two hundred members. The voting process at the Vatican in Rome is known as the papal election.

As Angela and I were wandering around the city, walking along the Tiber River, we were drawn to the sound of music wafting through the air. We found ourselves standing in the massive St. Peter's Square. People were gathering, being coaxed by the same melody we had heard. Then our eyes, staring, witnessed the momentous event. The heavenly white smoke the world was waiting for came from the Sistine Chapel's smokestack. A new pope had been chosen. Angela, who was raised Catholic, filled me in on what we were witnessing. Within a few minutes, the jumbotron screen came to life in a corner high above the square. On the screen, the gigantic face of an elderly male came into focus, the senior Cardinal Deacon. He said, "We have a new pope," in Latin, of course. The chance of witnessing such an event may be one in a billion, who really knows. You see, there is no way to truly predict when the new pope will be chosen. I had committed to the Run Italy race four or five months earlier. Fate had led us to the square, or we too could have returned to the hotel or been wandering in the opposite direction. To this day, I still ponder this thought! I can only tell you things just kept getting more interesting.

Our 2013 Run Italy group had nine runners and five nonrunners— family or friends who had tagged along. Before breakfast, a few of us would get up early to run with Jeff. Each day was then filled with sightseeing the dozens of classic Rome sights. Our designated travel guide, whose name was Lylah, was super. She was American-born but had moved to Rome fifteen years earlier. Lylah, being of small stature, made up for it in her energy and passion for history. Always moving fast, she raced ahead of us, held up her group sign, bellowing, "Follow Lylah! Follow Lylah!" Now you would think a group of marathoners could walk fast enough to keep up with a short-legged sixty-five-year-old. "Follow Lylah!" but what she really meant was, get your slow asses over here. Man, this woman wore us out.

One particular afternoon, when we returned to our hotel, I noticed a well-dressed man sitting outside our room at a small table on the second floor. He seemed preoccupied with something or someone as he focused on looking out the window. On the table was an SLR camera with a large lens, like you would use if taking pictures from far away. He looked up as I passed by and spoke a very American hello, immediately returning his attention outside. We noted he was still there a while later as we headed out for dinner. Angela and I discussed how strange this situation was and wondered what there was to be taking pictures of. There were only the hotel grounds and a street below. You couldn't see that far.

In the hotel lobby, we met up with Val, who wanted to join us for dinner, so off we went. Val was the Run Italy organizer. As we walked through the streets, Val started telling us that the Secret Service had been to the hotel and asked for all of our passports. We laughed and joked about this, believing that the bottle of red wine we enjoyed at dinner was causing silliness. After a few hours of wandering the narrow streets, we returned to the hotel.

The following day it was apparent something was up at the hotel. Three or four men in dark suits were on the ground floor busying themselves by carrying electrical gear in from two black vehicles. The shiny SUVs had dark glass windows and were parked outside the del Gianicolo hotel. Hmm, was the Mafia taking over our small hotel? Later the same day, Angela and I saw two suspicious-looking guys in one of the hotel's back meeting rooms, and we noticed they had set up the electronic equipment. The door to the large banquet room was semi-closed like they were trying to be sly and avoid being seen. The weirdness continued. The guys remained about the hotel, including the one sitting on the second floor looking out the window. The management wouldn't answer any questions we had about who they were. It soon became evident that they had to be Secret Service guys when Vice President Joe Biden was seen having lunch in the restaurant next to our hotel. I don't know if he was staying at del Gianicolo as he was not spotted in the hotel, but he must have been hanging out nearby.

Sunday the seventeenth of March, race day. The run was to start and finish at the Colosseum, you know the one where chariot races took place and Romans fought lions to the death. This well-recognized landmark was finished in 80 AD, and it could hold 87,000 spectators. The distinguished broken wall represents the damage of a past earthquake. Thought-provoking fact—500,000 humans lost their lives here, and over a million wild animals, mostly cats, were slain for amusement.

I followed Jeff's lead and started the race with him and Barbara. He got to the very back of all the runners and let everyone start the race. Not until several minutes after the last of the corrals had left did we start running. I have run many races and have never used this method. There is a psychology behind racing like this. I will admit it was hard as a competitive person to start behind thousands of challengers. This was one of the theories I believe Jeff had—the mental game. Racers were given a timing chip to attach to their shoelaces, so it was about your time, not who you are in front of at the finish line.

The race went off great. The weather was perfect, a bit overcast, with a few drops of rain. At least a third of the 26.2 miles/ 42 km was run on cobblestone streets, and after completing fifteen miles I was starting to feel drained. I now needed to really focus on my footing to avoid an injury. It began to rain during the last few miles, making the cobblestones slick, so I cautiously proceeded. My last ten miles were probably the best ten I've ever run. Starting behind everyone meant I had now caught up to the stragglers. I was passing runners like crazy—great for the ego. I can honestly say no one ran by me in that last ten-mile stretch. Digging deep for the last bit of push I could find, I sprinted the last few yards to the finish line. My birthday marathon ended with a big happy grin.

Meanwhile, over at St. Peter's Square, Pope Francis was inaugurated into his duties. Angela had gone over to watch but returned in time to meet me at the finish line. I had raced well and was now feeling both exuberant and exhausted. It's truly an incredible feeling to finish an endurance contest, knowing that the hours and miles of training are remunerated.

Exhausted, wet, and cold from the rain, I was happy to shower and relax in our room. Angela left me to rest, returning later with the most beautiful assortment of mini birthday cakes you can imagine.

The day finished with our celebration dinner and awards ceremony, Roman style, of course. Our group shared a delightful Italian meal. We chatted and toasted our memorable day. Awards followed dinner, and the runners were called to the front one by one. Mr. Galloway did the honors by handing us our medals and placing a *kotinos* on our heads. This olive wreath represented the original prize for the ancient Olympic Games. We were all crowned winners. In addition, we also received a custom-made plate to remember our special day.

The next three days entailed more sightseeing. We had already been to the Vatican museum, the Sistine Chapel, Trevi Fountain, and the Spanish Steps. In addition, we visited the Colosseum, St. Peter's Basilica, the Pantheon, and the Roman Forum. A day trip outside Rome to the 3000-year-old hilltop town of Tivoli, stopping at Hadrian's Villa and Villa d'Este, finished our journey. Finally, the group divided and headed off in separate directions. I hugged Angela farewell, knowing we'd be rendezvousing in a few short weeks back in the sandbox.

Ski Dubai, an indoor ski resort in the Mall of Emirates

Angela in front of the del Gianicolo hotel, Rome

Just happened to be in the right place at the right time, Pope Francis

Follow Lylah, our energic tour guide in Rome

The Colosseum is the largest amphitheater ever built

Headed towards the finish line at the 2013 Rome marathon

Jeff Galloway and I, at the awards celebration

Angela, Val and me celebrating in Rome

Well, This Isn't Good

*Life is not always round, reflected the waning
moon. Be patient, beamed the waxing moon.*
                                    ~ *Jonea Mounsey*

From Rome, I flew back to Dubai via the Doha airport and then to Phoenix for a short two-week stint. I busied myself spending time with family and friends and packing. Again. Drew and Jocelyn had decided to sell their house and head east to be near Jocelyn's parents. I had been renting a room from them for the past two years.

I had no real clue where the hell I was going to call home next. Having an apartment didn't make sense, as I was in Phoenix less than a third of the time. But I knew things would work out; they always do.

Communication with Tane during my holiday had been very sporadic. He might check in a couple of days in a row and then nothing for days. Rome had been a great distraction. I tried to dismiss my want for his attention. I longed to hear the voice, the accent which makes "i" sound like "e." The charismatic personality that had me captured and waiting on the hook. An easy take. Only the man in the moon knew of my yearning, as the rest of the world was none the wiser. My lips held tight my arcane.

The day I was to head back to the Middle East, my flight out of Phoenix was delayed, which disrupted my whole travel itinerary. I had difficulty explaining to the airline agent at the counter, "No, I can't travel through Dubai;

I need to go through Turkey. The connecting flights through Dubai won't get me into Basra early enough to get a new visa." She preferred to argue with me than be understanding and listen to my explanation. Finally, it was decided that my best option was to reschedule for the following day. I contacted Frontier's office to let them know what was going on. ROO's security team and movements team would need to be updated on my new travel plans.

The following day I was off again, heading nearly halfway around the globe, a flying distance of 7,841 miles or 12620 km. Due to a long layover in Istanbul, Turkey, I was given a hotel room for a few hours preceding my last leg to Basra. I sat in my room, reflecting on my truly good fortune, traveling and exploring the world, meeting and befriending people from all corners of the globe. Wonderment flowed through my soul as I questioned my luck. Remembering words from my friend Mr. Sperling, "Not luck, my dear, but because of diligence and toil." That was what got me to where I was.

Randolph Sperling was eighty-eight years old when we met. He had just had a heart attack and was in the ICU where I worked. I had the honor of being Randy's nurse as he was recovering. I did the one thing that is frowned upon in the healthcare arena, become friends with my patient.

Randy and I connected almost instantly. His irresistible personality stirred my interest. If anyone should have a book written about himself, it was Mr. Sperling, except it would need to be a whole series. A short example: as a teenager, during his school break, he spent the summer jumping trains and traveling like a hobo around the US. He was a professional football player in the days of leather helmets for the N.Y. Giants. When Pearl Harbor was attacked, he fudged his age and joined the military. He became one of the youngest Navy men to become an officer, but not just any officer. He became an intelligence officer. Oh, and if that wasn't interesting enough, he survived not one but THREE sunken ships.

Randy became one of my truest friends. He even moved into my home and paid me rent before the bank took the house away from me. My engaging mate could relate to my adventuresome spirit. He once told me I had big balls that hung down to my knees. He was referring to my fearlessness when I took the position in Iraq.

My Turkish Air flight to Basra was set to leave at 0145. Standing at the gate, I recognized several other ROO employees heading in. A quick glance and a nod of the head indicated they had also recognized me.

The process for boarding was to have your ticket scanned, then get on a bus and be driven out to the aircraft sitting on the tarmac. When it was my turn, I approached the gate agents who were scanning tickets and checking passports. The attractive female gate attendant took my ticket, briefly looked at it, and said, "Wait here a moment," pointing to the side of the line. With the last of the passengers checked in, I presumed she had forgotten me. I tried to approach and was again told to be patient and wait. I couldn't imagine what was up, and I started feeling butterflies swimming in my stomach.

I watched as the bus with the last of the travelers drove off. "Well, this isn't good," I mumbled to myself. It was apparent something was wrong. I stepped back up and said, "Ma'am, I need to be on that flight," not allowing her to ignore me.

She replied without looking up from what she was doing, "Your flight was yesterday. You missed that flight!"

"Crap." I then explained the situation. The frustrated United ticket agent in Phoenix had not bothered to correct this leg of my flight.

Continuing to stay focused on the papers in front of her, she stated, "I'm not sure if there is any open business class seat available on this flight."

"Ma'am, I don't have to sit in business class." She didn't answer. Standing there feeling panicked, I was wondering when she was going to check to see. Everyone had already left, and how would I get to the plane? They're not going to wait on one lone American woman.

She picks up the radio communicating to the crew on the plane, and she then turns to me, "OK, there is one seat left." The oversized transit bus showed up, and the same elegant woman who confirmed my seat escorted me to the jumbo 777. Funny, they *were* waiting on me. As I scurried, red-faced, to get to my seat, my unspoken words were, *Yep, I am important, and you all can stop looking so annoyed. Besides, if you choke on your dinner, you'll be damn glad I'm on this flight.*

Qarmat Ali

I only told the moon.

I t had been a struggle and a stressful trip. Nevertheless, I was gratified to have my feet back in Iraq once more. For an exciting twist to my arrival, I wasn't being sent straight to RSB or HQ. Instead, I was escorted from the Basra International Airport to another of ROO's remote camps, COB. I was to cover as the medic here for a few days before I returned to the isolation camp at RSB.

COB, Contingency Operating Base, was a British military base during the Iraq War. Along with the British army, hundreds of American and other countries' military troops spent time here as allies. In fact, the COB was one of the last four bases to be evacuated in December 2011 when the US finished pulling out of Iraq.

At the time of my visit, a handful of ROO staff were staying here to support the Qarmat Ali Water Treatment Plant Project (QAWTP or QA Project). The QA Project was anticipated to last approximately two years. This project aimed to refurbish the existing run-down water treatment plant. The makeover would enhance the capabilities of the water plant, which in turn would increase the water supply. This precious resource was desperately needed for Rumaila's reservoir. Once QA was remodeled, there would be enough pressure and water to be pumped all the way out to the north end of the oil field, allowing water injection to come to fruition.

Enhanced Oil Recovery, or EOR, is a technique that increases the amount of recoverable oil. Water injection involves drilling injection wells into the underground reservoir and forcing water in, displacing the oil, hopefully making it more reachable.

Rumaila operations reported that the northside had the largest reservoir of anywhere on the field. Not only was the oil deep in the ground in this particular area, but to add to the challenge, it was underneath of a massive swamp strewn with land mines. Tapping into this reservoir was going to be laborious and expensive.

Not only would ROO benefit, but the local citizens would also benefit from the electricity the plant would produce. The people of Basra City were in dire need of electrical power. Ms. Anwar had talked of the hardships of life minus utilities.

New housing quarters were needed at the Qarmat Ali site in response to the latest project. Construction of the new fly camp was already underway. In the meantime, the expats working on this project lived at the ex-military base, located four miles away.

The QA workers would travel from COB to a makeshift office complex next to the QA water plant each day. The daily routine was after breakfast; the expats would meet in the car park, have a safety brief, and be transported to the QA site in our armored vehicles. The medic's duties here were much the same as mine were at Lion. Organize your required gear and drag it into the B6 Land Cruiser that had been made into a mini ambulance. I hated to think of having to care for an injured person in the back of this vehicle. Also, my long legs made it difficult to fit inside the truck's rear. QA's site used G4S as their security personnel, another private security company much the same as the one used at ROO. This meant the ambulance driver was a G4S employee. When the rest of the security team and expats were ready, we moved to the QA site, where I staged out for the day.

The people involved at this location were amicable and laid-back. Only a couple dozen staff were staying at COB, and the small crew proved to be nondramatic. No wonder Nicky liked it here. The food sucked almost as much as RSB. But the gym rocked, and there was a large area to roam around and explore. COB was a frickin' enthralling war zone ghost town. Many buildings had essentially been abandoned postwar after the 2011 evacuation. It was like being on a movie set. It made me kind of wish I could have seen it in its heyday. The medic's quarters were an old musty barracks room. Although clean, it was a bit spooky somehow. When you enter the doorway, you step down a foot. The ceiling was low and the room dark, with no windows. It was essentially a bomb shelter cave.

My time here was short-lived, four days. I was first told I'd be heading to ROO on Friday and then onward to RSB. Thursday night, Vic contacted me and informed me that no, I would be going straight to hell, I mean to RSB.

Packed and ready, I dragged my gear out to the truck. I was glad I got a look-see of this place. It had been a mini furlough, but I was still gratified that Nicky liked it here. Before heading away from COB, the procedure was to have a huddle with all personnel involved. Security would state which route we would travel, what radio channel we would use, and any other vital information. I stood with the others in our small circle as the G4S team lead gave us the brief. "We will be going to ROO to drop Jo off, not to RSB as originally planned." WOO HOO, I was doing the happy dance.

Bring Lunch
Next Time

I have late-night conversations with the moon. He
tells me about the sun, and I tell him about you.
~ SL Grey

I arrived at ROO mid-morning, and my transport
team to Camp Iso wouldn't happen until they finished their day up at Lion at approximately 1730. The
med team was pleased to see me. The new Ops lead had
arrived, and I was introduced to Cal. Doug had been cut
loose. I guess he had disagreed with Lilith one too many
times. GONE, not even going, going gone.

Angela was in the country, so we had great fun talking
about our grand trip to Rome. We shared our stories with the
gang. They raised their eyebrows when we spoke of the Secret Service guys
hiding in our hotel and Vice President Biden having lunch next door. While
chatting away with our industrial hygienist, Stan, he commented that his
daughter's friend was a Secret Service agent who traveled with VP Biden.
Curious if the strange men at The Grand Hotel in Rome could be one and
the same, Stan searched for a picture of the guy on his phone. Huh, it looks
like the same guy to me! Stan added, "I think she said he was going to be in
Rome for the Pope's thing."

Tane had only just returned from leave two days before. I shocked him when I informed him of my location as I had already told him I wasn't going to be stopping in at HQ. "Can you come over to my cabin at lunch?"

"Ok, sure."

It was a pleasurable thirty minutes. I could easily get used to these laconic lunchtime quickies. Upon entering Tane's room, I found him sitting on his bed waiting for me. "Hi babe, I'm on my break. We don't have much time."

"Yeah, I know, baby," I replied as I kicked off my shoes. Thirty seconds later, my clothes were on the floor. "Move over hon," I requested for Tane to make room on the narrow twin-sized bed.

Unfortunately, there was no guarantee we'd ever have another chance. Our one-on-one encounters had all been little miracles of unpredictable events.

Although Tane's lunch break was too short, I was thankful to see him. As I headed toward the door to exit, Tane reached out and grabbed onto my arm, turning me around. I expected one of his silly snide remarks. But, instead, looking into my blue eyes, he delivered a soft kiss. My heart hurt with joy. "Come back anytime, and bring lunch next time." I peeked around before stepping out the door, zig-zagging my way back to the clinic to await my transport to camp. That man was just too cute for my own good.

Things were off to a pleasant start. Being at QA for a few days shortened my time at Camp Iso. I had secretly gotten my way. The short meeting on ROO would keep me appeased for the rest of this rotation, or at least I hoped so. Plus, rumor had it I was finally going to be sent to a driving course at ROO sometime during this rotation. Hard to believe I would be allowed another visit to the main camp. But I was not going to hold my breath, that was for sure.

Life at RSB hadn't missed a beat while I was away. The guys welcomed me back, and I am sure most were happy to have a female living among them. However, you have to wonder who in their right mind would knowingly place a lone woman in a camp full of lonesome males. I have to say, putting shorts on and going to the gym made me feel awkward, but I wasn't going to give up exercising for anybody. Frontier's project manager contacted me several times to check on me. I didn't hesitate to describe the RSB camp scene. The office wasn't exactly pleased that I had been placed at this remote camp. They were responsible for my well-being as my direct employer. Lilith ruled everyone, and Frontier couldn't afford to rock the boat with their most profitable client.

I didn't particularly appreciate having to eat dinner in the DFAC at RSB. I felt so self-conscious sitting there among the fifty males. You would have thought I'd have gotten used to youthful Iraqi lads glaring in my direction every time I was within their sight. I tried to sit with my driver if he was eating at the same time as me. Nael and I always ate together. We would preplan a time to meet for dinner upon our return at the end of the day, but this only happened when our work schedules lined up. On some of my rotations, Nael would only be working a couple of days. Nael was sensitive to my uncomfortableness and would go out of his way to arrange to be my dinner mate. My other two drivers often ate with the other Iraqi guys, so I avoided sitting with them. Sometimes I would be invited to sit with the Turkish contracting engineers. These mature guys were not living in our camp but stayed outside our wall. They were in charge of the new pipe yard being built. Although their English wasn't the best, they were true gentlemen. If I sat with them and they finished their dinner before me, they always refused to vacate the table until I was done. Honestly, they had the best manners of any group I'd been exposed to while working and traveling in the Middle East.

Each day at Lion, there was more *eulim* or teaching. *Sitta* (six) days a week, it continued, except when we got interrupted to go out on an emergency call. Otherwise, class carried on. The first responders were steadily moving through their lessons. I delighted in watching them build their pride and confidence. It was satisfying instructing these men. I had created a good rapport with them. It had been a privilege to have the chance to interact with the local Iraqis.

Tane and I communicated nearly every day and sometimes twice a day. The joking and flirting kept me in a jovial mood. By some means, it made me feel more secure knowing Tane was not that far away. However, I'm not sure what the outcome would have been without Tane being in the picture, for better or worse. Would I have been more content and not care where I was located? Or would I have succumbed to loneliness?

I had been on the schedule to do the defensive driving course for a couple of months. Three different times I was set to go, only to be denied. Each time I would inform Tane I was coming to ROO for the driving course, then at the last minute I would receive disappointing news. I started to fret Tane would think I was bluffing. But, no, he knew as well as anyone how things could be around this place. This type of work required being flexible and expecting nothing until you were standing in the middle of it, and then still it would probably change.

It was Friday, April 19, 2013, and once more, my course was postponed. All movements on the oil field were stopped due to political unrest in the country. Government elections were in progress, and even though we were far from any major city, precautions were taken. The risk of some unknown act of violence outweighed the benefits of going to work. We were stuck in camp, which was different for a change—nothing to do but go to the gym or stay in my cabin and read.

A week later, finally, after the fifth time being rescheduled, I found myself on ROO. I was lucky enough to go down the evening before the course and stay the night in the tranquil high-rise. The evening was grand, and I enjoyed an appetizing meal with my colleagues Stan and Johannes. The food served at HQ was always plentiful and of good quality. I missed having such an assortment of fine cuisine. It was here I grew fond of lamb and discovered what the famous Yorkshire pudding was.

My dessert was enjoyed later in the evening when my discreet friend visited me. I cherished the wee bit of time together, laughing and teasing. I'd often get badgered about being American or about our crazy politics. Why do Americans always cry on TV? Why do you guys call chicken wings buffalo wings? Why is a soft drink called root beer when it contains no beer? Do they call you a cracker (because of my skin color)? Is collard green really nagger grass? He soon realized that I wasn't so easy to get a rise out of but did have a sense of humor. These things kept me laughing not only for days but for years to come. I am pretty sure no one has ever had me laughing so much.

The following day I went to the driving course taught by Roger, a stocky Brit who had relocated to Australia during his twenties. The idea was that after taking the course, I would be qualified to drive the armored ambulance I was managing. The class was only a few hours. Listening to Roger's accent was entertaining, and the information was engaging. But I still struggled to keep my eyes open due to the short night that I had spent being entertained by my sexy mate.

Roger was a professional driving instructor who knew his stuff. The course wasn't about ordinary driving skills; it was to teach us how to reduce our risks while operating a vehicle here in Iraq. Important information was shared: always stay on a track if driving off the main road. There were still plenty of UXOs lying around. Instructions on handling roadblocks and what to do in a crash scenario were given.

I was stoked to think I might actually get to drive the beast and think I'm a woman on top of it. I couldn't wait to see the look on the Iraqi faces when I drove up to the security point at Lion or was seen getting out from the driver's side. But I couldn't imagine I would ever be granted the chance to drive outside the gates of HQ.

While listening to Roger's lecture, I started thinking about how English accents differ. Hearing people who speak traditional English made it evident that Americans have butchered the English language. We've added our redneck slang, which I do think makes it more colorful. Seeing that Americans are the descendants of England, why did our tongues manage to torture the British dialect. An interesting fact is that Americans started changing the pronunciations of words only one generation after landing in the New World. For example, Americans pronounce "r," known as a rhotic dialect; we say "card," and Brits say "cahd." Too funny.

My four weeks in the country were nearly over. Two days after the driving course, I was back at ROO HQ overnighting one more time before changing out with Larry. He would arrive from the airport, and we would have five minutes to shake hands and add any last-minute details or updates to the current rumors and such. Official handovers were prepared and emailed prior to the incoming person departing their home, but with the never-ending changes, information always required some amending.

Getting to spend yet another night at HQ meant I also got to attend the daily prayers session. Daily events in and around Iraq were disclosed—bombing, kidnapping, murders, and other political unrest. The number of people killed and injured was reported, and any local or possible threats were exposed. It was also a time to give any oil field updates, current production totals, problems or issues, awards, pats on the back, and such. I loved attending prayers as I got to say hi to all my non-medical ROO buddies. Some people I would occasionally see up at Lion, but the vast majority never travel off the main camp.

My last supper was shared with the entire medical team. Our group usually sat together during the evening meal, except Lilith, who rarely joined us. I found it humorous to hear my coworkers express their guilt-ridden excuses for why they shouldn't find the dessert table, but their taste buds ruled 95% of the time. The temptation was at its highest with the numerous sweets to pick from. However, the self-condemnation of a few didn't slow down the second or third trip back for additional sampling. One person would return with some enticing item that got the next person curious, and then off they went to see for themselves—fun times for sure. I so much missed these evening rituals and fellowship. I hoped my colleagues knew how lucky they were to have this comradeship.

Déjà vu, I was once again cozied up in my quaint little room in the blue two-story dorm. Likewise, messages were transmitted to and fro. "What are you doing?"

"Waiting on you."

"How late are you working?"

"Maybe til 2200 or so. I'll message you when I'm on my way."

"Perfect."

I was feeling nervous as the building was active with other guests. This was the busiest I have ever known it to be. The recent news that Rachell had been fired after being caught spending time with one of the security guys made me edgy. Rumor had it that she was flaunting it, and that was how they got exposed.

A soft rap was heard. My handsome *sadiq* was behind the door. "Welcome, how are you?"

"Tired."

It was a quiet and relaxing evening. We sat on the bed and watched TV. Tane took my hand in his, and my heart warmed with his touch. Tonight, Tane's stories included war sagas while he was an enlisted soldier in the army. The scenes described portrayed atrocities. I listened intently. I wondered how these men endured the emotional torture. Then, of course, to lighten things up, some off-colored recounts were told.

From the second he walked into the room, we both knew a physical encounter would transpire. There was an unmistakable gravitational force between us. Tane was super patient and loved keeping me at bay. Yet, each time we looked into the other's eyes, there was no hiding our genuine desire.

We grew still, and soon I felt the warm body ease. The masculine man sleeping next to me now seemed much softer. I snuggled a little closer wanting nothing more than to feel his breath on my cheek. I watched his face, wishing the night would last an eternity. Tane wiggled slightly, briefly opening his eyes, his lips turned upward with a priceless smile. My heart liquefied.

We All Can Run

We ran as if to meet the moon.

~ Robert Frost

I walked over to the flight status board, scanning the arrivals until I spied the Fort Wayne flight arrival time—fifty minutes away. "Cool." I headed through the pedestrian traffic of Chicago O'Hare Airport to await the FWA flight. I wondered if my son was suspicious of his surprise artist mom.

I watched Jan's flight land then moved out of sight from the disembarking passengers. I gave it fifteen minutes and rang Jan's phone. "Yep" was his typical greeting.

"You made it to Chicago?"

"Yes, I just got here a few minutes ago."

I kept up with the questions and started giving little hints. "Are you wearing your red and black jacket?" I relocated to the seat directly behind him. He finally turned to find me sitting there.

I had arranged for my homebound flight to come through Chicago so that I could rendezvous with Jan. I had bought him a ticket to go from Indiana to Phoenix. We would sit next to each other for the four-hour jaunt to Arizona.

Over the next few days, sweet memories would be generated. Creative planning was involved, along with secrecy, to continue with the unexpected events that were yet to come. Startling folks is one of my specialties, like when I showed up at my niece's graduation party in Indiana wearing a brightly colored jester's hat carrying flowers, acting like I was a delivery person. The party was held in my sister-in-law's garage. My mother looked up and saw me coming and said, "Who's that clown?" Everyone was totally shocked, but my parents were most surprised and happy.

I've been a runner all my life. My mother says it started when I was four-teen months old. Supposedly I never would walk, and they thought something was wrong. But at fourteen months of age, I started running and bypassed walking.

All four of my kids had done some running in their lives either during their school years or as a pastime like me. We all had run organized races at some point, but one of my lifelong dreams was for us to run in the same race on the same day. This special time had come.

The 35th Annual Whiskey Row Run was held in Prescott, Arizona, on May 4, 2013. This race has always been one of my favorites, and I had only missed running the event twice since 1998. Both of these times, I was doing something more physically challenging than running 6.2 miles.

Jan was living in Indiana, and Brock was stationed in Florida. Angie and Drew were both living in Phoenix. I had convinced my gang they needed to run the Whiskey Row with me. Brock was the one in question; getting any leave time from the Navy wasn't so simple. Brock reported to his siblings he couldn't make it. Disappointed, they accepted the news knowing we would still be doing something we had never done, which was to race together.

I had managed to keep the secret squirrel quiet. But, ultimately, Brock and his girlfriend showed up in Prescott on the morning of the race. Oh, how I love surprising people. Watching my kids' eyes widen when Brock and Renaye appeared was indescribable. My heart was happy.

Miraculously every one of my kids stood behind the start line that sunny Saturday morning in the mile-high city of Prescott. Not breaking the tradi-tion, we were accompanied by three other family friends. My daughter's best friend Mindy, Jan and Brock's friend Arron, and Brock's future father-in-law. Every year since I started running Whiskey Row, a new person came along as either a spectator or a runner to Prescott.

Whiskey Row is known to be a challenging run. First, its elevation is 5,400 ft. Secondly, the course is not flat with a few big hills to pull. Although we all started together, this was short-lived once the gun sounded. Being highly competitive, I had a personal goal waiting for me at the finish line. I knew what to expect out of Brock. He was headed for the gold. He was out of my sight within the first couple of minutes. Jan and Drew ran together and got in front of me early. I knew the hills would deter their motivation to some degree. Angie and Mindy were there to have fun and finish. Not saying they weren't going to put up a fight, but these young moms hadn't been able to train as much as the rest of us.

I kept Jan and Drew in my sight. You know I wasn't going to disappoint them yet. I definitely had the advantage over all of them as this was the four-teenth time I'd competed here. Following the second downhill, I picked up my pace and sped past my two sons. A few minutes later and a mile out from the finish, we were competing with each other. Pacing together, we encouraged one another's lungs to burn as we sucked the oxygen-thin air. At this point, we could have been the only three in the whole race, each focusing on leading the other two. I must say I kind of felt a little guilty making my sons suffer. They didn't want to lose to their mom. But I didn't back down or let them win; I had enough in the tank to sprint to the finish. Jan finished ahead of me by a few seconds. Drew had crossed the line behind me. After catching my breath and guesstimating when Angie and Mindy would end, I went back out on the course and ran in with my daughter. Drew wasn't so pleased his mom beat him. A bit later, my good friends, Dave and Tracy, came by to say hello and see how the race went. Dave told Drew, "Your mom is as tough an athlete as they come." Dave and I had spent several years as adventure race teammates, so he knew my capabilities.

It was a grand day. Three of us stood on the podium that day. Brock took second in his age group and was tenth overall. Jan took third in his age group and sixty-first overall. I took gold in my age group—first, with a personal record time of 53:38. I placed sixty-third of the 716 runners. My goal had been met, and my dream had come true. I was proud of my family and overwhelmed with sentiment.

I had contacted Prescott's local paper, *The Courier*, and told them the story of the thirteen previous times I had entered the famous Whiskey Row race. I informed them that all five of us would take the course this year. They asked if they could interview us after the run. Sure enough, our story made the paper a few days later. We even had our photo published, all the runners, along with our four-legged family member, Sierra.

The celebration continued later that evening back in Glendale. We gathered at Drew and Jocelyn's place for a cookout. Brock's girlfriend Renaye and her family also joined the party. These two met in Phoenix before Brock went to boot camp. Renaye is as petite as Brock is tall. Both were enlisted in the Navy, and in fact, this is how they met in the first place.

During the party, these two disappeared, and it wasn't long before they were starting to be missed. "Where'd Brock and Renaye go?"

"Oh, they wanted to go get something," I said, covering for them. The crowd was getting impatient as the food was ready, but we wanted to wait for them. Soon they returned, and dinner was served. Suddenly, Angie gasped in surprise. Approaching Renaye, she grabbed her hand. Renaye had a candy blow pop ring on one hand and a shiny diamond on the other. As Brock had chosen his bride, more celebrating took place that warm Arizona evening.

Renaye was a native Arizonan, born and raised. She had enlisted in the Navy as a corpsman and was currently stationed in Texas. The two made a lovely couple—Brock was nearly a foot and a half taller than his beautiful blonde athletic fiance. Renaye might be short, but her personality made up for it. She is a strong, confident, and tough gal who can hold her own with anyone. I was excited to know she would soon be a part of our family.

It was full-on when I returned to Iraq in late May 2013. The ambulance training was up to *sab'aa* (seven) days a week. Not that I cared that much, it was more of a struggle for the translators than for me. I led them through the material, and they converted it into Arabic. Teaching only occupied half of my day, and after lunch boredom set in.

Angie, Drew, me, Jan, and Brock.
The first and only time we raced together as a family

Brock and Renaye

On the podium, Brock, me and Jan

The Wolf Is Out
of Fresh Meat

Sometimes the moon is all I have.

I arrived on Monday, May 27 and went straight to Camp Iso. I would be crazy to believe this rotation could be half as great as the previous one had been. What would my karma hold for me over the next twenty-eight days?

Vic reminded me of my upcoming blood draw scheduled for the following week. I had been advised I would go down Monday evening at the end of my workday and spend the night. Blood draws were done every six months. This was so you could get an exit visa. All contractors were required to be tested for HIV.

During my first day back to Lion, Lilith dropped in for a surprise visit. We were just finishing up the lesson for the day. I started being probed about a multitude of issues. Lilith eyed the layout of the training room, evaluating every detail. The room was unorganized and messy, which was not my doing. I found it in this condition when I walked in earlier that same morning. I was displeased that my back-to-back had been so disorderly. Unfortunately, I had no time prior to class to rectify the matter. I tried explaining the circumstances to Lilith but could tell she was ignoring me. She was going to hold me accountable no matter what. I could perceive her dissatisfaction. The timing of her stop couldn't have been worse. On the other hand, she seemed to be pleased with the fact that the north field medics were being utilized as instructors. Upon her departure, Lilith validated my visit to HQ for blood tests the following week.

I was in great hopes that I would at least get a quick hello and see the whites of those black eyes I yearned for. But Tane was constantly pushing the question, when are you coming down here? He was going on leave in nine days. Part of me would be glad he was gone so I wouldn't be disconcerted in trying to always get to HQ. But I had no control over making a visit happen, although I spent lots of time daydreaming up schemes.

My ears were so attuned to the sound of the cherished bubble that if I were asleep, it woke me. My head was programmed to the *bluurp*, wake up, Tane is messaging you. Tane was an organizer, and he liked to plan every detail out. But, of course, things hardly ever happen as one thinks they should. The perfect plans, more times than not, never got off the ground.

Nevertheless, his creative wit was entertaining. How could I not be lured into the net? Besides, what else was I doing?

My first week was wretched; insomnia had become an unwelcome companion. My brain desired unconsciousness, and I tried to find the black hole to bury my thoughts. It was unreachable. The monster called anxiety had made its home under my bed and came to pester me when I shut my eyes and turned out the light.

To finish off my frustrating week, I was told my trip to HQ for blood tests on Monday was a no-go. Crap, I'd confirmed with Tane that I was for sure coming, that Lilith had reassured me only a few days ago. But unfortunately, I had been dumb enough to believe I could count on her words. Yes, I knew better, but still.

I was stressed again to have to break the news to Tane. My stomach was sick with dread. It was beyond my control. "Hey baby, bad news."

"What, you're not coming down here on Monday?"

"Yeah, you guessed it."

He couldn't hide his disappointment, but his reply eased my depression. "It's ok. don't worry, things will work out." The way our rotations lined up, it would be at least two and a half months before we'd be in Iraq at the same time again.

When I communicated with Tane, I wanted to remain reticent. The flirting must have made the attraction obvious. I didn't want him to know just how passionate I felt. I was sure if he knew, he would run, and I didn't want to find out if this was true. I wanted him to take the lead; if he wanted more, I would follow. I knew my eyes were an easy read to my heart. All he had to do was look.

I was aroused to full consciousness by my favorite sonance, *bluurp*. It was our farewell chat. Tane was headed out for R & R. Good for him. He had been working up to twenty hours a day and was spent. I was unsure if or when I'd get word from him again. He often just seemed to disappear for days. Part of the mystery was his closed-book life. He denied having a wife or girlfriend on the outside. I trusted this.

Life didn't let up. My inner pressure was only fueled when Doc Angela informed me that Lilith said she was disappointed in me after her stop at Lion the previous Tuesday. Angela also told me that Lilith and Nicky had been doing lots of suspicious talking. Eventually, Ang shared that she knew the Frontier office wanted to talk to me! I was damn sure it wasn't because they intended to give me a raise.

The gym was a great buddy. I needed to be putting miles in anyway. I was signed up to run a multi-day ultra in Ireland during my upcoming leave in June. Running provided me with the best anxiety release. Digging in and pushing my body physically improved my endurance and let the steam out of my head.

Lilith and Angela both dropped in at Lion the following day. If Lilith thought she'd catch me off guard again, she was wrong. My internal informant had exposed the visitation. Ang, being her cheerful self, calmed my mood. Lilith seemed distant today and didn't seem to be herself, and she avoided eye contact. The training room was found to be in tip-top shape. The visit was quick and short-lived, no faults to be found. However, I could sense I was now her target, which wasn't a good feeling. Some species are known to eat their young.

Later the same day, I received an email from the project manager in Mitcheldean requesting to set up a time for a phone conversation. The fear in my chest warned me that things were going south. Negative thinking took over all thoughts. The wolf had run out of fresh meat and prowled for its next prey.

I mulled over how long it would take to find a new job. I could easily work anywhere I chose in the States, but that was not what I desired. Already a goal, I would push to get work in either Australia or New Zealand or look for another international contract. The fact was that this job wasn't going to last forever, and the end was imminent.

Paranoia saturated every cell in my body, and I would very likely never see Tane again. My core felt hollow. Tears would have helped to remove the toxins, but none came. I forced my lungs to inhale oxygen repeatedly until I reclaimed my mind. STOP.

Wait until you know for sure, until you talk with Frontier.

The day of the dreaded phone call came. Frontier informed me that Lilith was not firing me but was banishing me to an even farther location. It was decided that Nicky and I would trade sites, and she would take my place at RSB/Lion. It was agreed that Nicky had more teaching skills than I did; this was Lilith's excuse. I would be transferred to QA (Qarmat Ali) as the medic there. I was less than thrilled, but at least I still had a job and had already spent a few days there last rotation. It would have been fine if I could only take Tane and Ms. Anwar with me. QA was far from the core drama and practically a village to itself.

The plan was that I would move in one week. There were limitless good-byes to exchange. I had allowed myself to like and get to know many people, especially the local people, the Iraqis.

Don't Be Sad

When life is at its darkest, learn to love the moon.
~ Shubh Kain

There were many saddened souls when they heard I was being moved. My Iraqi drivers not only were heavy-hearted but downright concerned. They had had previous issues with my replacement. Feeling disrespected was one of them. If trouble arose, it would be a Westerner's word against an Iraqi's word; equality might be omitted.

Ms. Anwar, my *sadiqa*, I cherished our friendship. We were like any close friends, sharing our deepest secrets. She is the strongest, bravest woman I have ever met. I couldn't have admired her more if she was a world-class athlete or Mother Teresa. I was proud to be her friend, and it would be impossibly hard to give our final farewell, the double cheek kiss—right-right-left-left.

A week later, I did return to HQ for my blood test. I arrived the night before and sheltered in the blue high-rise. It felt too quiet and solitary. Flashbacks of previous stays generated both smiles and sulks. I couldn't help wondering if this was my last visit, as I wouldn't be staying here any longer for crew change.

Lisa, Lee, and Angela had my back. They were supportive and encouraged me to hang in there. Things are constantly changing around here. "Heck, you might be back in a few rotations," Angela exclaimed. They knew I had been stepped on, and they felt my ache.

Ali reminded me, "Be happy. Allah will provide for you if you provide for yourself. Don't be sad."

A week came and went, and I was still living at RSB. The news came that I would stay in Camp Isolation for the rest of this rotation. I would go directly to COB/QA on my next trip back. I was to have my belongings packed and stowed. They would be taken to my new location, where I would rendezvous with my stuff upon my return.

I had not enjoyed my time at RSB. I had wished since the beginning that I could still be living at HQ. I'm a social animal and needed to interact with others whom I could connect with. I was already thousands of miles away from family and friends. Socialization is an essential aspect of our lives. It boosts our sense of well-being and increases happiness and contentment.

In prison, people are placed in solitary confinement to punish them. Ok, I wasn't in prison. I did get out every day, but I did feel like I was being punished. Now I was getting moved even further from my friends. I had befriended Mark, Davy, and Seth, my former drivers, but now they had been removed from the driver's seat and replaced with LNs. My island had become deserted, except for my native friends who spoke a unique language.

I came to Iraq to work. I had a role to fill, which needed to be my priority, and it was. Along the way, I became entangled ardently with not only Tane but also the LNs, the drivers, and even some of my coworkers. A big, mushy heart can get you caught up in the barbed fence—a painful encounter. So I asked myself, is this a strength or a weakness?

I was grateful for my job and the opportunity to be here. However, I still needed to keep myself positive. Living at RSB caused me to go somewhere emotionally I didn't want to be. I could manage notions during the day, but the nights were most often rough.

The gym was my friend. I was training for the longest ultra I had ever run. So having an athletic goal was an excellent incentive to keep me motivated. In the gym, there was a large TV that was loaded with music videos. The same ones played over and over. Pink had some awesome music out during this time. The guys were so infatuated with her and her animalistic sexy videos. As I pounded one foot after the other on the treadmill, my eyes filled with tears as I lipped the sentimental infused words.

On the one hand, the physical exercise was strengthening my body. On the other, the music lyrics were crippling my heart.

I know everyone does it, takes the words as their personal own. I was bound to get burned. Yes, I will survive. Tane, please stop leading me on.

Thank You and Goodbye

The night walked down the sky
with the moon in her hand.
~ Frederic Lawrence Knowles

It was my last few days at Lion. I felt like it was "my" Lion. I had been the first Frontier employee to work here and had built a rapport with the Iraqis, from the office managers, secretaries, IT personnel, and guards to the cleaning staff. It crushed my heart to be leaving my Iraqi *sadiqs* behind. Knowing that I would never see these people again was a terrible feeling. Coming back for a visit was 100% impossible. The amount of sadness can't be described in words. I spent nearly every day with these people over the past twenty-three months. A fair number of these guys and gals spoke little or no English. I had only mastered a handful of Arabic words. I greeted them in the morning with a smile, "*Assalamu alaikum.*" I could thank them, "*Shukran,*" and expressed "*Ma'a as-salaama,*" goodbye, at the end of the day. I learned you needn't have to speak the same languages to communicate friendship and respect.

My aim from the first time I encountered the Iraqi citizens, both those skilled and non-skilled laborers, was to have a harmonious relationship. I hoped they all would realize I was a kind and caring person who was sympathetic to their adversities.

343

I had a particular fondness for one certain lady in the black abaya (cloak). She was one of two local women whose duty was to keep the women's toilet clean. For most of the day, this woman sat in the restroom on a hard-plastic chair, tidying up the squat toilets and sinks after their use. Ninety percent of the time, I was her number one customer. One of the Iraqi doctors told me she had five children at home and no husband. He had been killed in the war.

"*Esme Jo.*" (My name is Jo.)

"*Esme Mariam.*" Mariam was like having a personal maid. I always felt guilty that she cleaned the bathroom every time I left. Having someone sitting in the loo listening to you splatter pee into the porcelain bowl wasn't always the coolest thing. I know Mariam was thankful to have the small wage she received.

I would savor the memories of these unforgettable people, their shy smiles and questioning eyes. I felt like I was letting them down by leaving. Who would continue to share a friendly smile, show gratitude, or even notice them? I had refused to treat them any differently than I did the expats. The fact is the LNs had always been much more appreciative than the foreign nationals ever were.

I needed to protect them. They knew I respected and cared about them. I wanted to prove to them that they had worth, to show we are all equal, that their jobs were necessary, and that I appreciated each of them.

I decided to honor my Iraqi friends with a farewell party. With the help of the new receptionist I had befriended, I accomplished my goal. On one of my last afternoons at Lion, June 20th, I gathered everyone into the oversized conference room. I first went to bring Mariam, the lady in black who attended the lady's WC. I took her by the hand and led her to the large room. When I tried to get her to sit at the beautifully decorated table, she bowed her head as if in shame and turned to leave the room. She didn't understand and thought it was inappropriate that she should sit at the distinguished table. I had to have Dr. Adel explain that she was invited. Finally, her eyes lit up. She blushed and took a seat. I could tell by her eyes that she had never been treated as equal, as a worthy person.

My guests started to arrive and each took a seat. I had to go and seek out the male cleaners, just like I did with Mariam. They too felt they didn't deserve a seat at the table. The girls from the reception had purchased beautifully decorated cakes with detailed flowers on the white frosting, along with dozens of juice boxes I shared with my guests. The two receptionists would not allow me to give them any money for the refreshments. While the treats were handed out, I stood and spoke to my audience. Standing strong and holding back my tears, I thanked them for the warm welcome two years ago, for everything they had done, and for teaching me about their culture, kindness, and friendship. Dr. Adel translated my words. "I will never forget you. You have made my time at Lion a memorable and happy experience." Under my breath, I asked Allah to please never let them forget me.

I received hugs and handshakes as the attendees made their way to the door. Ms. Anwar gave me two elegant, oversized rings, but neither would come close to staying on my fingers. When I tried to give them back, she wouldn't hear it. Finally, Anwar said, "Now we are engaged." She was not expressing a fricatrice meaning, but sisterly love, a forever friendship.

On my last day at Lion, I visited every corner of the compound. It was bittersweet. I was reminiscing, also visually absorbing and encrypting as much as my brain could hold. Deep in my core, I hoped that I would one day get to revisit "My Lion." But I did prepare my heart with the knowledge that this would never happen.

I remember that last day standing on the roof, gazing in all four directions. I wondered where I would be in a year from now. Will I still be communicating with Tane? Will I still be working in Iraq? My happy place had served me well.

I made my way slowly down the steps and back to my office. Our day was finished. I gathered my gear and all my belongings. I shook the LN doctor's hand goodbye and glanced back at the desk where I had sat for hundreds of hours. I walked through the lobby of Lion toward the exit. I wiped the tears as the door closed behind me one last time.

We drove south away from what would now be Nicky and Larry's Lion.

Mariam and Fatima

The going away party I had for my friends at Lion

Anwar giving me two rings

Hole in the Head

*I will never be a morning person, for the
moon and I are much too in love.*
                              ~ Christopher Poindexter

hy did Tane have to be gone this rotation? HET refresher training was held Friday, June 21 at HQ. I was blessed with an overnight in the high-rise, dinner at the DFAC with cohorts, and evening coffee at the shop with Mark and Angela.

This marked the start of my third year working for BP. The past two years had been quite the adventure. I was grateful to have the privilege of working for BP in such an unlikely locale. This ordeal had been more fun, less frightening, plus awe-inspiring. I planned to keep a positive attitude. There have been more good times than bad regardless of Lilith.

The Hostile Environment Training (HET) refresher course was required biennially. This was the short version of the two-day course I had attended in the UK before deploying to Iraq two years ago. The refresher included both lecture and demonstration of having the physical ability to escape from an armored Land Rover. I enjoyed learning about working and traveling in unsafe, challenging, high-risk zones. It's a bit of a thrill to get the chance to experience such a region, especially since I was non-military.

To pass the course, you had to sit in the back seat of the Toyota SUV. When instructed, you escaped through the top of the roof. The twenty-five-pound steel hatch had to be unlatched, shoved open, and then you had to exit through the roof. No problem, unless you don't get the hatch to lock in the open position, and it crashes onto your skull, as it did during my turn. "Whew, that smarted." I finished the maneuver and joined the others waiting their turn. With my fingers, I palpated the throbbing wound on my head, noting a moist three-inch laceration on my scalp. I decided I could wait till we finished to have the wound closed by the doctor. Standing in the hot sun, I started feeling queasy, wishing we would hurry and get on with it. That was until someone pointed to my face and said, "Hey, you have blood running down your cheek." I had thought it was sweat from standing in the sun at 115°. Everyone turned to look at the medic who was bleeding. I excused myself to the restroom and cleaned up my bloody head. I was red-faced about the situation, the medic injuring herself and all.

Luckily, I didn't require sutures. It was just a sore head and something to be occasionally mocked for by my classmates.

Hot in the Pants

There was a reason she was so romantic about the moon. It never asked her questions or begged for answers nor did she have to prove herself to it. It was always just there, breathing, shining, and in ways most humans can't understand: listening.
~ Christopher Poindexter

Only two days to go before my leave, I had withstood the dangerous waves. I had yet to be drowned. "She is tossed by the seas but does not sink."

I found myself back in the gym, mentally and physically preparing for the longest race I had ever run: the Celtic Traverse, a six-day ultra held in Ireland. I was going to be joined by three of my superhero running mates. Originally, Masha and I had decided we would run the 150k while the others had signed up to run the 300k race. Masha said we would make our final decision when we arrived in the UK. It was bound to be a memorable and painful adventure no matter what distance we chose.

On this particular evening, as I was finishing my workout, Liam, one of the security guys, stopped me and asked if I thought I was ready to race. Liam and I had chatted a few times when our paths crossed at the RSB's gym. He was intrigued that I was taking on the ultra challenge, impressed that it was taking place in his home country. He often quizzed me about my training and was captivated to hear about the many past adventures I had completed.

Liam was also a runner, but it was obvious he spent most of his time lifting weights. My eyes liked to survey his chiseled physique. What straight woman doesn't admire a handsome, well-built male? Solid shoulders and biceps are appealing. Gym rats, we all like to think that our hard-earned stature is respected and a motivator to others. I had been caught by his emerald eyes more than once, found guilty of peering in his direction, trying to play innocent. But of course, the blush on my face must have been a dead giveaway.

I replied to his question by saying, "It's tough to train for this kind of an event by only being able to run inside on a treadmill." My goal was to finish the race regardless of the distance we decide to run. Liam continued querying me about my visit to Belfast. He inquired about us possibly meeting up during my travels. I reported that I was unsure of our plans following the race but told him it might work out. Liam said he couldn't wait to hear about the run. He walked me to my cabin so I could hand him my business card with my contact information.

The following evening, I received a Skype message asking if I cared for a gym session. It was my last night in Camp Iso, so I figured I might as well join him. We met at the gym and did more talking than working out. However, we were having a good time, laughing and joking around. Chatting away as we performed a few chest presses, Liam spouted, "Hey, I have some better weights in my room. Let's go grab them." I followed him out the door, wondering what was wrong with the ones we had been using in the gym. As we approached his room, I noted several young Iraqi males were sitting on the steps of their cabins a few doors down, laughing and bubbling in their native tongue. I was relieved that they never looked up or noticed our existence.

Liam unlocked and opened his door ahead of me. I felt a bit unsure of why we left the gym. We seemed to be having a fun time. The bedside lamp dimly lighted Liam's room. I cautiously stepped in behind him. Catching me off guard, Liam quickly turned to face me. He grabbed my left arm and forced me tightly against his chest. Towering over me aggressively, he crushed his lips on mine. My eyes dilated with shock, or was it fear? WOW, I didn't remember asking for this. He held me so close I could sense his lust for me. Was I in trouble here? My mind was confused. His superior body had control over me, at least for a few seconds. Did I want this, or did I not? Was I going to have to fight to remove myself? Had I led him on to think this was OK? No, I was sure I had not.

His embrace held me tight against his masculine chest. With his right hand, he pulled my shirt over my head. Finally, he released me from his lips. I had eight seconds to decide—give in to his want or who knows what. My words of shock included, "You're wearing a ring." Thinking this would alert him, I knew he was a taken man, and I didn't plan to walk across that line.

"Yes, but."

Thinking silently, *Here we go. Of course, there is always a but when adultery conspires.*

Things cooled down, and I stayed to listen to Liam's story of his unsatisfying home life. The life of being a rotator puts strain on relationships on both sides. Everyone ends up with their needs and desires unmet. Wives are left at home to raise the kids, and men miss their women and family. Loneliness is felt by all, a dangerous mix.

Leaving his room, I peered cautiously toward the adolescent LNs. The coast was clear. I stealthily headed back toward my room, stopping to share my emotions with the only one I felt I could tell, my distant friend. As I peered up into the moon's glow, I felt he already knew my thoughts. I felt safe in releasing my reflections. This latest event could not be shared with anyone, period. It was a good thing I was vacating this camp. Liam had an attraction for me. He even wanted to meet up in Belfast.

My concerns about living at this camp had been genuine. I was exiting this place and remained mute, keeping the night's event to myself and the moon only. There was enough drama already. I would probably be the one at fault anyway. Lilith seemed to be hot on my trail as it was. If this were found out, no doubt we both would be given a one-way ticket home.

Visit to the Office

Gonna chill with the moon for a while.

Prior to arriving in Ireland for the race, Frontier asked me to come by the office for some training. In the two years I had worked for FrontierMedex, I had only been to their headquarters once. It was strange to me that you could work for a company and be 100% managed remotely. In addition, I heard several employees had never been to the office.

During this occasion, Frontier had arranged my travel from London Heathrow to Gloucester via bus. Harrison, the driver who had retrieved me two years earlier, again chauffeured me to the village of Ross-on-Wye, dropping me at my hotel, The Kings Head. Interestingly enough, this was a different hotel and location, but it had the same name as the place I stayed on my previous visit to Frontier's office. Confusing really. England has 229 pubs/hotels named The Kings Head.

In the year 1393, during the reign of King Richard II, pubs were first ordered to hang a sign outside to make them easy to find. During that period, most of the population was illiterate, so pubs were identified with a picture. Many names were intended to reflect history or honor whichever king was on the throne.

Ross-on-Wye is a small town that sits along the River Wye, a beautiful, peaceful location. The Kings Head hotel, old and quaint—everything in England is old—was rumored to be haunted. Decorated in warm, rich earth tones and wooden beams, the hotel included a restaurant and a pub. The place had character for sure. No, I didn't experience any hauntings.

I stayed two nights at the King's Head and spent two and a half days at Frontier's office. In my free time, I explored the village of Ross-on-Wye. The most intriguing thing I found was an old cemetery near the river. Coming from the brown Iraqi desert walking around the green tree-lined river was delightful. A light mist of rain started to fall, and a distinct aroma filled my senses. I missed this sweet, earthy smell.

Frontier's staff were accommodating as usual. I spent time with the educator getting checked off on thrombolytics, a clot-busting procedure used when a patient is diagnosed with a stroke or heart attack.

I met with both the project manager and her assistant. The ROO project team wanted to hear how things were going in Iraq. They were aware that I was struggling with being located at RSB. I was asked if I was excited to be moving to QA. Gingerly, I shared my thoughts; I expressed my sorrow for leaving my teaching position at Lion. I was questioned about Dr. Angela's and my concerns relating to the treatment of the LN drivers and their association with my replacement. The drivers were now employees of Frontier, so their contentment needed to be considered. At least one of the guys had threatened to quit if I was relocated. This was how unhappy he was that someone less sensitive would be filling my boots.

"How do you get on with Lilith?" I was asked.

"Well, since you asked," I explained, "in the beginning, everything was great. She was friendly, charming, and supportive of everyone on the medical team. This seemed to last the first year, with the exception of Joc. But as our team started to grow, her attitude and demeanor changed. It was as if she needed someone to pick on. As if she wanted everyone to know she should be feared."

The news I had feared was laid on me. I was informed that Lilith planned to eradicate the medic position at QA. I was stunned, but only for a few minutes, as I knew this wouldn't last forever. "Are you sure?"

"Yes, this is for sure going to happen. The Iraqi doctors will be the medical coverage at Qarmat Ali starting in January. You and Iggy will be out of a job."

I felt a sudden onset of nausea and chest tightness. I know the color must have gone out of my face. I tried to take a deep breath but I felt like I was suffocating. I wanted to cry, to scream, but most of all I felt hatred for the one person who controlled us all. The speaker apologized as she gave me a few minutes to process the news. Totally shocked, I wasn't.

I could hear their own disappointment. I was a good employee and had been an asset to the ROO team. I felt bad for these ladies having to deal with Lilith's manipulative behavior. They worked hard to keep their staff happy, but Lilith was the one who had the authority over all decisions. Frontier's office was required to make Lilith's wishes become a reality or risk losing this precious contract.

Well, now what?

I was told if I was still interested in working for Frontier, I could meet up with Adriene from HR. She was the same lady I had met up with in Las Vegas before starting my international career. So, of course, I wanted to learn what my other options were.

Adriene informed me once I finished the current contract to notify her, and she would start looking for a suitable position. Next, she went over some of the other projects that Frontier was contracted with. The majority were offshore on ships and oil platforms. I wasn't sure I wanted to work offshore, but I said I would consider it and would stay in touch.

I left feeling numb. Honestly, part of me was excited to think about moving on and finding another adventure to pursue. I was being removed from the people I enjoyed hanging out with. I expected Tane to become impatient and lose interest now that I would seldom get to see him. I became anxious thinking about delivering the news. It was out of my control. Unless Nicky or Lance decided to give up their position, I was doomed.

After I had finished my business with Frontier, I decided to spend two nights in the city of Gloucester. I had a few spare days until I needed to meet the girls in Belfast. I had chosen to stay at the fourteenth-century old New Inn Hotel, which featured a medieval courtyard and authentic ale pub among its four bars. This place was spookier than the King's Head and was also known to be ghostly.

This was a great time to explore the area and allowed me to meet up with my ex-colleague Ginge. On my previous trip to England in 2011, I was on such a tight schedule I never got to do any sightseeing. Gloucester's 2000-year-old history makes it an interesting place to wander around. For one thing, it hosts the country's most inland port.

Ginge had been my first ambulance driver on ROO. Gloucester was where Ginge called home. It was a sweet deal as he was available to meet up. We made plans to have dinner together and catch up on our current lives.

Ginge and his ten-year-old son picked me up, and we drove to a cozy and charming restaurant a few kilometers from Gloucester. We reminisced about the days together back in Iraq. I caught Ginge up on the latest gossip and drama, including my hot-off-the-press news regarding my dim future.

The trend for leaving or being ousted from Rumaila was never that of a happy tale. Many people I knew who had left had done so on sour terms. Ginge, like myself, had been a subcontractor and not a direct BP employee. Hardly anyone was a direct BP employee. Ginge left six months after I had arrived. He had a falling out with the contract company that hired him. I liked having Ginge as my ambo driver and was disappointed when he decided to return to England permanently.

Ginge's passion was military antiques. He had established his own online business, selling and buying vintage items. His life now focused on his son and his company.

The following day, Ginge took the afternoon off and drove me to some local sites. I had yet to see a real castle, so our first stop was Sudeley Castle and Gardens. Sitting on 1200 acres of immaculately groomed landscape, the fifteenth-century castle held many tales within her walls. King Henry VIII's sixth and last wife, Catherine Parr, died at the castle soon after she gave birth. Catherine was laid to rest on the property.

After roaming around the castle, we headed off to check out one of the historic Cotswolds villages. Visiting the Cotswolds village of Stow was like stepping back in time. Thatched roofed houses and shops built from ancient limestone reminded me of hobbits' homes. I think it's because these villages are set within the beautiful green rolling hills. The villages are the image of fairy tales.

The blue sky turned gray;, and we found a cheery pub to enjoy a late lunch just before the rain started. With the change in the weather, we voted it was best to drive back toward Gloucester. It had been a lovely time hanging out. I appreciated Ginge taking the time to show me his corner of the world. It was very much like my first few days on ROO when he had been so kind to usher me around. I hoped that our paths would cross again. Having good friends definitely increases the value of life.

Runners, Take Your Mark

Born to chase the moonlight.

T
wo days later, I was in yet another new country. I arrived in Belfast half a day ahead of the girls. I checked into our hotel, then headed out to explore the streets of Northern Ireland's capital city. Before coming to Ireland, I looked up interesting and must-see places. I felt my duty was to dig into the country's absorbing past. A branch of my family tree is rooted in this country.

Who's not intrigued with the story of the *RMS Titanic*? It was built in Belfast in the late 1800s. Since I had time to burn, I visited the *Titanic's* impressive museum. The museum's historical collection was eye-opening yet sobering, from the *Titanic's* beginning to its tragic sinking.

In more recent times, from 1968–1998, Belfast and Northern Ireland were faced with violent times. This period of conflict was known as The Troubles. The IRA (Irish Republican Army) and the Catholic paramilitary groups wanted to end the British rule over Northern Ireland, but the Protestant paramilitary wanted it to remain. I remember as a young adult seeing reports of the hostility on the news. During this time, Belfast was considered one of the most dangerous cities in the world. More than 3,600 people were killed and thousands injured as bombings, kidnappings, and murder spread through the area. Who would have thought that thirty-plus years later I would find myself walking the once-deadly streets?

Belfast is known for the hundreds of artistically designed wall murals scattered throughout the city. These creative drawings display a symbology of Ireland's intense history. Many represent the sectarian argument, and others commemorate historical events or people who have died. Viewing them in person is a very surreal experience. This made the hair on my neck stand up.

I was glad I had a bit of time to do some sightseeing, but I was in Ireland to compete in the Celtic Challenge with my teammates.

I was thrilled to see my dearest friends. Hugs were shared all around. We had once again enlisted ourselves to face physical pain by running an inhuman number of miles over six days. Who in their right mind would abuse themselves with such craziness?

Melissa, Louise, Masha, and me, that's who. Actually, the girls had started this. They had been doing insane physical events long before I had. I met Melissa while I was in Tanzania to climb Mount Kilimanjaro. I knew we would be friends for life within ten minutes of meeting her.

In 2007 I traveled to Africa to climb Kili and do a wilderness medical conference. On the first day there, during the introductions, I met Melissa. I learned she was a paramedic, a runner, and loved to travel. I instantly picked up on her kind, caring, and magnetic personality. Melissa doesn't know a stranger, and if you are one, that's bound to change. Because I was traveling alone to Africa, Melissa took me under her wing. It was through Melissa I became acquainted with the other ladies.

This was going to be the third distance running affair I had joined them on. I lived through the other two—the Coastal Challenge in 2009, 230 km over six days, and the Namibia Challenge in 2010, running 220 km in five days. So, let's go for broke. This time we were to run 300 km over six days through Ireland's lush countryside.

These types of races are known as staged races. Each day of the race, we had to cover a certain distance. The races are held in remote places, generally in harsh environments. This race course, although my longest, was environmentally the friendliest and safest one yet. We wouldn't be facing 120°-plus temperatures, deadly critters, or dozens of miles of remoteness like in our past events.

Masha and I originally had planned to run the shorter of the two distances offered. Both of us had suffered greatly with the past two races—infected feet in Costa Rica, severe tendonitis, dehydration, and blisters in Africa. Being the tough women we are, DNF (did not finish) isn't acceptable. The only way that would happen was if our life was at stake or if there was a chance of permanently damaging ourselves. The pain we endured was temporary. Blisters, tendons, and muscles would heal. Conquering these feats empowered us. Be it a blessing or a curse, our human drive led us, not only to the starting line but to the finish line, even if on our hands and knees. Such enriching experiences cannot be understood by those who have never personally taken on an overpowering physical act.

From Belfast, all the race participants traveled together on a bus to Newcastle, a small community south of Belfast for the start of the race. The accommodations for the Celtic Traverse were very upscale compared to the other places we had traveled to run. The Slieve Donard Resort, a Victorian hotel, was our lodging for the first two nights. The impressive resort sits on six acres at the edge of the Irish coast and at the foot of the Mountains of Mourne. This was a nice treat coming from the dry desert of Iraq. I thought that maybe I would change my mind and not race but just hang out in the luxurious lodge for the next two days while my friends tore it up on the local forest trails.

On race day one, I stood at the start line with thirty-some runners. My stomach was in knots, and my blood pumped with anxiety. My goal was to do my best and finish the 300 km race. Today's leg would be 34 km long. As with each race I've ever run, you don't know how the race will go. You might often finish stronger than you had hoped, but sometimes it's just not your day.

The gun went off, and we took off across the lawn of the hotel and headed down the road until we came to the marked trail indicating for us to turn and climb into the forest. I had started near the back of the pack, knowing I was one of the less-talented runners. I didn't want to slow the serious contenders. But I was holding some deep emotional blues and needed to release some steam. A mile into the run, my spirit was flooded with power, my engine shifted into overdrive, and I started passing everyone in front of me. When I passed Melissa and Louise, they cheered me on, "Go Sha Naa Naa!" The name was given to me by one of my past running mates.

My daughter, Angie, had two days before asked if I had heard about the Granite Mountain Hotshot crew. I replied, "No." She continued to tell me that nineteen wildland firefighters had perished when a fire overran them outside of Yarnell, Arizona. I had in the past worked as a medic on wildfires with these guys. I didn't know any of the guys personally but had been in the same fire camp. My heart hurt for these brave men and the families they left behind. The only way I could grieve was to run, and run I did.

I caught up with the guy leading the pack and stayed with him the entire day. We ran up and down trails in the forest, striding along sheep paths in the meadows. Then it started to rain and turned cold and blustery. Our shoes were wet and muddy and we slipped and slid in the water-soaked fields, stopping only to find our rain jackets and pull out a power bar, eating as we continued onward. The last two miles before the finish line, Bill excused himself and picked up his pace, and only then did I run alone. At the end of day one, I was in second place. Who knew I truly had it in me? My saddened heart had released energy from within.

That night I had my first ever Guinness, which was dark, thick, and flavorful. You can't go to Ireland and not experience the local brew. I was told in this country that if you're going to tap a Guinness as a bartender, you must go to a course on how to do it properly. After a hearty meal, it was off to get some sleep.

On day two, our course was more urban and shorter distance-wise. We had to meander through the streets of Newcastle, trying not to get lost. The race director had given us a poorly designed map and also told us he had marked the turns on the street with chalk. Now that I was in the running, I felt compelled to have another successful day. Keeping in view of the leader was a great goal to have. More competitors had decided to chase the leader, so a group of us was hanging together. This can be good or bad, and it definitely motivates you to work harder but increases the pressure. We found ourselves at the curve in the road that was supposedly marked. Not seeing any marking, we continued. A few miles later, we decided we must be going in the wrong direction. The more we debated, the more confused we were, some turned around, and some of us kept going. Well, needless to say, we ran farther than we needed, and finally, the race director came and turned us around. The marking at the curve had been unseen as vehicles were hiding it from our view. We finished two hours after the rest of the group. So much for being at the top.

On the same day, we moved by bus to the next area where days three and four would take place, Wicklow. Our lodging here was in a lovely little hostel in a rural area. This was my first stay in this type of lodging—dormitory-style rooms lined with bunk beds and shared bathrooms. It was like having an adult slumber party.

Day three's race began on the doorstep of the most famous pub in Ireland, Johnnie Fox's. Driving out to the start seemed to take forever, over an hour's ride. Masha and I looked at each other and agreed it would be a long day of running.

Masha and I had decided to pair up and run together today. I actually prefer having someone to run with during this type of race. It's pretty easy to take a wrong turn and find yourself lost, plus the pain would no doubt set in soon, and having someone to keep you moving helps. I was over the need to push hard and was ready to slow down and enjoy some company. The Wicklow countryside was gorgeous. We cruised along forest and emerald green moorlands, passing along Glendalough Valley, traveling on a high ridge overlooking the deep blue Glendalough Lake.

Tiredness and stiff muscles were setting in as the third day was over, and twenty-five more miles were out of the way. Words were not needed; body language said it all. Everyone's slow movements were proof our bodies were all rebelling. The next three days were going to hurt. The actual test was about to begin.

Day four, more of the same terrain, our path followed along much of the well-known Wicklow Way walking trail. We trod over farmland and through the rolling Irish countryside. The weather was perfect. Masha and I ambled along, occasionally meeting up with fellow racers. We both appreciated the endurance our adventure racing past had instilled in us. I was grateful to have Masha as my running mate. She was a superb athlete, and I learned a lot from her. She bestowed on me the power of digging in and pushing through pain, keeping me moving, and we did.

For the last two days, we again moved locations to the southern peninsula of Ireland, to the town of Seems. The longest days were going to be the final two. We would be running the Ring of Kerry, a scenic circular route in County Kerry. Many Hollywood movies have been filmed here: *Excalibur, Harry Potter and the Half-Blood Prince, Star Wars: The Force Awakens*, and one of the weirdest films I've ever seen, *The Lobster*. Check it out!

These last couple of days were brutal. First, the course was nearly all on pavement, which was terrible for muscles and joints that have been pushing the limit. Second, I was starting to experience a lot of pain in my right Achilles tendon, so I was moving with a limp. I was unsure if I was going to be able to finish. I'm sure I consumed enough ibuprofen and tramadol to shut down my liver.

On day six, Masha had decided to push hard. She and her husband, Rob, had to catch an evening flight, so if she was going to finish, Masha couldn't lollygag around. On the other hand, I spent the day hobbling along the 56 km or 35 miles. The pain increased with every mile. I knew I wouldn't die from the injury but wondered how long it would take to heal. I was yet to return home from an ultra-race unbroken.

I was near the back of the pack. I'd gone from second to nearly last place. I kept telling myself, "Don't stop now. Keep on, keep on, running. Keep on, keep on, running," to the tune of *Finding Nemo*'s "Just Keep Swimming." I was wobbling and not running, feeling frustrated that my heart wanted to run, but my body was saying STOP. We compromised.

That last afternoon seemed to go on forever. Every once in a while, one of the race crew guys (an Irish dude) would ride up on a scooter and ask how I was doing. He tried encouragingly saying, "You're doing great!"

"No, no, I'm not!"

"You only have 3 km to go." An hour would pass, and he'd come by, "You're almost there." I knew damn well I wasn't almost there. This went on for probably four or five hours. I kept thinking to myself, *These Irish guys are full of it. Little leprechaun liars, they are.*

The sun was sinking low in the sky. I was so over being in pain and struggling to put one foot in front of the other. My legs had turned to rubber hours ago. I reminded myself that it was pretty impressive that I was still moving and would soon be finished. I was going to conquer this challenge, another notch in my holster, medal for my collection, and a more profound admiration for my physical and mental power.

It's so much more than reaching the finish. It's the steps between. Hours and hours of thinking, focusing on putting the physical labor aside and letting your mind distract you.

Believing in myself and forcing bravery to override the fear—this was the recipe for my success. Digging deeper into my soul than I ever knew I could. I learned more about who I was and what I was made of. When you have incurred hours and days of physical anguish, only to ask your body to please keep digging, reassuring your nous that this is possible. I surprised myself. I had incredible endurance and more strength and inner power than I knew was possible.

I made it to the finish line. Relief flooded my soul. It wasn't an impressive sprint to the line, which I usually prided myself on, but I was able to get there under my own resourcefulness. Three hundred kilometers was a respectable distance. Although every bit of my body was hurting, I wondered in the back of my mind, *Ok, what's next?*

Me, Louise, and Masha ready for day one of the 300 km Celtic Challenge

Jim in the front, left to right- Masha, me, Louise, lady X, Melissa

Wicklow Way, where day three and four was run

Last day of the Celtic Challenge, only 54 km's today

Louise, me, Melissa and Jim

David Kennedy and I in Northern Ireland post-race

Grinning like a Cheshire Cat

In my defense, the moon was full
and I was left unsupervised.

~ *Word Porn*

My past two years in Iraq had been an adventure. Initially arriving in July of 2011, I had been a part of many changes, met dozens of people, and increased my lifelong friendship list. Iraq had been a fantastic experience. No matter how I exited, my nostalgia episode could not be stolen. I had expanded as both a professional and a person. I would never be the same.

The Celtic Transverse was done and dusted. After a brief seven-day trip to Arizona, I found myself sitting in business class, heading back to the Middle East. I never got tired of flying in luxury, even after more than twenty-six international flights coming and going across the globe. However, the snooty businessmen's attitudes had not changed. I still received the evil eye while standing in the queue to board my flight. However, my confidence had increased enough that I would wrinkle my brow, put on my most serious face, and glare right back at them. I didn't care if this seemed disrespectful. How dare you try to intimidate me?

The worst part was how tiring traveling made me and dealing with days of jet lag on both sides. I arrived exhausted, whether I had slept or not. There seemed to be no getting around it.

Another new adventure was starting. I had accepted my latest remote camp assignment. Qarmet Ali had to be better than RSB. For one thing, there were fewer people, and the camp managers were very laid-back. We could basically do whatever we wanted, and no one cared. Although I was now more than one hour from the main camp, I was only about three miles from Basra International Airport. We were virtually on the other side of the tarmac. I had already spent a few days at the COB during my last rotation at work, so I knew what to expect.

Tane and I frequently chatted during my leave, so he was aware of my arrival back into the country. As a matter of fact, Tane was scheduled to do some work at QA himself and had hoped he could delay it until I arrived, but it didn't sound promising.

Friday, July 20, I was back in Iraq. I was taken to the Dust Bowl along with the other incoming expats. Instead of moving into the regular armored van for the transit to ROO, I was met by the Qarmat Ali security team. A bit sad, thinking I wasn't going to get to see the ROO gang or my Lion friends, I wondered if I would ever see HQ again. Yet, I wouldn't miss Lilith's regular visits. I knew she did come to QA occasionally but not too often.

The trip from the Dust Bowl to my new living quarters at COB was on dirt roads. It was nice to see a different area of the Iraqi desert. Along our route was the Qanat Masnab al Am canal, where locals could be seen fishing, swimming, or just hanging out. Herds of water buffalo waded in the marshlands near the channel. Iraqi children stood by the road waving at the white people as we drove by.

Upon arriving at the Contingency Operating Base or COB, I was led to my room, where I found the belongings I had prepacked before exiting RSB twenty-eight days ago. It was midday, and the workers had just returned from their duties at the worksite. It was currently Ramadan, and with the extreme heat this time of year, the crew was only working half days.

I was instructed to head over to the daily prayers meeting as soon as I put my gear in the room. So I opened the door and stepped into the dark, damp space. It had to be thirty degrees cooler than the sweltering outside heat. I was exhausted and just wanted to shower and relax, but that would need to wait.

Walking the short distance to the meeting, I thought I must be exhausted and hallucinating. The back of that guy in front of me looked just like Tane. But it couldn't be; he said he had already been to QA and had finished his duties here. Tane had said he could not stall the job, and his boss had sent him the week before I arrived.

Wishful thinking, I guess. I found a seat near the door and looked around the room. Holy shit, it was Tane. He sat across the room from me, grinning like a Cheshire Cat. My face lit up, and I smiled back; I nearly peed myself. The small group numbered no more than ten, so much different than the 150 at HQ's meetings.

I was welcomed and introduced to the group. At the same time, I tried not to be obvious. My eyes kept wanting to drift in Tane's direction. We all sat in a small circle listening to the speaker. During the short fifteen-minute security brief, my demure grin repeatedly found my secret inamorato's shy smirk gazing back in my direction. I perceived that at least two people in the room weren't focusing on the intelligence report being delivered. Instead, I was intoxicated with excitement. How had this come to be? In an instant, my emotional agony vanished for the time being. If only this could last, but nothing great ever does.

I was asked by Tyler, the camp manager, to stay after the briefing so he could spend some time filling me in on the daily routine. Our team would leave COB at 0700 after breakfast and then travel to the QA water plant. Here I would sit in a small office that I alone would occupy. The return times to the COB might vary but would generally be around 1230, in time for lunch. The rest of our day was free time, and I was to keep my company phone with me in case I was needed. Tyler shared that the complex had a small shop and a gym. I was surprised at how much freedom we had. This was a good deal for me as I was only working five hours a day, whereas, before this move, I easily put in twelve-to-thirteen-hour days. Plus, I was making eighty bucks more per day.

COB was a large, deserted military settlement, with a maze of abandoned buildings and structures everywhere, including warfare equipment left to rust. It was a captivating place, like being on a movie set or in a museum after dark.

I returned to my quarters and started unpacking. The afternoon passed into evening. I fell asleep waiting for Tane to reach out and message me, but he never did. I figured he knew I must be tired and didn't want to bother me. Still, I was disappointed.

The following day I was surprised by the number of people in the canteen. I learned that another security group (Grada World) was staying in the same complex, and we all shared the dining room. I only saw Tane in passing until we returned from our workday. He was an extremely patient man and liked to be a tease. He knew that I would be anxious to see and talk with him. So when he didn't contact me, I decided to make a move. I followed him out of the dining hall at lunch. "Hey, how are you? When did you get here?"

"Hi, how was your trip?"

We chatted for a few minutes and decided to message each other later.

At first, we were cautious about being seen hanging out together. Soon we realized no one gave a crap, nor were they paying any attention. Tane was only going to be here for a few short days. He then would be replaced by someone else from ROO. I didn't want to think about how lonely it would be when he left or when I would ever get to see him again. Plus, there were no plans for me to go to ROO during this rotation, and who knew if I would be allowed to go during my subsequent rotations. My mind wandered with thoughts of the future. I had been informed that my time on this project was ending. Actually, I might only have two or maybe three rotations left. I was already starting to feel stressed. I hoped Frontier would find me a new contract, and I would be able to create a new voyage. Getting work stateside was no problem, but that wasn't what I wanted to do. I was still currently connected with the Abrazo registry program. Maybe, I would try and get my Australian nursing license. Working as a rotator was addicting, and I didn't want to give up this lifestyle. I wanted to travel more and see new and exotic places. New Zealand was on the top of my list.

Tane started feeling at ease hanging out with me. He didn't shy away from being seen by the rest of the camp members. For one thing, none of the administrative personnel lived here. We started going to dinner together, but this was always after everyone else had eaten. We often were the only two in the dining room. I thought this was quite romantic, and the canteen workers always gave us special treatment.

Tane had been here during wartime when a few hundred troops lived on base. He walked me around the campus, telling stories of what it was like just a few years ago. He showed me where his quarters were, recalling various incidents of attacks on the base. Tane was my personal curator, and this was as close as I would probably ever get to an actual combat scene. As I listened and asked questions, I hoped these memories wouldn't stir up old wounds.

A week had passed, and I couldn't believe my good fortune. Tane was still here. He was having some of his belongings from ROO sent over. He was getting extended. I'm sure it was because he had asked if he could stay longer as his work wasn't complete here. He had only brought a couple of sets of clothes as he was initially supposed to have been at COB for four days. Guess he was enjoying being away from the hustle and bustle of ROO.

I treasured the time we had been given here at COB. Every added day was a gift. My soul felt rapt for every minute collected. Some afternoons we spent watching TV or chatting, but some days we didn't meet up at all. This was Tane's decision and not mine. I gave him space when he wanted it.

As far as I could tell, our friendship was only superficial to Tane. We never discussed our future in-depth. We were having fun for now, and we both knew the future was highly unpredictable for either of us. Tane wasn't a man of many words, especially when talking about feelings. I could read his eyes when he discussed accounts of his past.

Tane's room was directly behind mine. While I lay in bed at night, it was a warm and reassuring feeling knowing he was just on the other side of "that wall." It was too funny; we would flirt via Skype, messaging back and forth when we were only fifteen feet apart. Then, some evenings I would be invited to come over for a visit. Although I cherished our time together, I also was a bit on edge. I feared someone would come searching for the medic, and she wouldn't be in her room. Looking back now, I know that the laid-back camp managers wouldn't have cared as long as they could contact me on my phone.

On one particular day, we never left COB as protesters were near the QA site. The local Iraqis were demanding that ROO give them jobs. The QA Project had hired Turkish contractors and very few Iraqis to provide the staffing to rebuild the water facility. The local villagers wanted a share of the *masarri*, money. Residents had their fill of the lack of essential services, suffering from chronic power outages and lack of clean and safe water, not to mention the corrupt government. The LNs saw it as unfair that billions of oil dollars were not benefiting their citizens.

Ms. Anwar talked about the power outage issues in this province. Some days they would only have four hours of electricity. Imagine fasting all day, it's 50°C or 122°F, and you have no air con available. You can't depend on your refrigerator to cool food, so you will need to go daily in the heat to the market to feed your family. Your drinking water is known to be polluted, while your corrupt government lines its own pockets and forgets about its people.

The QA Project was currently moving slowly and behind schedule. The first step was to build a new fly camp to house the expats and security personnel now living at COB. Once the fly camp was finished, the focus would move on to remodeling the worn-out water plant. Being in brand-new quarters would have its benefits, but I liked living at the museum and getting to ride around the countryside, going and coming. Once we moved to the new QA camp, we would have no reason to travel anywhere. This would, of course, be safer by not exposing us to a dangerous confrontation outside the walls.

Although my workdays were short, I did have a list of duties to complete besides tending to patients. I was responsible for hourly temperature checks with a WetBulb Globe Temperature (WBGT) device. Using the WBGT, I measured the heat stress in direct sunlight. I recorded the results on a whiteboard outside my office so everyone could come by and get an update.

A few yards away from the new fly camp was an outdated Southern Oil Company (SOC) medical clinic staffed by assistant doctors. This small clinic served the general area. The clinic was additionally staffed with ambulance drivers, who piloted an antique, bare-to-the-bones ambulance. ROO's plan was in place to take over and manage this clinic. The QA medics, Iggy and I, would be a big part of this operation. First, it would be our responsibility to build a trusting rapport with the clinic personnel. The second step, provide them with training; third, get them to call us for backup emergency medical support.

I can tell you this was easier said than done. Lilith wanted us to go over to the clinic daily. She had little patience for all the roadblocks we dealt with along the way. This facility had been there for decades, and so had most of the staff. Then, along came these Western-trained medics who want to push their ways on them. I'm sure these men had more years of working in their profession than Iggy and myself combined.

When I first started visiting the clinic, I was warmly welcomed, and the guys were proud to show me their operation. However, I was astonished at how minimally equipped the place was. They had no basic life support equipment, no BMV (bag valve mask), AED, airway equipment, suction, and any advanced drugs they did have were expired. Their glucose testing meter was broken. They didn't even have a proper examination stretcher, nor was there any linen available. How oh how did they do it?

On the one hand, it was exciting to think of being able to provide the new and necessary equipment. But getting these health care workers to skill up and accept these changes would be like catching a feather in a windstorm. On the other hand, I liked the idea of this challenge. I felt if the right people were involved, it could be accomplished. These men needed to be shown respect and praised each step of the way.

Prior to my arrival, Iggy had given the SOC clinic a blood pressure machine, BVM, and some other airway equipment. Unfortunately, they had no intentions of using it. Note my message to the on-duty Ops lead.

Sunday, 28 July 2013

It was a good morning. I visited the SOC clinic today. The ambulance and drivers were there, and the Assist Doc. I inquired about how they handled emergencies and was told they bring them to the clinic and, if needed, transport them to the hospital via ambulance. I asked about the phone and was shown a mobile phone. When asked about calling in an emergency, he pointed to the SCCC number on the wall. I was told that the mobile would work to call this number. I reminded him that I'm here during the day to assist with any emergency or other needs he might have. I asked about where the equipment was that was sent to them, and he pointed to a cabinet in the resus room. I only saw one O_2 mask hanging on the O_2 tank. The BP machine was there, and he said it was good. But I'm not sure if this is one we gave them. I don't think so. He did ask for a glucometer as theirs is not working.

I didn't spend too much time as he had a few patients to see, and my translator had trouble understanding me.

I tried to convey that we are here to improve things for them and give them more training and equipment. I also told them they are doing a good job with the equipment they have to work with.

I don't think they understand why we keep showing up. I was told that the other Doctor (Ignatius) had already been there.

Cheers

Jo

Interestingly, a week later, I found the missing airway items locked in a cabinet. I trained the staff there that day on how to use the equipment. I left feeling unconfident. I believed that showing them on actual patients would be more promising.

The days were moving too quickly. I wanted this era never to terminate. Life was GOOD.

One hot afternoon, Tane and I decided to check out the little shop located on the base. I wondered how this place stayed open with so few people around. The shop was larger than the mall at ROO HQ. It was stocked with the same junk, sweets, cigarettes, toiletries, soda, random clothing, etc. Tane bought us a soft drink and himself a hat. He asked me repeatedly if I wanted anything else. There was nothing intriguing to want. Honestly, I wished there had been a nice souvenir, but there wasn't.

Tane surprised me one afternoon when I returned to the COB for lunch. I walked into the canteen and collected my food from the buffet. I looked around, hunting for a seat, and saw Tane pointing to a chair across from him. After I took my seat, he pushed a plate in front of me and said, "Here. I made this for you." He had created an impressive hamburger sandwich for me.

"Hey, thanks. I just made my plate." I was instructed that I should eat my plate of food and the sandwich he designed for me. You see, Tane's passion was cooking and creating appealing meals. Today he had built a mile-high burger loaded with items from the salad bar. I remember it was scrumptious. It was the first time I had a sandwich with beets on it.

Master Chef Tane often talked about the food he created and showed off the pictures of the final products. For example, he was working on a sandwich he named Juicy Lucy. It was amusing that he recorded his ideas on paper so that he could assemble the artwork when he went on leave.

The time had come. It was Tane's last night, and we had had nearly two weeks of hanging out. It had been twelve days. Tane knew my time working on ROO would expire in the coming months. He was looking to change jobs and spent part of his downtime during the past two weeks upgrading his CV.

At 2300 I received instructions to rendezvous with my companion. To avoid being observed by the smoking crowd that sat outside at night, I squeezed myself along the small space at the end of my accommodation block and the T-walls. I was instructed not to knock but just come in, which I did.

I slowly opened the door to find Tane watching TV in the dark. I kicked my shoes off and sat next to him.

We reminisced about the wet, rainy night eight months ago and about the Christmas Eve phenomenon. One bold phone call, and now here we were. We laughed, snuggled, kissed, and shared the deepest intimate passion I had ever experienced.

Look into my eyes; can't you see all the way to my heart? You must sense the craving I have for you. I kept begging him mentally, hoping that he would be able to decipher my feelings. But unfortunately I was too timid to verbalize my inner thoughts.

The following morning he disappeared as quietly as he had mysteriously appeared. That evening I ate my meal in solitude. I missed my mate, yet I was smiling inside.

I received a Skype message saying he had arrived safe and sound. The moon kept me company as I took a stroll in the darkness. I stopped and stared at the crescent face shining down on me. I envisioned that just maybe someone out there was looking skyward and thinking of me too. Who knows? Life is so full of wonderments.

Masnab al AM canal near COB

Inside the Contingency Operating Base (COB)

COB, the last US base to close in December 2011

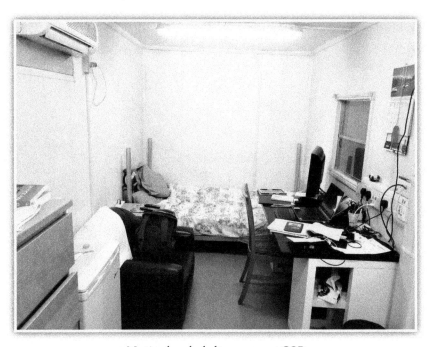

My tiny bomb shelter - room at COB

Forever Is a Lie

*I feel a little like the moon who took possession
of you for a moment and then returned
your soul to you. You should not love me.
One ought not to love the moon. If you
come too near me, I will hurt you.*
                        ~ Anaïs Nin, Delta of Venus

I had fifteen days left on this hitch, then I would be off
again. I had numerous things that should have kept my
mind distracted.

I was anticipating my upcoming trip to Alaska. My
holiday was comprised of a backpacking excursion with
five of my mates. I had masterminded this Alaska venture,
having invested more than a year of planning. However, final
details needed to be set so that the five of us could complete our
goal: to conquer the famous Chilkoot Trail.

I quickly realized my work at QA was going to become a bit challenging
as there seemed to be resistance from the local SOC clinic staff, where I was
to teach. I would need to use my charm to build trust with this bunch. I had
easily connected with the Iraqis at Lion and became well thought of there. I
hoped, with time, I could do the same here. I was concerned that management
would start getting too impatient and pushing too hard, too quickly. On top
of this, every twenty-eight days, I would step out, and Iggy would step in. He
seemed to be a laid-back, easygoing guy and, as far as I could tell, got on OK
with the LNs.

With this said, I knew I needed to keep my head down and focus on making Lilith happy and keep her at bay. But, unfortunately, being out of sight didn't mean she wasn't keeping score.

With all of this preoccupying me, I needed to give some attention to planning my next career move. Frontier had discussed the possibilities of other positions that they might have in the future. It seemed most of their contracts were offshore jobs on ships or oil rigs. I wasn't totally sure if I would like being so confined for weeks at a time but hadn't crossed it off as a possibility.

It had been only *ywmaan ma* (one day) since my *Habibi* had vanished to ROO. I still wondered if the whole thing was just an illusion of wishfulness. I recently started creating utopian scenarios in my head. These were fictional fantasies where I controlled the outcomes. It was my mind's way of satisfying the part of my being that wasn't dealing well with certain manipulators. The professional description of such wandering thoughts is known as maladaptive daydreaming. This condition is when you have intense daydreaming events triggered by real-life situations. The bad thing is it can disrupt daily life.

Different symptoms can exist in this rewarding mental activity, although most people only experience a few. My phantasms were highly vivid and involved characters I knew as real people; they were story-like. I always had an overwhelming desire for the dream to continue. A secondary symptom is difficulty sleeping at night, and I also suffered this.

Luckily, I didn't talk or whisper while dreaming, nor did it stop me from completing my daily tasks.

Our team returned to COB after a typical day spent at QA. I couldn't wait to get out of the oversized coveralls we all were required to wear while working at the active construction site. My body was soaked with sweat. The summer sun worked long, hard hours. She seemed to be attempting to break a heat record as our daily highs climbed to the 50°C mark and beyond. However, once the sun set, the evenings were quite perfect for sitting outdoors or going for a walk.

I was excited to go to prayers, as I was expecting another of my comrades. Mark was coming to camp to finish up Tane's work, so having another familiar face around for a few days would be good.

I headed out the door toward the meeting room, hoping Mark had arrived. Seeing old friends would surely ease the loneliness. I fell in line behind others walking toward the gathering. The guy ahead of me sure reminded me of—No, stop it. But, wait, can it really be?

Sure enough, Mark hadn't been sent. Tane had returned. I would have been on the ground if I were one to faint. Thank God I'm not. Tane somehow managed to be allowed to return. I was told he had convinced his manager to let him finish the project. Tane was a wise and likable guy. I'm sure he had little trouble convincing the boss to let him come back. Ha-ha, he sure had thrown me a curveball.

Tane must have been proud of himself for successfully surprising the heck out of me. Unlike when I arrived two weeks ago, this time I sat across the room, making eyes and gestures at my smirking mate. I had no clue how long he would be hanging around, but it would be fun no matter what.

We started up where we left off, sharing dinner and spending time hanging out. One afternoon I even convinced Tane to join me in the gym. This was an impressive accomplishment as I never knew him to set foot in the place.

I realized the more time we were together, the harder it would be for me to say *mae alsalama*. Tane knew I was soon going to vanish from this assignment. I wondered if he would forget about me and move on or would we continue to stay in touch? *Inshallah*, I hoped so.

August 8, 2013, Tane's last day at QA was here. Tomorrow he would walk out the gate and head back to ROO. There would be no more surprise visits. Tane had completed his task.

We had made plans to share the evening after the moonrise. I was to stealth my way over to his place. He would never come to my place as he was nervous someone would come knocking on my door. Sometimes he could be bashful and a bit shy. He didn't like being out of his comfort zone. On the other hand, I enjoyed the adventure and liked being somewhat risky.

We had an amazing time, laughing and teasing. We chatted about how fortunate it had been to have had nineteen days of this amatory affair in the same camp without the restrictions of peering eyes or suspicious minds. Allah must have listened when my Iraqi friends said they would pray for me.

Tane left on his white stallion riding off into the sunset, like the ending of a great movie. Nothing lasts forever. Forever is a lie. All we have is what's in between hello and goodbye.

North to Alaska

Love is like the moon: now full, now dark.
~ Polish Proverb

I touched down in Phoenix on Sunday the eighteenth, and four days later I was back at Sky Harbor Airport heading north to Fairbanks. Chris and I met at the airport and flew together from Arizona. Upon arriving in Fairbanks, we were to meet up with my longtime friend Debbie who had come ahead of us from Minneapolis. Excitement was in the air as we headed to the rental car desk.

Debbie was my first friend when I moved to Phoenix in 1996. She was also a nurse on ward 4C when I started working at Boswell, which is how we met. Deb was a girl after my own heart, a runner, hiker, and an outdoor enthusiast. I credit her for getting me back into running shoes.

Chris and I, well Chris was my ex. Ex-husband, that is. We had met through a singles group and hit it off right away. Chris was one of the organization's hike leaders. We dated for a short time and got married. Unfortunately, our marriage only lasted a year before I panicked and pulled the plug. There was some missing information disclosed after we were hitched, which I worried would affect my financial future.

Chris and I were able to remain friends and forgive each other. We put the past behind us and went on with our lives separately. We were still getting together once in a while to hike or have a beer.

Debbie and I had thought about returning to Alaska to trek the Chilkoot Trail while we visited Skagway during an Alaskan cruise in 2010. However, the thirty-three-mile-long trek required permits which needed to be obtained months in advance. The passes allowed us to stay at the various campsites along the way. It was a one-way hike that started at the beginning of the famous Klondike Gold Rush trail. The trailhead was located ten miles outside the town of Skagway, near the village of Dye. We would catch the train to return to Skagway, concluding the experience.

My adventurer racing friends Yvonne and Brad decided to come along. They would join us in Skagway, bringing our clan to a total of five. A perfect number. Unfortunately, they were limited on time and couldn't hang with Debbie, Chris, and me for more exploration of this great northern land.

The three of us stacked our gear into the back of the rented SUV and headed east to the small village of Tok, Alaska. My brother Thad and his family called Tok home. Thad had moved to Alaska when he was a senior in high school. My brother had also been gifted with adventurous blood from our lineage.

We had arranged to crash at Thad's gorgeous cabin for a few nights, allowing me to catch up with my younger sibling and his family. It had been a few years since we had sat down and chewed the fat as the saying goes.

This was Chris's first trip to Alaska and Debbie's third, all of which had been with me. It was great fun sharing this experience with the two of them. Alaska is a unique land.

Alaska is big, remote, and on the wild side. It's the land of mountains, wildlife, and wilderness, an insanely beautiful topography. I had been fortunate to have traveled here four times before this trip.

My parents visited here for the first time in 1978 and fell in love with this countryside. A year later, they returned, purchased a property, and became partners in a trading post in the village of Tok. There are few places better than Alaska if you love hunting, fishing, and the great outdoors, which my parents did.

Moose stand along the roadside, grazing like cattle. The occasional bear can be seen crossing the road. If you're fortunate, you might even spot a wolf. During the summer months, the sun never really sets, so it is light out for twenty-two hours of the day, making sleeping difficult. It is remote enough that there are stretches where you can drive more than two hundred miles without finding a fuel stop.

On our four-hour drive to Tok, I reminded Chris and Debbie to keep their eyes peeled for wildlife. Sure enough, off the road, Chris spotted a cow moose and her calf grazing in the tall grass. It was our first wildlife spotting, but it wouldn't be our last.

I was excited to see my northern family; it had been too long since our last visit. However, it was a short catch-up as the three of us needed to keep moving. We were 500 miles from our destination. The plan was to return to Tok and spend a few more days hanging with my family after we finished our tramp.

The next morning we set off for a long day's drive filled with incredible scenery and more wildlife sightings. A grizzly bear was detected on the side of a mountain, and Chris barely missed running over a lynx as she crossed the road. We stopped along a river to stretch our legs and snap a few pictures. Debbie pointed to the sky. "Hey guys, look at those eagles."

It was impressive to see dozens of golden eagles searching for their dinner.

Two days later, we arrived in Skagway, where we met up with the Poes, collected our hiking permits, and watched the mandatory bear awareness video. We spent the evening sharing a meal and chatting like a group of juveniles. Stories were exchanged throughout our small gang.

I designed the trek to be broken up over five days and four nights. We each would be toting a hefty backpack loaded with the essential gear needed to complete the thirty-three-mile hike safely. This was a remote trail where there would be nowhere to purchase a sandwich or a can of fuel. Our gear list: tent, sleeping bag, water filter, stove, food, clothing, rain and cold weather gear, plus any extras we were willing to carry.

There were nine campgrounds scattered along the walk. Hikers must decide which campsites they want to stay at when applying for permits. Starting out in Alaska, USA, we would be crossing over into Canada on the trail. This required us to have a valid passport on us.

I first became intrigued with the Chilkoot and Klondike trail after seeing the 1991 movie *White Fang*, a story based on the Jack London novel. The main character, Jack, heads off to find his deceased father's mining claim in the Yukon. Of course, Jack starts his adventure in Skagway, following the Chilkoot Trail into the Canadian province.

The history of the area is remarkable and fascinating. The discovery of gold in the Yukon in 1896 got the attention of thousands of people all around the world. It was the beginning of the Gold Rush Stampede, 1897-1899. The migration of an estimated 100,000 prospectors attempted to make their way to Dawson City, a 600 mile/966 km march over rugged terrain in hopes of striking it rich. These miners were required to bring a year's worth of supplies. With this knowledge in our heads, carrying five days of supplies would surely be a simple task for our fit troop.

Gear checked and packs loaded, off we went down the trail through the forest toward our first campground at Canyon City, 7.7 mi./12.5 km up the trail. It was not a lengthy nor strenuous day of hiking. I had planned our trip to allow us to take our time and enjoy our outing the best we could. The walk to our campsite was enchanting and primarily flat through a vibrant boreal forest ecosystem, surrounded by alder, white-barked birch, fragrant pine, and large cottonwoods. The path brought us to a large beaver pond which we crossed over on a raised boardwalk. Our eyes scanned the water until someone spotted one of the critters gliding silently through the reeds.

Arriving at camp, Debbie and I chose a level area to build our nylon house. Within ten minutes, our housing was set up—the tent erected, sleeping pads inflated, complete with sleeping bags and pillows, "Ta-da."

Next assignment, dinner. Camp food isn't always so wonderful, but when lightweight and with plenty of carbs it can fill you up. After dinner, we sat around chatting. I had picked up some flavored cigars in Dubai to share with Debbie. We had a tradition that we smoked a foo foo cigar whenever we girls got together. You know, the petite girly ones, with flavors like vanilla, cherry, or Kahlua. Neither of us was a cigarette smoker, and it was our time to be a bit silly and naughty. We conned Yvonne into having one with us. It was so fun laughing and being kookie. Deb and I loved to let our hair down. We have been known to embarrass our families on more than one occasion. I'm pretty sure I've never laughed harder than when I spent time with my crackpot friend.

On day two, with our houses on our backs, we were off for another few hours on the trail. As we continued through the temperate rainforest, the path started to climb. Sheep Camp was our destination for the day. This campground is the last one on the trail before climbing up to the summit and crossing into Canada.

Back in the day, during the Gold Rush, Sheep Camp was a bustling, mile-long town supporting saloons, hotels, restaurants, and even an aerial tram. For the 100,000 prospectors traveling the Chilkoot Trail, the journey was treacherous and required immeasurable physical and mental fortitude.

On the third day of our tramp, we clawed our way toward the summit, walking up the infamous Golden Stairs, passing by the rusty old scales that were used to weigh the gold-seekers required one ton of supplies. The Chilkoot is known as the longest outdoor museum. Strewn along the route are gravesites, abandoned towns, and lost personal items, a reminder of the history that went before us.

We left the tree line behind as we made our way up the 3000 ft. ascent. It started to spit rain and a mist of thick fog settled in around us. With every step up, the temperature seemed to drop another degree. I guided the team as our trail turned into crawling over wet boulders of gray granite. The path was marked with orange flags every few hundred feet to keep hikers from getting off-trail. The flags soon started to disappear in the fog. Chilled and wet with heavy packs, we slowly made our way toward the Canadian border and the top of the mountain. I was literally on hands and knees a few yards ahead of Chris, Debbie, and a dozen other hikers, when I put my hand on a good-sized rock to pull myself up. The two-foot-in diameter stone pulled loose and started to slide downward.

I grabbed the rock, trying to hold it in place as I felt myself being pulled backward toward the scree and rocks below me. A feeling of panic overtook me. Chris and the others were in direct line with the rock I was attempting to brace into the hillside. I was standing on loose and slippery stones. If I lost control of this large piece of granite, it would tumble down the mountain. It was highly likely someone below would take the impact. I screamed to Chris to hurry and help me as I couldn't find a way to secure the stone. Between the weight of the boulder and my fifty-pound pack, I was being pulled backward. I was terrified I would be flipped off the steep wall of rock. I tried to warn the others below me, but no one paid any attention. Finally, Chris made his way up to me, and we moved the deadly fragment into a safe zone together. I was pissed that no one seemed to realize how dangerous this could have been.

Finally, on top and much relieved that the most challenging part was behind us, I was exhausted and freezing. Disappointed that the fog hadn't lifted, we remained in a cloud, which blocked the scenic views of the two countries from high on top. I was miserably cold. After snapping a quick picture of the blurry scenery, I didn't feel like hanging around. Leaving the others at the summit marker, I set off to find the warming hut a half-mile down the trail. There was nowhere to sit when I arrived as it was full of gleeful noisy Germans. Forcing my way in, I stood in the corner of the small shack until Chris and Deb showed up. Once my hands had stopped throbbing, we headed north, where the trail descended further into the Yukon Territory. The sun found its way through and started to vaporize the misty gray fog, allowing us to see more than the ten-foot distance we had been swallowed up by for the past four hours. Shortly, we came to a steep icy glacier that we had to cross before continuing on the well-trodden path. I must have fallen half a dozen times while crossing the icefield. Debbie had to help me to my feet each time I tumbled. My legs were weak and shaky from climbing up the Golden Stairs and boulder field. Unable to regain my balance while sporting my heavy pack, I had to unstrap the bag and leave it on the ground next to Debbie, who kept it from sliding down the ice without me. With my hiking poles in hand, I would slowly push myself from a kneeling position to a standing position balancing on the wet ice sloping downhill. Steadying myself, I cautiously lifted my bag back in place. Taking a deep breath, I stepped slowly forward. Boom, down I went. Replay. Eventually, I made it across the glacier, happy to be standing on a stable dirt path.

From here, the hike to our campsite was gorgeous. We trod through a valley with snow-capped mountains and subalpine terrain dotted with turquoise blue lakes. The sun shining in full force warmed us to the point of being hot, compelling us to peel off our jackets and gloves. The scenery surrounding us is what postcards are made from. Far from civilization, deep in the wilderness, I was still unable to forget the woes of Iraq. Thoughts of my recent rapture and wonderment of where my future was headed slushed around in my brain.

Night #3 found us setting up at Happy Camp, and we were. Debbie and I took to the cascading river to bathe in the frigid water. It's a tricky process to wash your hair while living on the trail. I have adapted the procedure to find a perfectly sized, semi-flat rock at the river's edge, one on which I can lay on my back and dip my hair into the rushing river. Using environmentally friendly soap or baby shampoo, I lather up and rinse—a refreshing way to bathe.

I remember our group sitting in the camp that evening, looking out over the landscape, hoping to spy a bear across the river. It was part of the adventure, knowing we were deep in grizzly territory. We watched the bear safety video at the visitor center and learned how to behave while spending time in their domain. Trampers often saw bears on the Chilkoot Trail. We needed to stay alert.

It's all good until you're lying in your tent in the dark and listening intently or when you can't wait for the sun to come up before you need to pee. Unzipping the tent fly and crawling out into the night to relieve yourself is unnerving when you're in bear country.

All backpackers needed to use the bear boxes at each campground to store their food as bears have a great sense of smell. Everything had to be put away, including canned goods, drinks, soaps, cosmetics, toiletries, trash, sunscreen, bug repellant, and even fuel. Instructions were given never to leave your food scraps behind, and they had to be packed out.

By noon on day five, we arrived at Bennett Lake, the trail's end and where we jumped the train back to Skagway. After a celebration meal and a beer, we said our goodbyes and parted ways. Brad and Yvonne were heading home to Arizona. Chris, Debbie, and I had more exploring to do. First, we were off to check out Dawson City. We had experienced Skagway, the jumping-off point for many of the Klondike prospectors. Now we would explore the town that had been the center of the Gold Rush.

On August 16, 1896, three Yukon "Sourdoughs," George Carmack, Dawson Charlie, and Skookum Jim, found gold at Rabbit Creek. Word of the discovery spread like wildfire. Rumors had it that shiny nuggets could be found in the local creeks. This sounded like an easy solution to the world suffering from a recession.

Most of these gold-seekers left with little knowledge of what they were up against. The 600-mile trip involved treacherous routes and uncharted landscapes in reaching Dawson City. On their arrival, many met disappointment, discovering the best claims had already been chosen. However, others did find their fortunes. Between 1896–1899, $29 million in gold had been recovered. Dawson City's population topped 40,000 by 1898 at the peak of the migration.

Modern-day Dawson City is a bit of a tourist site. The now-small town with a colorful history is lined with interesting places to check out, such as museums, Gold Rush tours, a dance hall, shops, and plenty of bars and restaurants. It's home to the world-famous Sourtoe Cocktail, which features a REAL dehydrated toe and alcohol. Look it up sometime.

This remote town could keep you busy for a week, but we only had one afternoon and a night to spare. Regrettably I wasn't able to join the Sourtoe Club, as that particular bar was closed when we were there. Maybe next time I get to Dawson City.

Up early, we caught the George Black ferry across the Yukon River. Our next objective was to drive the Top of the World Highway. Sixty-five miles of winding, narrow, washboard-gravel road connected Dawson City to Chicken, Alaska. Ignoring the rental car agreement, this was one of three roads I wasn't supposed to drive on.

My dad had talked about how beautiful the drive was, so it was one of the must-dos on my list. The highway stays on top of the mountain range, giving you a 360-degree view of the spectacular landscape.

We couldn't miss a stop off in Chicken, Alaska for lunch. The remote community of seven residents has a restaurant and gift shop, and the toilets are a three-stall outhouse. If you're scratching your head as to why it was named Chicken, when the town was established in the 1800s, the gold miners couldn't spell Ptarmigan, which is a ground fowl about the size of a common chicken. Following our brief stopover, we returned to Thad's place in Tok.

I felt somewhat guilty that I wasn't getting to spend much time with my distant sibling. I had moved Thad to Alaska in the summer of 1984. He was seventeen years old and had decided to finish high school in Tok. That trip is a chapter in itself. Since then, we have spent little time together.

Thad is six years younger than I am. Our age difference was enough that we had never been playmates or very close as kids. However, Thad follows in our dad's footsteps in several ways. He not only loves hunting and fishing but is highly talented at it. Much like Dad, Thad can fix any piece of equipment and has inherited superb carpentry skills. He had built his current house and wisely installed in-floor heating.

Thad married Sara in 1989 and now had three kids of his own. At the time of my visit, Thad was running his own logging business. I had invited him and his family to join us on the Chilkoot trip. Being the workaholic that he is, he declined the offer. As the saying goes, time and money often stand in the way for all of us.

Two days and nights were all the time we had to devote to my younger brother and his family. It's most enjoyable to catch up with loved ones, reflecting on a time gone by and enlightening each other on our current doings. So, with hugs shared among everyone, with goodbyes said, off the three amigos went, headed for Fairbanks so Debbie could catch her evening flight back to the Twin Cities.

Then there were two. Chris and I still had two and a half days left in Alaska. We debated going to Denali National Park or heading north up the ice road to Cold Foot. I had been to Denali three times before, so the decision was made to head north.

The 414-mile-long road heads north from Fairbanks. The Dalton Highway, also known as the North Slope Haul Road, leads to Prudhoe Bay near the Arctic Ocean. Initially, the road was built as a supply road to support the Trans-Alaska Pipeline in 1974.

We decided that there was only time to go as far as the village of Coldfoot, 250 miles up the road. We would drive up, spend the night and return to Fairbanks to fly home. The Dalton Highway was another one of the three forbidden roads per the rental car agency.

I was elated to be en route to latitude 66° 33'. Not even my dad had driven up as far as the Arctic Circle or Coldfoot, which is essentially a truck stop and the only place between Prudhoe Bay and Fairbanks to have any service, which in and of itself is minimal. A fuel station, restaurant, visitor center, and limited accommodations aren't cheap. Located at the edge of the Brooks Mountain Range, the village got its name when mining prospectors in 1900 got cold feet walking up the nearby Middle Fork Koyukuk River. In 1902 Coldfoot had two roadhouses, seven saloons, a post office, and a gambling hall; by 2010, the population was ten. The *Ice Road Truckers* reality show has often featured Coldfoot on TV.

We found the gravel Dalton Highway in much better condition than had been forecast. In addition, the terrain north of Fairbanks was much different than we had experienced to this point—an open treeless prairie until we approached the rugged Brooks Mountain Range.

It was awe-inspiring to have the opportunity to be this far north in the world, above the Arctic Circle. On the other hand, Coldfoot was pretty dull. A muddy pothole-infested gravel parking lot with a simple truck-stop-style restaurant and simple sleeping quarters. I remember it being quite cold up there and snowing. Being the doofus I am, I had to get Chris to take a picture of me holding my bare foot on the signpost saying Welcome to Coldfoot, Alaska.

It was time to fly south, back to Phoenix, where we were met with temperatures in the triple digits. It's incredible how far you can travel in twenty-four hours.

My time off this trip was crammed full. My wings were on fire. I arrived back in Arizona on Friday morning and flew out thirty hours later. This time I was taking my daughter Angela and my eight-month-old grandson to Indiana for a short three-day visit.

My parents would be delighted to see us, and my dad would want to hear all the details of the Alaskan trip. At this time in his life, he lived vicariously through his children and grandkids. With ill health upon him, he was limited to rides to the cancer doctor and short drives around the local countryside. He loved checking out how everyone's crops were doing. His heart longed for the days when he sat in the tractor seat, laying the seeds into the soil and then having the satisfaction of reaping the harvest when the crisp fall days came.

Our time together was inestimable. I was fortunate to have a great-paying job where I could afford to travel and make these frequent jaunts to visit my Indiana family. Dad quizzed me with a hundred questions. He was fascinated with the details of the Chilkoot tramp and about my trip up the Haul Road. How far north did you get? Was there any caribou? What was the condition of the road? We talked for hours.

Baby Christopher was a hit. Everyone came by to see the newest member of the family. His aunts, uncles, cousins, and his great-grandparents displayed their love for the baby boy. Angie caught up with her cousins, who were her best friends at one time.

Angie and I were sad to be heading away so soon. But time can't be controlled, and we had places we needed to be. Angie had to get back to her teaching job, and I had less than twenty-four hours to, yet again, be on another jet heading east. It was always emotional, a ripping, painful feeling when I gave my pop a tight hug and peck on his cheek as I made my exit. He would always repeat, "I love ya, kid," and "Thanks for coming." Both of us were trying to avoid wet eyes. Thanks for coming! Heck, I'm the one to be thankful for having amazing parents who have always been there for me.

Alaskan moose

My Alaska family, Ellie, Thad, Becka and Sara

Debbie welcoming us to Whitehorse

Golden eagle

Chilkoot trailhead, Brad, Yvonne, me, Chris, Debbie

Along the Chilkoot trail, artifacts from the gold rush era can be found

Brad and Yvonne chilling out at Happy Camp

Bennet Lake on the Chilkoot trail

Dalton Hwy has been featured on the Ice Road Truckers TV series

Latitude 66 33, the Arctic Circle

800-mile-long Trans Alaska pipeline

Antigun Pass on the Dalton Hwy, the highest pass in Alaska

One muddy rental car after driving 2400 miles

I Just Fired a Bullet

She was like the moon. Part of her was always hidden.

September 11 is a perfect day to fly unless you're superstitious after the 9/11 attacks of 2001. I am not, so no problem. I was ready to go back to work after having an incredible leave. Tane and I Skyped several times, keeping up with each other's activities during my time off. I was looking forward to returning to work but held little hope of getting to ROO or seeing any of my buddies.

The flight was grand as always with no hiccups. Hours in the air brought a time to relax and enjoy being pampered by the flight crew. I had flown so many times that I started to recognize some of the flight attendants. Once I was on board with my glass of bubbles in hand, I would search the entertainment screen, deciding what movies to watch for the next fifteen hours. I loved flying now that I was sitting in business class. It was a relief once I was seated; I felt at peace. I always fell asleep while the jet was taxiing down the runway and lifting into the sky.

Iggy and I had a few hours back at the COB to discuss our situation. Lilith determined that Iggy and I would be replaced with LN doctors in January. Iggy informed me that the security managers for QA weren't very happy with this idea. The two of us discussed several other problems that this change created, many of which were safety-related.

Iggy headed out on his leave, and I was left to deal with the topic. I would take a hard look at our list of concerns and planned to discuss them with the camp managers.

The newly constructed fly camp was ready five days after arriving back in Iraq. We packed up and moved out of the ex-army barracks at COB and into the brand-new accommodations at Qarmat Ali. It was fantastic to have everything new, including a clinic that I, again, was to set up and organize. The worst part was there wasn't any gym yet. Although I missed it as a way to de-stress, I can tell you there was plenty to deal with.

On our last night at COB, a small group of us went on a walkabout of the base. We were sad to be leaving this historic place. We tried to imagine how the site must have been only a couple of years earlier. We explored the graveyard of vehicles that had been forsaken; some were noted to have bullet holes, a reminder of the destruction that wars bring. We snapped photos of ourselves standing atop the broken remains. Then, with the sun setting, we photographed our last memory. The graffitied wall behind us read "We Like It Loud" in large print. A message left from others that had been here before us. It was anyone's guess what significance the message had.

Besides managing the regular daily workload, I was now asked to detail the concerns regarding the expat medics being replaced by the local national physicians. It seemed ludicrous to be replaced by the same people I had helped train. However, our goal was to get their medical skills up to meet the level of Western values.

At the same time, I was trying to maintain my emotional composure. Thoughts of Tane weighed heavy in my heart. I was terrified it would be months before we would reconnect. Would this even be possible? Would he lose interest? All I knew was I was willing to do whatever I needed to make it happen. Tane kept reassuring me, "Babe, it will be OK." Communication was difficult at times, as the Wi-Fi was shit. Whenever we tried to Skype, our connection would get dropped over and over until we would be forced to give up.

Sleep seemed to be impossible. Along with the typical time switch, I had so much going through my brain that it refused to pause. I was engrossed in outlining my future, fighting to try and save my current job or prolong the end. Part of me was excited about the new possibilities, a subconscious safeguard to buffer the grim destiny. Where would I be a year from now? I was addicted to the rotational work lifestyle—a few weeks of work followed by a few weeks of free time. My goals included getting to travel more. I liked the idea of living in a different country for a year or two. Maybe I would try to get a nursing license in Australia and spend some time there. One thing was for sure—I would never earn the income I did now.

As planned, I sat down with the security supervisor and discussed the issues of concern. The expats working and now living at QA's fly camp were uneasy with the idea that their medical care would soon be placed in the hands of the LN Doctors once Iggy and I were removed. The plan was that the doctor would be working and staying at the SOC clinic a few hundred yards away from the main fly camp. This didn't make sense. If Lilith felt they were qualified enough to provide medical care to the expats, why weren't they considered trustworthy enough to live in the same camp? I felt this was disrespectful to the doctors. They were good guys.

The second issue that was put on the table was that the Iraqi docs were not experienced prehospital providers. This meant they hadn't spent any time dealing with accidents and situations outside the clinic (scene calls). The QA water projects' premises were found to have so many hazards that the chances of an incident happening seemed very possible. Walking around the old water plant, I was amazed at the threats it held. If this was in a Western country, where job site safety matters, 90% of the place would be draped in yellow hazard tape. I wondered how a well-trained, fit medic would manage a rescue from one of a dozen enclosed spaces, let alone an unprepared stout person. Allah, please watch over these poor workers.

It is noteworthy that Stan, Lilith, and Frontier's Ops lead knew about these conditions. I discussed the situation in detail with Stan, as he was the industrial hygienist. His hands were tied as a higher power chose to look the other way.

The camp managers asked if I would please write my findings up so they could have something on record. I was terrified and said I would think about it. I first wanted to discuss the matter with my coworkers back at ROO. They all agreed that keeping the ALS medics in place was the safest thing, but no one would verbally stand against Lilith. They feared her control and power, even willing to let the safety of employees be overlooked. Angela warned me against getting involved. My heart told me this was wrong. No one should have to be afraid of doing the right thing. Look at how many lives were affected by past events where large corporations looked the other way.

There was a reason why I received extra hazard pay, $80 per day, since being relocated to QA. One evening I was lying in bed when the security siren sounded. I thought at first it was just another safety drill, where we practiced running to the main building that provided us with hardcover from potential incoming ballistic missiles. But on this particular evening, we were taking cover for real. It was reported that there was gunfire coming from our front gate. We sheltered for an hour until it was all clear.

What if someone had been injured and the medical provider was stuck over at the SOC clinic? Then what? Just a perfect example of why that scenario wasn't going to work. A few days later, we again had an incident where shots were fired into the air from a nearby village, and bullets were dropping outside the wall of our camp—forcing us again to seek hardcover protection. The locals liked to fire off their rifles during celebrations. This wasn't a hostile event toward the Westerners, just a group of Iraqis expressing themselves.

It didn't take me long to make my decision. Besides, I had been heavily backed and also reassured that the information I was to produce wouldn't be given to Lilith. So I informed the QA managers that I would be sent to the guillotine without a fair trial if the conspirator laid her eyes on it.

The actual letter I wrote:

September 19, 2013

As one of the Qarmat Ali ALS medics, I believe it is my responsibility to bring the following concerns to your attention. First, I would like to state that I have discussed these concerns with my BTB, Ignatius, and several of the FrontierMEDEX team.

It has been proposed that an LN doctor will replace the ALS medic here at the QA as of January 1, 2014. I have been informed that an LN doctor will be moving into the QA South Oil Company (SOC) clinic as the primary medical provider. The current plan is that the LN Doctors will stay there and work a 24-hour shift, then switch duties with another on-coming doctor. The SOC clinic is to be soon remodeled and supported by BP. The LN doctor will become the primary care provider for all the QA staff, including all expats. Personnel seeking medical attention will need to go to the SOC clinic.

We have also been informed that we are losing our armored ambulance. The plan is that the ALS medic from RSB camp will provide emergency backup and evacuation assistance as needed.

There are several other things to keep in mind about QA and the fly camp. First, security is being taken extremely seriously here. There is an increased risk of living off the COB inside the fly camp. We are currently doing daily lockdown drills. The risks are real here!

Qarmat Ali work site is overflowing with hazards. Chemicals, electrical, falls, unstable buildings, faulty equipment, pipes under pressure, the list goes on and on.

With the above items in mind, let's look at some concerning issues.

First, if the primary medical provider is outside the fly camp wall and staying at the SOC clinic, there will be NO advanced medical provider available if the fly camp is attacked. It would be unsafe for him to attempt to get into the fly camp.

If an expat needs to evacuate to ROO, no immediate armored ambulance will be available. The MERP standard is to have required care in less than 60 minutes. I understand that the LN doctor should be available in most cases, but what if he is transporting an LN patient to Basra. What happens when there are multiple patients? What if there was a vehicle crash close to QA involving expats?

If the situation arises that the QA fly camp needs to evacuate back to the COB, there would be no ALS medical person available. I have been informed that the LN doctor wouldn't be allowed to enter the COB.

It is not uncommon once or twice a week for roadblocks to take place close to QA. This could delay or prevent the armored ambulance from being able to access the QA site. In addition, the LN Doctors may also have issues trying to come to work at QA when roadblock activity is going on.

The LN Doctors aren't currently trauma certified, and they have little prehospital experience. This means that if

*there was an accident on the QA site, an expat, or an LN,
the doctor responding might not be competent to deal with
these overwhelming situations. They need to have hands-on
experience and not just classroom training.*

*The LN Doctors recently achieved their E-ACLS
(Advanced Cardiac Life Support). The E- means they did an
online course. This is not up to Western medicine standards.
This means if you ask anyone on the medical team if they feel
the LNs are competent in Advanced Cardiac care, the answer
would probably be no.*

*Nowhere else on the ROO are the LN Doctors providing
sole care to expats. The QA expats have verbalized their concerns about the medical changes coming to the QA. This sets
a negative Safety Culture for this site.*

*Please understand that I respect the LN Doctors. They are
working hard toward improving their standard of care. They
do a good job; it's been great working and educating them.
However, they need more training and experience in certain
areas. I think they could eventually be prepared to take on this
role with further training.*

*The QA Project is one of ROO's top focuses now. As a
result, there will be an increasing number of personnel living
and working here. Unfortunately, this will also increase the
risks of injuries, illness, and other medical needs for both the
QA and SOC clinics.*

Sincerely,
Jonea Mounsey
QA Medic

I was a pistol, and I just fired a bullet. There was a cloud of smoke rolling
out of the barrel. Would I be arrested? No doubt. I bravely handed the document over to the QA manager. These were my feelings.

The information was the facts as Iggy and I saw it. It was not only our
job to give medical attention to the sick or injured but to point out risks and
educate everyone on the importance of safety. For example, does a guardian
protect the child from pulling the boiling pot onto themselves?

BP boasted that safety was the Rumaila Operating Organization's number one priority! Maybe the HS overseer felt it was easier to ignore the concerns at the remote camp of QA. It made one particular person look good, having had the Western-skilled medical team train the local physicians and then replacing the expats with the Iraqi physicians. This was BP's long-term goal throughout the field. They possessed the bold idea that one day the management of this ginormous reserve would be handed back over to the Iraqis. Off the record, most oil field personnel felt this was inconceivable. Regarding the QA medics, some higher power refused to be proven wrong and could sway the top dogs into seeing things her way.

Feeling like I might have braided my own noose, I sought to distract myself by flirting with Tane. The time we had spent together last rotation seemed to make Tane more enticing. Now that the internet had improved, we communicated more regularly. He was verbally making it known that he had feelings for me. We didn't know when or where, but we would hook up somewhere on the outside one day. Unfortunately, I was not going to be given a chance to come to headquarters this rotation. The wondrous hours we shared a month ago were now but a mirage, a never-to-be-lost souvenir of our souls.

My stature felt as though it was constructed of butter. If I weren't punctilious, I would lose my form and become a puddle of salty liquid soaking into the sand. I must stand stiff as if I was built of marble. Resilience baby, don't let the inner fear surface.

I couldn't let the enemy know my weakness. Instead, the light of the moon caressed my mood. I understood no matter my fate, I would endure.

If things were to play out as they should have, I should not have had to sweat it. Tyler, the security manager, had promised to protect me. He would take the concerns up the chain of command but wouldn't disclose where the information came from. Instead, he was going to use the list as evidence to prove removing the expat medics was a poorly thought-out scheme.

But hold on, as you may have guessed, this was not how it ended. Cal, the current Ops lead at ROO, knew I had written the letter as I had discussed the issue with all of my coworkers, hoping to earn their support. Cal got nervous and, without confiding with me, decided to go to Lilith, alerting her!

I was devastated. I can tell you I felt ambushed—nothing like being wounded by friendly fire. Cal was fearful for himself. I presume he thought if Lilith found out he was keeping this cannon in the closet, he would be thrown under the bus.

I have always wondered what would have happened if all the Frontier employees had stood together and at least let us democratically discuss the issues. But, no, there was a dictator on the throne. One day she would fall as they all do, but not soon enough.

Cal did at least call me and let me know I had been handed over to the firing squad. Cal had only been working in Iraq for a short time. He and I never really spent time getting to know each other since his arrival. I could only presume he would believe me when I told him that Qarmat Ali's management was going to keep the letter confidential. What was done was done. Now I just had to wait for the hammer to come down.

A few days later, I received word that Lilith and Cal were coming for a visit. Of course, they were. They would also be discussing it with Tyler. I was prepared for the worst and expected nothing less.

The others who I had known to stand their ground against the autocrat were no longer employed on ROO. So my only question was, would I last until December or not? Would I be allowed to finish this contract by completing my last scheduled rotation? It seemed silly to hire someone new for one month of work.

Cal had said the only way I might survive this was if I would write a letter stating all of the concerns were **my** ideas. This would protect everyone who had agreed, including Iggy, Cal, and the other Frontier team members. This would be the same as falsely pleading guilty to a crime you know you will be convicted of, then hoping you will get a shorter sentence. It is sad when you realize who does and doesn't have your back.

Lilith and Cal showed up as scheduled. I found it interesting that the mighty Lilith couldn't look me in the eyes when talking to me. Her behavior seemed off, and she appeared to be uncomfortable and distracted. Lilith verbalized in so many words she didn't give a damn about the issues of concern. I was told it was a done deal, and she was the winner. The conversation implied how dare I go around her and not include her directly. I explained that my concerns were safety-related, and I had been instructed to record my findings. I was told this was her and Stan's job, and I needed to keep my nose out of it. Lilith didn't say she was firing me; I got the impression she didn't intend to. Instead, she told me to focus on managing the QA hospital and training the SOC clinic staff. The topic was closed, done, and dusted. Her demeanor spoke it all. I could tell she knew that I knew she was wrong. I could see right through her.

Although on the outside, it may have looked as if I lost, I knew in my soul I had scored. I did not back away from doing the right thing. As Tyler told me, I did my job. I was sick and tired of watching my workmates either be axed or turn into craven puppets. No one wanted to lose their jobs, and some were willing to kiss arse to keep them.

Standing on a war relic

Some like it loud, our farewell photo at COB

New fly camp at QA

QA water plant, one of the many hazards

Barrier wall at QA fly camp

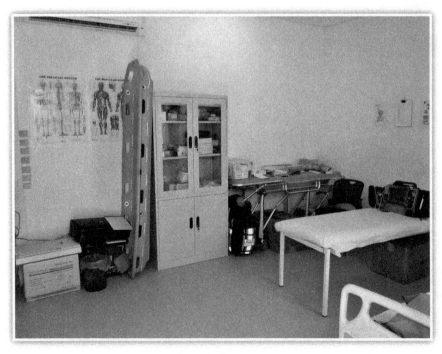

The new clinic at QA

Abyad

My heart beats differently when the moon is full.

British Petroleum has an excellent reputation for participating in humanitarian efforts worldwide. Often, they focus on the communities near their worksites. Iraq was no different.

The Rumaila project used the profits from two coffee shops located on the main camp as a way to support the local people. These funds were spent on purchasing school items for the Al Khora village near the Qarmat Ali water plant. Al Khora was only two klicks from our new fly camp.

When I heard that Tyler and the assistant GM were going to be delivering the school supplies, I inquired if I might be allowed to join them. He was happy for me to come along. I was elated that I was being permitted to travel into the local village. After more than two years of working in Iraq, I had only been to the edge of Al Sekak village near Lion. I had always hoped to get a chance to actually see more of Iraq. I was keen to learn more about how the local people lived.

Specific oil field staff were occasionally allowed to go into Barsa for meetings, and some even had the opportunity to travel to various villages around the oil field. I had always envied them.

Visiting the schools was enlightening. The classrooms within the stone buildings were simple. Desks lined both sides of the small pale green room. Students sat with two and three pupils at each desk designed for one. The floor was uneven from the broken concrete and mix of stone. The windows were cracked and in poor condition.

We had come to deliver a collection of school supplies to the children. The students were instructed to line up to receive their gift packs. Their eyes expressed gratitude as their teachers reminded them to convey a verbal *shukran* or thank you.

At first, the kids were very bashful and hid behind their timorous smiles. I assisted with handing each child a packet. Soon they wanted to approach me and touch my white skin. I love the thought that they had never felt the skin of an *abyad* person. One little girl took my hand and held on to me until the teacher made her let go. I asked the kids if they had any questions for me. "Why is your skin like that?" I could tell the teacher was embarrassed, but I reassured her I didn't mind the question. How else were they going to know the answer? One little girl told me I was *jamila* (beautiful). I repeated back to her *jamila* as I pointed to her, reassuring her she was also *jamila*. She blushed and hid behind her teacher.

The children were in grades one through four. The school's curriculum was similar to that of a Western school, math, science, writing, and even English. I was told the kids walked or their parents brought them. The school session started at 0900 and finished at 1:00 p.m. The kids went home for lunch and didn't need to eat at school.

The Iraqi Ministry of Education controls Iraqi education. Public education is free from primary school to obtaining a doctoral degree. However, primary education had suffered due to the difficult economic situation, which had led to parents not sending their children to school or caused the kids to drop out at an early age. Postwar child labor had also affected the attendance rates. In addition, teachers dealt with low salaries and a severe shortage of books and teaching aids.

According to a report published in September 2013 by the Ministry of Planning and Development, the literacy rate among Iraqi youth fifteen years and younger is 74%. Twenty-six percent are considered illiterate, having dropped out of school or were unable to attend due to financial obligations.

The first school we visited had 300 students. The second one had 800, and I was shocked upon arriving at this facility to see the children were less groomed. It was obvious they came from the wrong side of the tracks. The classrooms were overcrowded. The students were less outgoing and appeared to be socially and emotionally behind the first group of curious children I had met.

The trip to the schools was the high point in my rotation and one of the coolest things I had done since I had started working in Iraq. Interacting with the Iraqi people has opened my heart and mind. I was sure going to miss this delicate culture and humble populace.

Al Khora village near COB

Al Khora village school children

Iraqi school girls

School boys at the village school

A Changed Person

Mysterious as the dark side of the moon.

P lanning my future was invigorating. I set my schemes in motion. I started reaching out to international employers as I was hoping to find another position outside the United States. Bingo, a well-known international organization asked for a phone interview.

Frontier had encouraged me to do a BOSIET course in case I decided to work offshore for them. The program was mandatory for anyone who worked on a vessel or platform. With this in mind, I enrolled in the basic offshore safety induction and emergency training course to align with my upcoming leave. With a BOSIET certificate, I would be prepared if an offshore gig came available.

While working in Iraq, I started dreaming of working and living in another foreign country elsewhere. This then gave me the aspiration to seek an international nursing license. I knew I would be limited to an English-speaking nation. This left me with Canada, the UK, Australia, and New Zealand. I started researching how to go about getting an Australian Nursing Registration. I added this to my wish list.

I was sure my ambitions would eventually lead me to an exciting future. Regardless, I was nervous about having to re-enter the life of normalcy when I returned stateside after I finished this contract—a complex topic to explain to those who have never lived the life of an expatriate. You are no longer a regular citizen of your native land. You have become a changed person. Life in Iraq had been an adventure every day and a flood of drama, some amusing and some we all could have forgone.

Tane messaged me nearly every night: sweet dreams, xoxo. I would be awakened in the morning to that beloved bloop bubble alerting me my admirer was awake. "Morning babe, are you up?" It was the best time of the day as he often called me before he went to work. This wasn't making it any easier with regards to vacating soon.

In the back of my mind, I knew trying to keep a long-distance romance alive would be difficult. We're not talking about a few states away but literally halfway around the globe. The time difference alone had already proved challenging, as I discovered during my leaves.

Boom, the days were gone, and my rotation was over. The entry from my journal.

Thurs Oct 10th, 0530. HO (handover) day. Iggy will be here today. Tonight is my last night in QA this rotation. I'm not 100% sure they are having me return. So I have packed nearly all of my belongings and am taking my giant suitcase home! I'm still waiting for flights for my next trip. A bit concerned as I normally have received them by this time. I am excited to be going home with many events planned, but my second home is here. Tane is a few K's up the road, even if I can't see or touch him. I must stay strong.

The Verdict

The moon has eclipsed my sun.

I was back in Phoenix only a day and a half when I found myself strolling around terminal four at Sky Harbor Airport. I was traveling to Houston, Texas, to complete the BOSIET course, as I had mentioned before. While pacing the halls, my phone rang. Before responding to the call, I looked at the screen and saw Frontier was on the line. My heart sank, and I felt a wave of nausea take over my soul. Before even saying hello, I knew. I knew. I knew. I knew. I felt dizzy as I heard Allison's voice.

"Hello, Jo, Allison here. How are you? How was the trip home?" sounding as cheerful as ever. "Hey, I need to let you know that you're **not** going to be needed back in Iraq next rotation."

Yep, the hammer has dropped.

"Jo, I am really sorry. You've done a great job for us, but, as you know, Lilith is not the easiest person to deal with. She was angry about the letter. Sorry for the news. If you're still interested in working for us, give us a ring in a few days."

Well, ladies and gentlemen, the verdict was out—no more Iraq.

I was not surprised and truly expected it. Still, my heart fell heavy. The door may have been slammed, but I was prepared. My foot stopped it from closing enough that a ray of moonlight could still peek through.

Seven months later, I did return to Frontier, working offshore on a seismic vessel. This opened the door to many new travel journeys. Tane and I did reconnect more than a year later. I pursued an Australian nursing license unsuccessfully but did obtain one for New Zealand. Unfortunately, my father passed away in June 2014. I have remained close friends with Dr. Angela, and we have met several times. In December 2018, I attempted a reunion for my coworkers and friends of ROO in England, and only four of us attended. Currently, I'm back working in Iraq on a different contract.

I have carried resentment and bitterness toward Lilith for all these years, knowing her narcissistic behavior afflicted so many innocent people, not just me. However, completing this book and sharing my story has given me the freedom to forgive.

I have plans to write a second book detailing more adventures and details about my life both before and after ROO.

Glossary

abyad - Arabic for white

alnisa - Arabic for woman

Allah - God in Islam

altitudinous - high, towering, tall

armament - military weapons

amatory - passionate, sexual, sensual

arcane - mysterious, secret, obscure

ardent - passionate, loyal, devout

assalamu alaikum - Arabic greeting meaning "peace be upon you"

atrocious - nasty, vile, awful

audaciously - bravely, boldly, daring

badgered - harassed, teased, tormented

beguiling - cunning, devious, deceitful

charismatic - charming, attractive

coltish - lively, playful

contemptible - vile, delvishish, ruthless

demure - shy, timid, bashful

despotic - narrow minded

diorama - scene, landscape, view

discomfitment - feel uneasy or embarrassed

disconcerted - distracted, distressed, worried

Du'a - Islam private prayer

enervated - lazy, lifeless

esme - Arabic for "my name is"

ethnological - unfamiliar cultures

execrate - loathe, despise

exigency - crisis, hardship, jam

expatriate or **expat** - a person living or working in a country other than their native country

fricatrice - female homosexual

gaol - jail

guffawed - laugh loudly

habibti - Arabic for good friend, colleague

humongous - very large, super big

inamorata - beloved, admirer, lover

inestimable - priceless, precious

inimitable - unique, uncommon

iniquitous - immoral, sinful, evil

Inshallah - Arabic for if Allah (God) wills it

insolent - brazen, audacious, mannerless

impish - playful, teasing, naughty

jinn - Arabic for spirit

jovial - happy, jolly, cheerful

kahuna - person in charge,

keffiyeh - scarf

laconic - brief, short and sweet

limerent - obsessive thoughts, involuntary desire

mae as salama - Arabic for goodbye, go in peace

mawt - Arabic for death

mesomorph - very muscular, brawny, strong

milieu - environment, surrounding, setting

nous - mind, brains, intellect

pantomath - a person who knows everything

punctilious - careful, attentive, studious

queue - line up, form a line

query - to question

Quran - the sacred scripture of Islam

remunerated - work done, satisfied, awarded

resettle - relocate, move, migrate

reticent - composed, reserved, dispassionionate

sadiq - Arabic for friend

sadiqa - Arabic for female friend

saeid alhazi - Arabic for happy, lucky
shukran - Arabic for thank you
solicitous - gracious, unselfish, warm-hearted
succor - support, aid, encourage
supplication - request, prayer, plea
tenacious - steadfast, determined
thaumaturgic - special, spellbound, miraculous
timorous - shy, skittish, timid
triumvirate - group of three people who share power
tumultuous - deafening, thunderous, loud
utopian - romantic, hopeful, imaginary

Acronyms

ATP - Advanced persistent threat
BC - Base Camp on Mount Everest
COB - Contingency Operating Base
CME - Continuing Medical Education
GC - Grand Canyon
HQ - Headquarters
HET - Hazardous Environment Training
IED - Improvised explosive device
LOI - Letter of invitation
NBA - National Basketball Association
NFL - National Football League
LN - local national (host country national)
NS - normal saline
Ops lead - Operations leader
QA - Qarmat Ali
QAWTP - Qarmat Ali Water Treatment Plant
QRF - quick response force
ROO - Rumaila Oil Operations
SOC - Southern Iraq Oil Company
TL - Team leader
UNESCO - United Nations Educational, Scientific and Cultural Organization
WMS - Wilderness Medical Society

Acknowledgments

My children, Jan, Drew, Brock, and Angie, and my parents, were all tremendously supportive and forgiving of missed holidays, celebrations, and family get-togethers while I traveled, worked, and adventured my way around the globe.

My heartfelt appreciation goes out to my biggest encouragers. Alicia Valentyn, or AJ for short, your endless support has been invaluable. You never gave up on me, with countless messages prompting, cheering, and influencing me to push on. My daughter and best friend, Angela Bihn. Ang, thanks for listening to my frustrations, answering my questions, teaching me to be a better writer, and motivating me. My son, Brock Mounsey, you believed in me from the beginning. I'm much obliged for all your support and your ears.

Carmen Davis, my fabulous co-worker, thanks for routinely asking, "*How is the book going?*" and then listening to my challenges and excitement as this has come to fruition. Oscar Marumure, a fellow nurse in Iraq, your kind words and interest in my progress have been a true blessing. Jamie Ratcliff, you came into my life at just the right time. Your support through these last few tedious weeks is very much appreciated.

I would like to thank each of my beta readers. Your input opened my eyes to weaknesses that I could not see myself. With your help, I was able to view my manuscript in a different light. From the bottom of my heart, thank you so much, Shelley Hoffman, Ryan Murphy, and Kerris Harvey. An extra big thanks to you, Kerris, for staying on and proofreading and mentoring me for a few additional weeks. Also, I want to express my gratitude to Jasna Cizler for designing the map of Iraq. I'm so pleased with how it turned out.

I want to give a shout-out to Pamela Jane for your eyes and advice. You encouraged me to take a deeper look into my content by showing and not telling.

Paula Wiseman, as my editor, you have helped me shape my manuscript into a flowing piece of art, smoothing the edges and making it possible for me to publish a book I'm proud of. Thank you so very much.

Wez Van Zyl, thank you for sharing your fantastic photography skills and capturing the perfect author photo of me at the beautiful Pukekura Park.

Witi Ihimaera, reading your beautifully written books has sparked my own creativity. Getting the opportunity to meet and talk with you was a dream come true. I have never forgotten your advice and encouragement, telling me that my first book needed to be well done.

Author's Note

This is my personal story told from my own experiences.

It has taken me more than ten years to fulfill my promise to my treasured friend and advocate, Bob Titel, to write and publish a book.

I'll never forget walking into Bob's room that April morning back in 2011. After receiving the patient handover from the off-going RN, I approached Mr. Titel to introduce myself as his nurse and complete a patient assessment. Lying in bed in the ICU was a fifty-eight-year-old man who had been airlifted 130 miles to Phoenix after having a heart attack. Although the previous nurse had shared Bob's medical history, I was shocked when I laid eyes on my patient. Bob stared across the room, unable to notice my presence, for he was legally blind. My eyes were quickly drawn to the fingerless hands at the end of his long arms. The poor man was missing **all** of his fingers. Later, I was told the story. A camping trip gone bad. Several years earlier, Bob had been camping alone when he tripped while wearing his prosthetic legs and landed in the fire pit, severely damaging his hands. You see, diabetes had robbed the man of his lower legs and, years later, his sight.

I was immediately drawn to Robert's incredibly optimistic attitude and will to keep living his life to the fullest. When Bob was finally discharged to rehab, I asked the social worker to find him a facility near my house so I could look in on him. How this man remained upbeat was bewildering. In the school of hard knocks, Bob was an A+ scholar. During my biweekly visits, I listened intently to Robert's compelling stories. In return, he listened to mine. Soon we became pals. Before returning him to his family in Quartzsite, Arizona, we vowed to each other to write a book. Unfortunately, my dear friend passed away a few weeks later. Regretfully, his story may never be heard.

Although the events in *I Choose the Moon* mostly took place following Bob's death, I know he would be pleased with my accomplishment.

For months I procrastinated. I was unsure how to go about creating a book. All I knew was that it was something I felt compelled to do. Then the day came when suddenly, out of anger and emotion, I picked up a pen and started scratching out my story.

After doing my damnedest to keep Tane's interest and my hopes for us alive, I was told there was another woman. I was heartbroken. Writing allowed me to express my feelings on paper and not just to the moon.

Writing this book hasn't been easy, aside from the thousands of hours it's taken me. Riding on the emotional roller coaster has brought me oodles of both joy and tears each time I relived these chronicles.

Many of the characters gave me permission to use their real names. Other names have been changed to keep the mystery alive and the guilty or innocent undisclosed. For example, neither Lilith nor Tane are real names—Lilith, for obvious reasons, and Tane, due to the fact he still works in the security sector. I chose the name Tane because it means the "God of the Forest." Between my passion for both nature and the man behind the name, it felt befitting.

I spent many years despising the woman I named Lilith. First, she had unfairly governed the Frontier team. Then, with a swipe of a hand, she ended my Rumaila career, the opportunity I had long hungered for. Finally, she tore me away from the man I was smitten with.

Over the years, I have slowly let go of my hatred. Nevertheless, I would not go out of my way to throw her a lifeline.

Thank you so much for taking an interest in my story and buying my book. I want to encourage you, the reader, to believe in yourself, roll up your sleeves, and climb your way to whatever summit you are inspired to seek.

Why the glossary? To make your reading more straightforward, especially with my use of Arabic words and many acronyms.

This story doesn't end here. Book two will have more adventures, drama, and an update on Tane.

About the Author

Jonea Mounsey, mother of four successful adults and grandma to six rowdy grandkids, has spent the past twenty-seven years as an RN caring for people in the United States and abroad. She has cared for patients in the hospital setting, in a burning forest, in the air as a flight nurse, on a seismic ship, in an emergency department in New Zealand, and in the desert of Iraq.

Making a promise to a friend that she would put her life undertakings and daring experiences into print, she has written her first memoir, *I Choose the Moon.*

Jonea likes living on the edge and is a true adrenaline junkie. A competitive athlete, she has participated in three ultra-races on three continents.

Her soul thrives on keeping fit and spending time outdoors camping, hiking, climbing mountains, or exploring nature.

Her favorite things are traveling to foreign lands while experiencing local customs and cultures and making new friends along the way.

These days, she splits her time between (Arizona) and (Iraq), carving out a little time to work on her next book.

CPSIA information can be obtained
at www.ICGtesting.com
Printed in the USA
BVHW051930080623
665636BV00009B/508